W9-BGA-330

Pope John Paul II
and the Church

Peter Hebblethwaite

Sheed & Ward
Kansas City

Copyright© 1995 by the *National Catholic Reporter*

All rights reserved. No part of this book may be reproduced or transmitted in any form or by any means, electronic or mechanical, including photocopying, recording or by an information storage and retrieval system without permission in writing from the Publisher.

Sheed & Ward™ is a service of The National Catholic Reporter Publishing Company.

◆

Library of Congress Cataloguing-in-Publication Data

Hebblethwaite, Peter.
    Pope John Paul II and the Church / Peter Hebblethwaite.
        p.   cm.
    Collection of articles originally written for The National
Catholic Reporter published between 1978 and 1994.
    Includes index.
    ISBN: 1-55612-814-2
    1. John Paul II, Pope, 1920-   . 2. Catholic Church—Doctrines.
3. Catholic Church—History—20th century. I. Title.
BX1378.5.H39 1995
282'.09'045—dc20   95-9251
                                                  CIP

◆

Published by: Sheed & Ward
                    115 E. Armour Blvd.
                    P.O. Box 419492
                    Kansas City, MO 64141-6492

To order, call: (800) 333-7373

Cover illustration by Maureen Noonan. Cover design by James F. Brisson.

Contents

Postscripts

Dedicated to
Margaret Hebblethwaite
and
Peter and Margaret's three children,
Dominic, Cordelia, and Benedict

Preface

Peter Hebblethwaite died Dec. 18, 1994. As the saying goes, we shall not see his like again. This book is a tribute to his memory by the staff of the *National Catholic Reporter*.

Three key aspects — Jesuit priest, Vatican journalist and papal biographer — overlapped to give Hebblethwaite intellectual and moral heft (for biographical details, see obituary on page 301). He resigned from the priesthood but the church remained his focus, one might say his passion. He was perhaps the world's leading Vaticanologist. His coverage of the papacy and the worldwide church for *NCR* has colored how a generation of Americans view those institutions.

Meanwhile, he wrote several books about popes and papacy, most notably biographies of John XXIII and Paul VI. Those were universally acclaimed as definitive studies.

A biography of Pope John Paul II and his church would, logically, have been Hebblethwaite's next major project, but time ran out.

Since the day Karol Wojtyla was elected pope, Hebblethwaite wrote hundreds of articles about him and his pontificate for *NCR*. This book contains a selection of the most significant pieces. Deprived of the advantages of hindsight, they may lack the cohesion and polish Hebblethwaite would have brought to a finished book, but they still constitute a comprehensive picture of the church of John Paul II.

It is intriguing to retrace the journey and see how quickly Hebblethwaite "read" the little-known Polish prelate who was about to become one of the most fascinating and controversial leaders of our age. Hebblethwaite's analysis of the man and pope, the trends and changes and atmosphere and power shifts and theological shifts sometimes seem almost prophetic. Hebblethwaite the former Jesuit steps back and sees it as an ongoing drama, with highs and lows and plateaus that make sense only in context, and providing context was where Hebblethwaite excelled.

A fine storyteller, he saw the church as the best story of the day and loved to tell it. What glows through these articles is Hebblethwaite's love for the church and the papacy. Because he did care, he wanted the pope to get it right, wanted the pope to be a hero, and he was not afraid to criticize when reality fell short of the ideal as he saw it.

We decided to keep the style as well as the substance of the original *NCR* articles. Only a few small changes have been made, for the sake of consistency or other editorial reasons. We have arbitrarily broken down the material into the rather obvious "early years," "middle years" and "later years." We kept the chronological sequence of the *NCR* articles, so that the author returns, over the years, to several central themes. He plays the variations on those themes like a conductor does with an orchestra.

Many people contributed to turning the articles into a book: Tim Finn and Antonia Ortiz typeset much of the material; Robert Folsom proofread and organized it; Nancy Vaught did extensive photocopying; Toni Ortiz massaged it in her computer; Leslie Wirpsa, Jean Blake and Patty McCarty provided editorial backup; Arthur Jones and Tom Fox had the idea in the first place; the Sheed & Ward staff made it a book.

From all of us, Peter, this one's for you.

Michael J. Farrell
Kansas City, Missouri
April 1995

Part 1

The Early Years

1

From Poland, a pope

(October 27, 1978) This time there were three surprises: that the new
pope should be so young — 58; that he should be a non-Italian; and
that he should come from an Eastern European country. Though
there has been noticeably less talk about the Holy Spirit, once again
the cardinals have said how satisfied they are with their choice.

Cardinal Karol Wojtyla was better known than his predecessor,
Cardinal Albino Luciani. He took part in all four sessions of the
Second Vatican Council, was on drafting committees for the "Constitution on the Church in the Modern World" and the marriage sessions of "The Church in the World Today." He also took part in
every synod from the first in 1967 to the most recent in 1977. His
position papers were appreciated for their solidity and clarity.

No one would call him an adventurous theologian. As he made
clear in the speech the day after the election, he is wedded to the
theology of Vatican II and thinks it should be applied still further
and developed. He particularly stressed collegiality and its instrument, the Synod of Bishops. Though these would not be called "progressive views" in Holland, in Poland they represent the best and
most advanced thinking available.

Cardinal John Krol of Philadelphia, who knows the new pope
well, was right when he commented that in the United States, Vatican
II "has meant adaptation rather than spiritual renewal." Still, Wojtyla
organized a synod in his diocese — it is still going on — in which
more than 500 groups of 15 to 20 people work together on texts.

In his first speech to the cardinals, Pope John Paul II committed himself to ecumenism without any of the hedging restrictions his
predecessor introduced. It is difficult for a Polish Catholic to find a
partner in ecumenical dialogue — the Orthodox number 500,000 and
move among themselves while the Protestants number only 200,000.

---

* Dates identify original dates of publication in the *National Catholic Reporter*.

3

But the Octave Prayer for Church Unity has been held in Kraków ever since Wojtyla became archbishop in 1964. Liturgies were celebrated in the Dominican church, with Wojtyla presiding in person, and on the last evening the service was followed by an agape (love feast) in the medieval Dominican refectory.

One of the most significant stages on Wojtyla's road to the papacy came in 1976 when Pope Paul VI invited him to preach the Lenten retreat for the Roman curia. His discourses were published last year in Italian in a book called *Sign of Contradiction*. It is classic enough material, but enlivened with literary references to Shakespeare and contemporary authors. But the real importance of the 1976 retreat was that the cardinals of the curia came to know him better and liked what they saw.

Another clue to his election is that three Latin American bishops bought copies of the *Sign of Contradiction* two weeks before the conclave began. They had him on their short list. True, he has said little about the Third World and does not know much about it from firsthand experience — though there is a delightful picture of him with feathered warriors in New Guinea — but a Polish bishop can do nothing about the Third World. No money may be sent out of the country. Even food and medicine parcels may be stopped and have heavy export duties. Poland's contribution to the Third World has been through her missionaries.

After the indiscretions of the last conclave, lips have been more tightly sealed this time. One hint, however, was provided by Cardinal Avelar Vilela Brandao, who revealed that in the first ballots, the Italian candidates blocked one another and that a foreigner was needed to get them out of the deadlock.

Cardinal Giovanni Benelli of Florence, who at first seemed rather brusque with the journalists, confirmed this when he said, "We did not have the necessary convergence on an Italian candidate. But that does not really matter since there are no foreigners in the church."

Cardinal John Carberry of St. Louis unhelpfully said, "I would like to tell you everything — it would thrill you. But I can't."

Pope John Paul already has conquered the people of Rome. His opening few words, while not having the quicksilver wit of Luciani, delighted them, especially when he apologized — quite unnecessarily — for speaking their language so badly, hoping they would correct the mistake "in your language — no, in our language" (Italian). After that, they cheered everything.

When, the next day, he emerged from the Vatican to visit Bishop Andre Deskur, the Polish head of the Vatican Commission for Social Communications, who is ill in a Rome hospital, their delight was even greater. The pope rode through the streets in an open car and was cheered along the route. Pope John Paul I also had tried to get out of the Vatican but had been advised against it for protocol reasons. Pope John Paul II evidently swept such reasoning aside. He will be his own man.

He has learned tough-minded independence the hard way. Few priests can have had such an unusual preparation for ordination. Just before World War II, he was a student at the famous Jagellonian University in Kraków (apart from Prague the oldest university in central Europe). There he studied Polish literature and tried his hand at poetry.

He belonged to a theatrical group called Rhapsodic Theater (a loose translation). They did verse dramas on heroic, medieval themes from Polish history, sometimes in modern dress. They were regarded as avant-garde. When the war came, the theater was abolished, along with all other signs of cultural life, but the group continued to perform in private apartments before groups of 20 to 30 people. Wojtyla belonged to the "cultural resistance movement."

He was by then doubly an orphan. His mother had died when he was a small boy. His father, a noncommissioned officer in the Polish army, died in 1941. His only brother, who was much older than he, was a doctor who caught an infection from one of his patients and died before the war.

At 21, the young Karol Wojtyla was on his own. He found work in the Belgian-owned Solvay chemical factory (it still exists in Kraków but under a different name), partly to stay alive and partly to have an *arbeitskarte* (a work permit). Anyone caught without a work permit risked deportation to slave-labor camps.

In 1942, he vanished from his factory and was not seen until after the war. During this time he was in the archbishop's residence in Kraków pursuing his philosophical and theological studies. He and four other students there were directed by Cardinal Adam Sapieha (known as Prince-Prince Sapieha because he was a prince by birth and a "prince of the church"). For security reasons they never left the palace. From this period the rumor of his supposed marriage and widowhood dates. It is false.

Wojtyla was ordained in 1946 and managed to leave Poland for Rome, where he did a study of St. John of the Cross at the Angelicum University in Rome under the direction of French Dominican

Fr. Réginald Garrigou-Lagrange, who was famous for the intransigence of his Thomism.

But his influence was balanced by his doctorate at the Catholic University of Lublin, Poland, which was a study of Max Scheler (1874-1928), a Catholic philosopher with leanings toward existentialism and personalism (phenomenology). Wojtyla is a serious reader who likes to keep up with all the latest books.

It was the time of Stalinism. Wojtyla was successively assistant priest and pastor and also taught theology in secret (the faculty of theology in Kraków had been suppressed). He kept a low profile. He wrote a good deal of poetry in this period.

His poetry was published in the weekly publication *Znak* (Sign), the movement of Catholic intellectuals in Poland. He never signed any of the poems because he thought this would be incompatible with his priestly ministry. He used instead the pseudonym of Andrzej Jawien.

Jerzy Turowicz, the editor of *Znak* then as now, told me the poems were long, written in free verse and dealt with philosophical and moral themes. They certainly were not pious and not always religious. *Znak* has high standards and rejects 90 percent of the poetry it receives.

But why Andrzej Jawien? It was the name of the hero of the popular prewar novel *The Sky in Flames*, written by Jan Parandowski. It was the story of a young man who lost his faith. (He recovered it in a later postwar novel.)

After this unconventional background, the rest of the Wojtyla story is less dramatic, though there were the usual struggles with the authorities, normal in communist countries. The Russians had insisted — against all economic logic — on building a new town, Nova Huta, where the new socialist individual was to be forged along with steel. Revolts broke out in 1966 when the authorities tried to stop the building of a church. In 1977, Wojtyla opened that new church, which rises like a vast ship.

The idea was that Nova Huta should counteract the sleepy Austrian-Hungarian empire provincialism of Kraków. It failed. The people of Nova Huta are saved from boredom in their gray city by the closeness of Kraków with its café society and satirical theaters.

Wojtyla was named auxiliary bishop of Kraków in 1958 and became archbishop in 1964. Turowicz told me that when Wojtyla became archbishop, he wanted to remain in the two-room flat he had as auxiliary bishop.

He managed to hold out against the vicar general for four weeks until he came home one day and found that the vicar general had removed his belongings into the episcopal palace.

Wojtyla turned the palace into a hive of activity. Every month he organized two-day symposiums for young people, actors, workers and priests and always took part himself. His curia thought he should have been busy about other things. Every morning he received visitors on a first-come, first-served basis. He was known familiarly among Kraków students as "uncle."

Many inaccurate reports have circulated that he was appointed cardinal to counterbalance the influence of Cardinal Stefan Wyszynski, primate of Poland. Wojtyla is 20 years younger then Wyszynski, does not share his anti-intellectual approach and does not reduce theology to Mariology. But they have remained friends, and Wojtyla has always remained perfectly loyal to Wyszynski. The unity of the Polish episcopate is the basis of their entire policy.

Questions are being asked already about the political implications of this election. If the cardinals wished to embarrass Polish President Edward Gierek, they could not have found a better way to do so. Yet Gierek, a patriotic Pole, will not be wholly displeased.

The real problem will come if John Paul II makes a return visit to Poland. He already has indicated he would like to go back for the May 8, 1979, celebrations to mark the ninth centenary of St. Stanislaw, an early bishop of Kraków who was murdered in circumstances similar to those of Thomas Becket in Canterbury. The question is whether a Polish pope could go back home without a demonstration of popular feeling that could be explosive. The idea that Our Lady is queen of Poland makes a political point: The current users are temporary usurpers.

Italians on the other hand see the implications for their own situation and are anxious about the future of the "historic compromise," an agreement between the Christian Democrats and Communists. At the 1977 synod, Luciani quoted a "Polish bishop" who had remarked to him that Italian Communist Party leader Enrico Berlinguer's promises of respect for the church and political pluralism were "no more than fine words." The Polish bishop was Wojtyla.

The rest of the church will be more interested in his approach to other controverted questions. There is little joy for progressives. His book *Love and Responsibility* defends *Humanae Vitae*, which, he says, "provides luminous and explicit norms for married life."

To those who talk about a crisis in the priesthood, he cites the example of Blessed Maximilian Kolbe, the Franciscan who gave his life in Auschwitz to save the father of a family. Wojtyla has the traditional Polish attitude toward women, though slightly softened by his regard for Blessed Hedwig, the queen of Poland who founded the Jagellonian University in the late 14th century.

But past performance is not necessarily a sure guide to future actions. Pope John Paul II is a thinker. He already has shown he has great respect for the local churches. His pride in the ancient diocese of Kraków will enable him to respect the rights of other churches, including the newer ones.

It is difficult to imagine, for example, that he would want to interfere with preparations for the deferred meeting of Latin American bishops, now that they have revised the documents in the light of the storm of criticism to which the previous draft was subjected.

Perhaps the best symbolic expression of Wojtyla's new style came last Wednesday when he spoke to the college of cardinals. Instead of blessing them at the end of his speech, he asked them to bless one another. He could hardly have found a better way of saying he will think of himself as not above his fellow bishops but with them. ❑

2

Papal vote deduced

(November 3, 1978) How did the 111 cardinals reach their surprising decision in the October conclave? After the indiscretions of August, Cardinal Jean Villot, secretary of state, had exhorted them to complete secrecy, and lips were sealed more tightly this time. The inquiring observer was rather in the position of an intelligence officer who has to interrogate captured troops determined to give away nothing more than their names and serial numbers.

So I cannot — nor can anyone else — tell you what happened in the conclave. "None of the figures given for the August conclave," said Belgian Cardinal Leo Joseph Suenens, "were even remotely correct." Guesses about the October conclave are even less likely to be accurate. What follows moves from a single nugget of fact on to reasonable suspicion.

The only solid fact is that the conclave elected Cardinal Karol Wojtyla after a number of ballots (which may have been eight). The smoke signals, if the rules were followed, certainly indicated eight ballots. But some of them could have been a sop to the waiting crowd. Cardinals showed an extreme reluctance to commit themselves on the precise number of ballots.

Cardinal Maurice Roy of Quebec, with whom I shared a radio studio for the Canadian Broadcasting Corp. three days later, was asked how he felt after the eighth ballot. "After the *last* ballot," he cautiously began, "I felt very relieved." Cardinal Basil Hume of Westminster was equally wary. I asked him what conclusions could be drawn from the fact that this time eight ballots were cast compared with the four (or three) of August. "If there were eight ballots," he replied with a smile of great charm, "then there must have been twice as many as last time."

The number of ballots is not important in itself. But if, as some suspected, Wojtyla had asked for time to think and pray and had asked for a confirming ballot, this diffidence on the exact number of ballots would be explained.

Interviews with the cardinals as they emerged from the Vatican provided a few further clues. No one claimed that the virtual unanimity asserted in August had existed in October. There was much less talk about the Holy Spirit — not that he was felt to have been absent, but there was a keener sense that he works through human agencies.

The basic outline of what had happened came from Cardinal Avelar Vilela Brandao from Brazil. He said the cardinals had failed to find a consensus on any of the Italian cardinals and, to resolve this deadlock, had been obliged to look for a non-Italian.

Cardinal Giovanni Benelli supported that. He was looking rather tired, had lost his suitcase and was somewhat testy with Italian journalists who asked him stupid questions. ("Is this a significant event?" "Of course it is a significant event.") But he was more open in an interview the next day in *Gazzetta del Populo* when he said, "There was not the convergence of votes on an Italian needed to be elected pope, but this did not matter, for in the church there are no foreigners."

True enough, but that glossed over the novelty of the event. Pope John Paul II himself in his speech to the cardinals in the Consistorial Hall on Oct. 18 recognized they had done something surprising that required explanation: "Venerable brothers, it was an act of trust and at the same time an act of great courage to have wished to elect a 'non-Italian' pope as bishop of Rome. I can't say more about this, other than to accept the decision of the College of Cardinals." Thus, from the most authoritative source, we learned that the departure from precedent required courage and that, therefore, it was not a step easily taken.

So Wojtyla was not the man they had in mind when the conclave started. Brandao and Benelli's witness is that a non-Italian was considered only after the Italian candidates had been tried and had failed to gain the 75 votes needed.

Fabrizio de Santis (in *Corriere della Sera*, Oct. 19) claimed to know that in the early ballots, Cardinals Ugo Poletti, Corrado Ursi, Pericle Felici and Giovanni Colombo each gained 20 to 30 votes and that with none of them making any significant headway, they gradually were abandoned.

The Italian cardinals thus canceled one another out. There are two objections to the de Santis speculation. First, it does not suggest the "thrilling story" that Cardinal John J. Carberry of St. Louis said he would have liked to tell but could not; and second, it ignores the roles of Benelli and Cardinal Guiseppe Siri.

That would have been the point at issue in a Siri-Benelli contest. One suggestion is that Benelli reached 70 or so votes and thus came close to being elected but that he constantly was opposed by 40 cardinals from opposite ends of the spectrum.

The Siri group would continue to veto him, while some progressives, knowing his authoritarian ways, in no circumstances would vote for him. I prefer not to name the curialist who said that "a Benelli papacy would mean 20 years of dictatorship."

The quality called "spirituality," which Cardinal Francis J. Dearden of Detroit said could be felt instinctively, was not Benelli's strong suit. He seemed to some more like a manager in Church Inc. than a man of God.

But Benelli also is a *bon prince*. Now that a candidate in his 50s had been seriously considered and the Italians had effectively destroyed one another, the way was open for the leading non-Italian. The imaginative leap could be made.

Indeed, a number of cardinals had already made it. For Wojtyla was well-known and popular. He was much better known than Cardinal Albino Luciani. According to Cardinal Carlo Confalonieri, dean of the college, Wojtyla had received a number of votes in the August conclave. Despite his comparative youthfulness — which now seemed a positive advantage — he had taken part in all four Second Vatican Council sessions (unlike Benelli). And he was at all five meetings of the Synod of Bishops between 1967 and 1977. In 1971 he was elected a member of the secretariat of the synod, and in 1974 he presented an important theological report on evangelization.

Those who had sat with him on the Congregation for the Sacraments — for divine worship, for the clergy and Catholic education — valued him as a patient listener who could sum up positions with clarity and fair-mindedness. His intellectual stature was not in doubt. His grasp of languages was another positive factor. He quite plainly was wedded to the council. And there could be no question about his strength of character: Anyone who had to deal with the Polish authorities for 20 years would have to be robust, patient, clearheaded and subtle.

Moreover — and this was decisive in his election — though he had stressed the importance of the local church and was intensely proud of his own ancient diocese of Kraków, he had never thought in terms of opposition between the local church and the Roman curia.

In 1976, Pope Paul VI invited Wojtyla to preach the Lenten retreat for himself and the curia. This task usually was entrusted to a Franciscan or some other Roman member of a religious order. By this retreat, later published under the title *Sign of Contradiction*, he became known to the curia — and the curia liked what it saw.

Such *post factum* rationalizations do not mean his election was inevitable, but they do help make it intelligible. The reason almost all observers overlooked Wojtyla was that they underestimated the College of Cardinals' courage and imagination. It was thought mistakenly that they could not elect a pope from Eastern Europe because of the incalculable political consequences. But they took a risk, seized the initiative and, in so doing, had the Polish government floundering.

One of the most astute brains in the conclave was Cardinal Franz König of Vienna. He knows Eastern Europe well, having been charged with various missions (which he always insists are pastoral rather than diplomatic). Vienna has a historic relationship with the entire Danube region, and the southern part of Poland, including Kraków, was part of the Austro-Hungarian empire from the end of the 18th century until after the First World War. Moreover, König always said quite openly that the time had come to consider a non-Italian as pope. It was clear he had Wojtyla on his list.

So had the four Latin American and Spanish cardinals, including Cardinal Juan Landazuri Ricketts of Peru, who bought copies of *Sign of Contradiction* on their arrival in Rome for Pope John Paul I's funeral. To read a man's book is the simplest way to find out what he's like.

One also recalled that Cardinal Joseph Ratzinger of Munich had warned, before the conclave and rather superfluously, against "Italian left-wing pressures" on the College of Cardinals. Wojtyla's intelligent opposition to communism would commend him to the German cardinals. The Poles had just been publicly reconciled to them, thanks to Cardinal Stefan Wyszynski's visit to West Germany, where he said Mass in the concentration camp of Dachau. The Wojtyla constituency was building up.

One should add that the U.S. cardinals, especially Cardinal John Krol of Philadelphia, had been cultivating good relations with the Polish bishops and had been on spectacular visits to the shrine at Czestochowa. But even Krol admitted that the result was a surprise. He said rather cryptically: "If one or another of you did not guess what would happen, then you have a lot of company; we have again witnessed the presence and activity of the Holy Spirit."

Krol also painted a touching picture of Wojtyla just after his election, seated alone at the table beneath Michelangelo's "Last Judgment," his head in his hands, his body slumped — the loneliness of the long-distance pope. This hint gave rise to the unsubstantiated story that Wojtyla had asked for time to pray before accepting the papal office.

But the pathos of the papacy was a theme Hume stressed the day after the election. Asked how he had reacted, he said: "I felt desperately sad for the man. But somebody has to carry this tremendous burden and be confined in this small area. There comes a time when all the clapping stops, when the pope ceases to be news, and that is when the truth dawns."

But he added that Pope John Paul II had the strength to cope. Few who have seen him in action will doubt that. ❏

3

Pope elates crowd, acts cautiously

(November 17, 1978) In his first four weeks as pope, John Paul II has aroused the enthusiasm of the crowd and quietly set about keeping the Roman curia guessing.

At his audience Nov. 8, he was lost for a time among the milling 5,000 who surrounded him. Buttons were torn off his cassock, his hands were bruised and scratched from countless handshakes, and there were lipstick stains on his sleeves. John Paul is the despair of his protocol-minded entourage. It looks as if he will not take refuge on the *sedia gestatoria* (portable throne). If he continues to insist on plunging into the crowd, he must expect to get mauled. He does not seem to mind.

He cheered the Roman curia by giving them their usual gratuity on the election of a new pope and an extra day's holiday. All Saints and All Souls are traditional holidays, and as Nov. 3 was a holiday, they were given that day off as well.

But the curia still are being kept on tenterhooks about the future. Only Cardinal Jean Villot, secretary of state, has been officially reconfirmed in his office. This was unexpected, as it was assumed a non-Italian pope would need an Italian secretary of state to help him through the tangled maze of Italian politics.

By reconfirming Villot, John Paul showed he approves of Villot's "pastoral" rather than "political" line, for Villot has made no secret that he sees his task as that of liaison among episcopal conferences of the world rather than one of political forward-planning. Still, the concordat with Italy remains to be negotiated.

All the other heads of Roman departments have been received by the pope and therefore reconfirmed, but only temporarily. John Paul is moving with extreme caution. His predecessor formally reconfirmed everyone within a week of being elected, thus denying himself the chance to renew the personnel. John Paul II has retained his freedom.

Cardinal John Wright, head of the Congregation for Clergy, was last to be confirmed. Though in a wheelchair, he told all who would listen that he had no intention of resigning and that "the head of a Roman congregation does not have to be able to walk — it is enough that he should be able to think." On Oct. 30, a few days after Wright's remarks, the pope visited Wright in his apartment.

It is not yet altogether clear what Pope John Paul intends to do about the Roman curia. He has on his desk two reports — both commissioned by Pope Paul VI. The first, written by the late Cardinal Luigi Traglia, concerns the effectiveness of the 1967 curial reforms. There is still a grave lack of coordination.

Marriage, for instance, can fall under the Congregation for the Doctrine of Faith when it is a matter of certain annulments, but the Congregation for the Sacraments also is interested in marriage; the Secretariat for Christian Unity is concerned about mixed marriages (or "ecumenical marriages" as they are called more positively); and to compound the confusion, there now exists a special committee on the family. All these departments work independently, often with different aims in view.

The second report — prepared by Archbishop Edouard Gagnon, vice president and secretary of the Committee on the Family and rector of the Canadian pontifical college — was inspired more by considerations of financial stringency. Every curia member, nearly 3,000, was interviewed. It is likely that an ax will be wielded. Offices will have to justify their usefulness. Conclaves are an expensive business.

John Paul II gives the impression of pacing himself much better than the rather frantic John Paul I. His Sunday excursions outside the Vatican — he has been to the Shrine of Our Lady at Mentorella and to Assisi — show he will not be a "prisoner of the Vatican."

He intends to take his role as bishop of Rome and primate of Italy seriously. He already is popular with the Italian people.

He will be able to use his popularity to deal with the Roman curia. ❏

4

John Paul in Poland: 'Among his own, pope spoke his heart'

(June 15, 1979) Warsaw, Poland — As John Paul moved from Warsaw into the country, he threw caution to the winds. In the capital, for the most part, he was prudent and diplomatic. But among his own people again, he let his heart speak. He started to respond to the crowds, and they to him.

In Gniezno, for instance, someone unfurled a banner that said: "Holy Father, don't forget about the children of Czechoslovakia." It caught the pope's eye, and he read it out in Czech. His sermon theme in Gniezno, first capital of Poland, was that his mission included all Slav peoples, including the Christians in the Soviet Union and Lithuania.

"We cannot forget these brothers of ours," he declared, and then added a phrase not in his prepared text: "We trust that they can hear us." The pope was referring to television coverage of his visit. The principal Polish channel can be received in parts of Lithuania and in Czechoslovakia and East Germany.

But it was unlikely that the Czechs and Lithuanians heard his appeal, for after Warsaw, the visit was relegated to the second TV channel, which they cannot pick up.

In any case, the television editing of the Warsaw event was cunningly devised to diminish its impact. The cameras focused on the pope and the ministers around the altar; they could have been performing their rites in isolation, for all the viewers knew. Shots of the crowd were rare, and they picked out the old rather than the young.

Anxious commentators relapsed into silence rather than depart from their prepared scripts. While waiting for the pope to appear at the Belvedere Palace, official residence of the Polish president, the cameras held a long shot of the classical facade for about 20 minutes. The commentators helpfully gave biographical details on the pope — as if we didn't know — and read, yet again, the pope's letter on the purpose of his visit, in which he stressed that he hoped to serve "the unity of the Poles."

None of the TV programs was announced in advanced. One simply switched on hopefully at what one surmised must be the right time. Poles have become used to taking potluck information.

Despite the television manipulation, Stalinist hard-liners in the media were said to be furious. One remarked: "This visit has undermined all our work in the last 25 years." He was right, for the pope broke ground rules in his speeches and sermons:

- He did not accept that some topics were taboo. Thus he referred to the Warsaw uprising of 1944, "when the city undertook an unequal battle against the aggressor, a battle in which it was abandoned by all the allied powers." Every Pole knows the Russian armies, on the other bank of the Vistula, cynically watched the city's destruction. But no one dares to say so in public. It would upset the "friendly Soviet Union." That this was said in the heart of Warsaw was astonishing.

- John Paul said quite plainly that Pope Paul VI had wanted to go to Poland for the 1966 millennium celebration but was refused permission. That had often been surmised before but never so clearly stated.

- He rejected the official view of Polish history. For the government, Polish history is divided into "prehistory" and the real thing, which began 35 years ago. "A new Poland" or "a second Poland" is supposed to have come into existence after World War II. The pope constantly ignored the anniversary and talked about an uninterrupted flow of more than 1,000 years of Polish history.

- He challenged head-on the atheistic basis of education in Poland. In Warsaw he won the greatest applause for the following remarks: "Christ cannot be kept out of the history of man in any part of the globe, at any latitude or longitude of geography. The exclusion of Christ from the history of man is an act against man." That resulted in a 10-minute interruption, with much spirited singing of Polish hymns and rhythmic cries of "We want God! We want God!" Victory Square can have seen nothing like it before.

Even in the presence of First Secretary of the Communist Party Edward Gierek, there were moments of frankness. To denounce, for example, "new forms of colonialism, whether economic or political or military" may seem unexciting, but many Poles feel the Soviet

Union uses COMECON (the communist common market) to drain Poland of its hard-earned wealth.

"The pope has been much more outspoken than anyone dared to predict," said a Polish Catholic journalist. "He used his position as pope to say what he liked. One has to reckon with the papacy's tremendous moral authority in Poland."

And the fact that a Pole is now in the chair of Peter has enormously boosted national morale. No other office compares to the papacy. "It is the highest office open to a human being," said a Warsaw engineer. "It means so much more than 10 U.S. presidents or five czars of Russia or two queens of England." The historical comparison may seem a little quaint but makes the point.

Since the Oct. 16 papal election, Poles have been asking: "Why, precisely, a Polish pope?" The pope, too, has asked. He gave a sort of answer during his Warsaw sermon in Victory Square: "Have we not the right to think that one must come to this very place, to this land, along this road, to read again the witness of Christ and his resurrection?"

The cryptic answer makes a lot of sense in the light of Polish 19th century poets like Adam Mickiewicz and Juliusz Slowacki, who identified Poland's sufferings with the passion of Christ. Slowacki even predicted that the 20th century would see a Slav pope. The pope was suggesting that the sufferings of Poland throughout history were somehow in part compensated for by his unexpected election. Most Poles are prepared to believe that.

And the government cannot do much in the face of such a conviction. It can attempt to erase the memory of the visit — and the temporary altar with its huge cross was removed within hours of the Mass, but it will find it difficult to persuade Poles nothing has changed. The balance of power has shifted in favor of the church. The long-term consequences could be grave.

Referring to church officials, he told the crowd that he could already hear them "telling the pope off for drawing out the sermon" and that he "knew that it was what the pope said off the cuff rather than from the prepared text that was the most interesting." But here the pope is wrong; the prepared text is of interest, too.

Church officials play down the implications of some things the pope has been saying. One said: "It's not what the pope has written down that could worry the authorities but rather the applause as the people pick up his meanings that will give them something to shout about."

One such moment was at the Mass in Warsaw's Victory Square, when on the first day of the trip the pope said, "Christ cannot be kept out of the history of man in any part of the globe" as the 250,000-strong crowd broke into applause and song. It waved across the square, dying down in one part to start up again in another for many, many minutes — so much so the pope decided to drop the next sentence in his text, which read: "The exclusion of Christ from the history of man is an act against man" — which would have drawn the same effect.

The text was general, but the people understood it as a reference to the communist authorities' attempts here and elsewhere to secularize culture to the extent that, for example, history books rarely acknowledge the church's role. But the Holy Father was happy to have the people clap and sing and told his companions nothing was wrong with it. "They are only expressing their feelings," he said.

By midweek last week, four speeches stood out. One was the Victory Square sermon, where the pope spoke of the link between Christianity and culture. The second was at Gniezno in western Poland (the country's oldest diocese). There the pope said he, as a Slavic and Polish pope, could never forget the people in this part of the world and in an ecumenical gesture reminded the world of the nature of the Christian tradition of East and West.

The third was his speech to the Polish authorities, in which he reminded them of their duty to the nation and to safeguard sovereignty and human rights, and told them the church worked for authentic stability in society and should be allowed the means to carry out its mission.

But the speech the pope made to the bishops' conference maybe was the most important for the future of church-state relations in Poland and in other countries where similar conflicts exist. In it, the pope made clear the church must push its quest for normalization of relations with the state and must struggle for its own rights, in the context of the rights of society as a whole. That freedom for the church must go hand in hand with freedom for the nation, for its people.

Reminding the Polish bishops of the death of St. Stanislaus — the 10th century bishop of Kraków who was killed for opposition by the king of the time — the pope said that "their calling sometimes exposed them to the danger of losing their lives and paying the price of proclaiming the truth of the law of God."

The pope also told them their quest for normalization of relations with the state must be "clear principle, a . . . source of moral strengths that also serve the purpose of true normalization."

His speech to the Polish episcopate also underlined the essential unity of the European countries despite their differing political and economic systems. The pope said Christianity, the church itself, had an important role in this work. It was a clear directive to Western European churches to express their interest in what goes on here. Europe's "spiritual genealogy" demands, the pope said, "that the church work for its fundamental unity."

Despite this European dimension, the pope repeatedly made clear that he came here to fortify not only the imprisoned church in Poland but also the Christians in other European countries.

One evening, speaking to Czestochowa crowds, he noted a sign that said in German: "Magdeburg, Germany, greets the Holy Father." And he replied: "The Holy Father greets Magdeburg."

He went on to ask: "Is there anyone here from Czechoslovakia?" There were cheers. "From Hungary?" Cheers. "From the East?" Cheers.

Scanning the pope's speeches and watching his tour through Polish towns decorated with flags and streamers, and through streets lined with people, it was clear this historic event would take time to digest. The speeches will have to be read and reread, and the Christians in this part of the world will have to be watched.

As the pope himself said at Gniezno, "This pope has come to this place to bear witness to Christ, the lives and the souls of this nation that once chose him as their own, the way, the truth, and life itself. And thus the pope has come to speak of these often forgotten people and nations to the whole, to Europe and to the world." ❏

5

U.N. talk: Muted tone

(October 12, 1979) In the curiously fishbowl world of the U.N. building, the sounds of the outside world are screened out and you need roller skates to get around efficiently. It is an atmosphere in which it is difficult to say anything novel or arresting about peace. The word has become threadbare from overuse. It has been paid the past compliment of vice to virtue: hypocrisy.

Pope John Paul knows this. Perhaps it accounts for the curiously muted tone of his speech, which, even with cuts, lasted a bit longer than an hour. It was delivered at dictation speed in an even tone. Never once did his voice rise with passion. Never once was he interrupted with applause. At the end, he still seemed uninhibited: his hands soared in the air in grateful acknowledgment of the ovation, but they were not allowed to give a blessing.

The contrast between his main speech and his remarks to the permanent staff of the U.N. secretariat later in the afternoon could not have been greater. With the secretaries and statisticians and lawyers, he let himself go. He compared their work to that of the builders of the pyramids of Egypt and Mexico, of the temples of Asia and of the great cathedrals of the Middle Ages.

They were architects but they also were artisans who toiled away at an individual piece of decoration and would never see the completed masterpiece. His audience loved it and loved him. Max Weber talked about the "routinization of charisma." Here the charismatic met the bureaucracy. And in the end, he gave them the blessing he had withheld from the delegates but only after they had asked for it.

But the speech to the delegates will remain on the record. Instant commentators were puzzled by its abstract tone and clutched eagerly at political straws. The pope observed that peace in the Middle East "cannot fail to include the consideration and just settlement of the Palestinian question." It was too hastily concluded that he was criticizing the Camp David solution as inadequate.

Even greater subtlety was expended on his remarks about international guarantees that would "respect the particular nature of Jerusalem" for Jews, Christians and Muslims (to put them in cautious chronological order of appearance). This, I was assured, meant he had abandoned the Paul VI policy of the "internationalization" of Jerusalem. Alas, it meant nothing of the kind. Indeed, it meant nothing at all, except that the three major religions should have access to Jerusalem — which they have, with complaints from Muslims.

John Paul II is better at communicating attitudes than ideas. His philosophical background means he utters without explaining. His ideas look like abstractions that can be "cashed" only with difficulty. The main thrust of his U.N. speech — as more patient study will show — is that neither Marxism nor Western liberalism possesses all the answers. There is a "third way" that draws on both but is bound by neither. His thinking is dialectical.

The central assertion of his U.N. speech was that of the primacy of the spiritual. He called it a constant "rule of history" (and I would love to know why his translators avoided the words "law of history"). But his statement was clear enough: "This rule is based on the relationship between spiritual values and material or economic values. In this relationship, it is the spiritual values that are preeminent, both on account of the nature of these values and also for reasons concerning the good of man."

This is a flat rejection of the central contention of Marxism. Though they differ among themselves, communists — whether Russian, Chinese, Albanian or Euro — all contend that material conditions determine what happens in the realm of the spiritual (which includes religion and literature and music and much else besides). Let *The Wanderer* heave a sigh of relief: Pope John Paul II is not a Marxist.

But then, while Western delegates might have been congratulating themselves on having the pope on their side, he sprang an ideological surprise. He began to talk about "human rights." But instead of putting in the first place, along with President Carter and the West, "civil rights" (e.g., freedom of speech, of assembly, of religion), he talked about more fundamental rights linked with the basic distribution of the world's goods.

This is precisely the answer of the communists to Western talk about civil rights. Civil rights, they claim, are meaningless, so long as more fundamental rights to eat and to work are not guaranteed. A hungry or deprived person may enjoy freedom of speech, but that freedom is abstract and illusory. That freedom is pretend freedom.

The pope does not go all the way with this argument, and he certainly does not believe that political rights are unimportant. He tries to hold together what others divide.

In this we can see an aspect of his quest for a "third way." He endorses the dominant ideology neither of the United States nor of the U.S.S.R. He seeks to be genuinely "nonaligned." The "common good" bounds his horizon and, together with the key concept of "human dignity," provides him with a criterion by which all societies can be judged and found wanting. The experience of Auschwitz has burned deeply into his soul and remains with him a reminder of what happens when people are subordinated to ideologies.

In his picture of the world, the East-West conflict has given way to a North-South polarity. He referred to this when he spoke of "economic tensions between entire continents" as one of the main threats to peace.

The U.N. speech did not tell us anything we did not already know. But it provided the theme for the rest of his trip. He did not come simply to flatter the United States. Though he admires the tradition of political freedom (Battery Park), his image of the United States is of a land of privilege that contains too many poor and marginalized people (Yankee Stadium).

He is particularly critical, too, of playing to sexual liberation: "No freedom can exist when it goes against man in what he is, or against man in relation to others or to God" (Philadelphia).

The natural enthusiasm of the big welcome should not blind anyone to the "hard sayings" of John Paul. He has come to discern the Spirit. It is not a comfortable process. In his version of Christianity, it challenges before it comforts. ❏

6

Pope unveils his papacy: 'Restoration' era begins

(October 19, 1979) What was the meaning for the U.S. church of Pope John Paul II's visit? Archbishop John J. Roach of St. Paul-Minneapolis, vice president of the National Conference of Catholic Bishops, was asked this question when he bravely faced the press in Chicago after the pope's 90-minute address to the bishops.

He prudently replied that it "had created a climate in which good things can happen," expressed the hope that they would not respond merely by setting up 95 new programs and that, for the rest, the bishops "would have to reflect on what this visit means." It was a confession of agnosticism. He didn't yet know what the visit meant.

Yet the pope's address to the 350 bishops was the most important of the week. It has the greatest, and gravest, implications for the future. In this address, Pope John Paul II revealed clearly for the first time what the strategy of his pontificate will be.

It will be *collegially conservative, socially progressive* and *doctrinally restorationist.*

The pope began by establishing that he was "one of them" — almost. He spoke of their "partnership in the gospel" and "our common pastoral responsibility." He recalled that he, too, had been a pastoral bishop who knew personally "the hopes and challenges of a local church" and who had lived through "the exhilarating experience of collegiality" in the Second Vatican Council.

Then came an apparently innocuous sounding phrase: "I desire to strengthen you in your ministry of faith as local pastors, and to support you in your individual and joint pastoral activities by encouraging you to stand fast in the holiness and truth of our Lord Jesus Christ." He sees his task not as being the source of all initiative in the church but as confirming, helping, enabling the local bishops to do their own things.

That explains the deeper purpose of his visit. He brought the prestige of his office and the charisma of his personality to the support of the wavering local bishops. Everywhere he went he was proudly introduced by the local cardinal (or the local bishops in the case of Des Moines). They caught something of the reflected glow of the pope's authority and human charm.

This is what Pope John Paul understands by collegiality. He does not appear to use it in the sense of consultation before decision-making. There is a lot to be said for the idea that the pope should support the local bishops in their best endeavors. The brief visits to Harlem and the housing project in South Bronx, to the blacks and Hispanics in Chicago were more than symbolic gestures: they will be a permanent encouragement to pastors and people battling for encouragement.

Perhaps the best instance of the positive value of backing up the local bishops was the visit to Iowa. Bishop Maurice Dingman and his National Catholic Rural Life Conference were given a powerful boost just when they were preparing their document *Strangers and Guests.* Their work has now been made known nationally and internationally. Urban dwellers are no longer the norm.

One good effect of the visit could be to prod the U.S. church into an awareness of the problems on its doorstep. It was a consciousness-raising exercise. But all these matters so far mentioned are practical and social. Though they may lead a *Chicago Catholic* correspondent to speak of "pinko" bishops, they are not all that controversial. They involve a certain view of the church's role in and impact on the world, a battle that has been largely won, theoretically at least.

On the doctrinal level, problems begin to arise. Here, the pope's stand was fiercely uncompromising. His position depends upon a reinterpretation of the Second Vatican Council. He quoted John XXIII's famous speech on the opening day: "The greatest concern of the ecumenical council is this: that the deposit of Christian doctrine should be more effectively guarded and taught." The concern of the council, then, was for a more effective proclamation of the council.

This is true. But if one leaves it at that, one has only a defensive, apologetic and conserving view of the council's work.

But Pope John XXIII added something else: "Our duty is not only to guard this precious treasure, as if we were concerned only with antiquity, but to dedicate ourselves with an earnest will and without fear to that work which our era demands of us, pursuing thus the path which the church has followed for 20 centuries."

In order to make possible the more effective proclamation of the gospel, he said, we need to distinguish between "the substance of ancient doctrine of the deposit of faith and the way in which it is presented."

This principle was at the heart of the aggiornamento. It was the key to all the conciliar reforms and the basis of all subsequent theological endeavor. It implied that there were new — really new — problems that had to be faced.

By omitting this second part of the conciliar programs as envisaged by John XXIII, John Paul revealed his conservative hand.

He then applied his defensive interpretation to certain controverted moral questions. Here he followed exactly the same pedagogical method as in the social questions. He was not laying down the law from on high, on his own initiative. He was commending the U.S. bishops for the line they had taken. Crucially on birth control: "In exalting the beauty of marriage, you rightly spoke against both the ideology of contraception and contraceptive acts as did the encyclical *Humanae Vitae*. And I myself, today, with the same conviction of Paul VI, ratify the teaching of this encyclical."

Abortion, premarital sex, euthanasia and the indissolubility of marriage were given the same treatment. You speak; I ratify. Homosexuality — male and female — was included in the same package. "As compassionate pastors," said the pope, "you rightly stated: 'Homosexual activity ... as distinguished from a homosexual orientation, is morally wrong.' " Here was an interesting nuance. The U.S. bishops as a whole had not pronounced on this question. The pastoral letter on the topic was the work of Bishop Francis Mugavero of Brooklyn, New York.

On the other hand, the pastoral program of Bishop Carroll Dozier of Memphis, Tenn., on general absolution was firmly rejected. Thus the commendation of an individual bishop depends on the pope's agreement with him. The ratification of the stands taken by the local church is selective and partial.

Two features about this procedure are worrying. The pope first builds up an identi-kit picture of a "dissident." That dissident ostensibly proposes a package deal of "reforms" in sexual matters. But this does not correspond with the facts. The questions need to be distinguished from one another. Those who have found a "pastoral" solution in conscience to birth control do not for that reason advocate a different approach to abortion or homosexuality. It is misleading and harmful to lump them together.

The second cause for distress is that a mere retaliation of principle does nothing to change the situation. The indissolubility of marriage has been asserted even by those who draw attention to the obvious fact that many hundreds of thousands of Catholics are separated or divorced.

The problem concerns not indissolubility but how these people should be dealt with pastorally, how they should think of themselves, whether they should be burdened with added guilt and banned from what they had hoped was a compassionate church. A reaffirmation of indissolubility may make the speaker feel he has "stood up and been counted" but it will not make the problem go away.

The U.S. bishops thus have a dilemma. They will be torn between loyalty to the man who outshines them so manifestly by his office and his personality, and the people they have to serve: the unchurched and the half-churched and the not-quite-sures.

The pope may seem to have tried to put the clock back to those happy days when Bing Crosby played the curate and won the hearts of the kids with his skills at basketball. But the clock won't be put back. The illusion from which one rudely awakes becomes a nightmare. ❑

7

Pope directs East European church affairs

(November 9, 1979) John Paul II has taken personal charge of the Vatican's *ostpolitik* — the whole complex web of relations with the Soviet Union and Eastern Europe. In the pontificate of Pope Paul VI the complaint of the East European bishops was that the Vatican did not understand their problems, acted above their heads and showed insufficient resolution in dealing with the communists. It was also charged that the Vatican was so anxious to come to terms with the Russian Orthodox church that it was prepared to sacrifice the Uniates of Ukraine and the Catholics of Lithuania.

None of these charges can be made to stick now that there is a Polish pope. John Paul has acted vigorously and decisively on all the fronts opened to him.

Administratively, he has set up a Polish section in the Secretariat of State. With a Polish pope, this became essential if only for translation reasons, but it also means closer attention to wider East European affairs. Secondly, the new No. 2 in the Council for the Public Affairs of the Church (in effect the foreign ministry) is Msgr. Andryas Backis, a Lithuanian whose father was the last ambassador of independent Lithuania to the United States. This appointment is not calculated to endear John Paul to the Soviets. But, once again, it means that the problems of Catholics in the Soviet Union will not be forgotten.

John Paul, moreover, wrote a soothing letter (March 19, 1979) to Cardinal Giuseppe Slipyj who had been fulminating for years against the Vatican's *Ostpolitik* as practiced by Cardinal Agostino Casaroli. The letter was a warm commendation of the Uniates and an assertion of their rights to religious liberty. The controverted points — the status of the Ukrainian synod and the claim to the title of patriarch — were not mentioned, but clearly the Ukrainians are going to get a more favorable hearing in the future.

Whether cause and effect, it is not possible to say, but the Roman Catholic/Orthodox meeting scheduled for Odessa at the end of April was canceled, said Moscow, "because of organizational difficulties." The Uniates have always been a source of friction between Moscow and Rome.

But the most striking instance of John Paul's seizing the initiative was his June visit to Poland. That the visit happened at all was dramatic evidence for the notion of "moral force": the Polish government had all the physical force needed to keep the pope out, but it could not morally keep him out without provoking an outcry. Stalin's famous question about the pope's divisions received a decisive answer.

The worrying thing, from a Soviet point of view, is not just that the pope is Polish: it is that in Poland he spoke as a Slav and made himself the spokesman of all Slavs, wherever they were. At Gniezno he mentioned by name all the Slav peoples and said: "I do hope that they can hear me, because I cannot imagine that any Polish or Slav ear would be unable to hear words spoken by a Polish pope, a Slav. I hope that they can hear me, because we live in an epoch when the freedom to exchange information is precisely defined, as is the exchange of cultural values."

The pope knew perfectly well that the Lithuanians and the Czechs and the other Slav peoples were not hearing his message, except indirectly through Radio Free Europe and the British Broadcasting Corp. The rebuke to the Soviets was plain. That the pope should go to Poland to proclaim his vision of a wider Europe, culturally and spiritually unified, was an enormity.

All along the line, then, John Paul has seized the initiative. Paul VI's *Ostpolitik* was a matter of reacting to government initiatives, trying to inch forward and secure limited guarantees of freedom; John Paul's *Ostpolitik* is aggressive, initiative-taking, and echoes the language of human rights used by dissident groups in all the communist countries. Now it is the governments who have to react.

There is some evidence that last month saw the first attempt to meet the new challenge. It was reported from Moscow that Cardinal László Lékai, primate of Hungary, has spent from Oct. 6-16 in the Soviet Union at the invitation of the Moscow patriarchate. This had never happened before. What was Lékai doing in the Soviet Union?

He had the usual round of meetings with the Orthodox leaders in Moscow, Leningrad and Zagorsk. But he also went to Lithuania and met representatives of the Catholic church in Zilnius. He may also — this could be neither confirmed nor denied — have gone to Kiev to meet Ukrainian Catholics (who, officially, do not exist).

Though a cardinal, Lékai was not in any sense an "emissary" of the Vatican. He is not suspected of unfaithfulness, but his readiness to praise life under socialism seems in Polish eyes to have compromised him unnecessarily. The same characteristic — political reliability — would make him a useful tool to be exploited by the Soviet government in an attempt to mend fences with the Vatican. For the Moscow patriarchates serve the purposes of Soviet foreign policy in the sphere of religion. It takes no initiatives on its own.

Lékai is in Rome for the consistory that started Nov. 4. No doubt he will be invited to give a report on his travels. What he will say is his own business.

But what the Soviet Union will expect him to say is that things are not so bad as they have been painted, that no one is ever charged for religious offenses but only for political crimes, and they may have a minor concession or two to sweeten the pill.

The last time John Paul met Lékai was at Czestochowa in June. He joked with the crowd and quoted an old Polish proverb which said that Poles and Hungarians were either getting drunk together or fighting each other.

There will not be many jokes at this meeting. The stakes are too high. ❑

8

Pope asks for 'self-mastery' in marital sex

(November 16, 1979) "One should not cheat with the doctrine of the church," said Pope John Paul on November 3rd, "when it has been clearly expounded by the magisterium, by the council, by my predecessor — and I am thinking of Pope Paul VI with his encyclical *Humanae Vitae*."

John Paul was speaking to the Liaison Center for Research (CLER is the acronym in French), a group of doctors, psychiatrists, marriage guidance counselors and others who have been working on a reliable "natural" alternative to artificial contraception. He strongly supported their work and at the same time delivered a broadside against his critics.

"One must constantly aim," he said, "at this ideal of conjugal relations which involves self-mastery and is respectful of the nature and purpose of the marriage act, rather than make any concession, more or less broad, more or less explicit, to the principle and the practice of contraception." The reason is, he explained, that "God calls spouses to holiness in marriage, for their own good and for the quality of their witness."

So-called "pastoral" solutions which bend the rules are not to be allowed. The claims of "conscience" were not discussed. The appeal to widespread disregard of the official teaching was sternly met in the following passage:

"It is good that they (married couples) should grasp how this natural ethic corresponds to a properly understood anthropology, and in this way they will avoid the snares of public opinion and permissive legislation, and even as far as it is possible contribute to the correction of public opinion."

John Paul, consciously and deliberately, challenges the conventional wisdom. He confronts it head-on. Characteristically, rather than state his arguments, he prefers to ask a series of questions. Here they are.

"At a time when so many ecological trends of sorts demand that we should respect nature, what should we think of the intrusion of artificial techniques and substances into this predominantly personal area?"

"Is not the attempt to replace self-mastery, self-renunciation for the sake of the other person and the common striving of the couple, by techniques, not a step backward in human nobility? Cannot people see that man's human nature is subordinated to morality?"

"Have people considered the consequences for the psychology of the parents, and for the future of society, of the ever increasing refusal of a child, while all along they have the desire for a child written in their hearts?"

John Paul's final question concerns the young people whom he has enthused: "And what can one think of an initiation of young people into sexuality which fails to warn them against seeking immediate and egotistical pleasure, divorced from the responsibilities of married love and of procreation?"

In addressing CLER, John Paul was speaking to the converted. They will give the answer he expects to the questions he posed. The search for a reliable, non-artificial method of spacing births is on. Science, so the theory runs, will eventually confirm what the church was saying all along and what Paul VI, risking unpopularity, prophetically announced in 1968.

It is only fair to add that John Paul sets his criticism of the "contraceptive ideology" (a phrase he used in Chicago) in the context of an exalted view of Christian marriage and its sacramental reality. Christian marriage is unintelligible except in the light of Christ's union or covenant with his church.

Marriage, says John Paul, "is a recalling, a making present and a prophetic anticipation of the covenant history." In marriage two people embark on an adventure — he uses the word three times — which inserts them into salvation history. They *recall* the grace-filled marvels of God; they *make present* to their children and the world the demands of a forgiving and a redeeming love; they *bear witness* to the hope of a future encounter with Christ.

It is a grandiose vision of married life. The "personalist" philosopher John Paul appears when he remarks that "married love is a totality in which all the elements which make up the human person are found — the call of the body and of instinct, the strength of feeling and emotions, the will and intellectual aspirations; it seeks a deeply personal union, beyond the union in one flesh, which makes of them one cell and one heart; it demands indissolubility and faithfulness in the definitive mutual self-giving; and it is open to fecundity."

This is the context, the only context in which parents should envisage their "responsible paternity" (the phrase is used).

So, on the eve of the meeting of cardinals, at 11:30 a.m. Nov. 3, John Paul issued his most direct challenge to the modern world and to Catholics who have been — in his judgment — suborned by it.

He added that CLER's work is particularly valuable when the 1980 synod — on the role of the Christian family — is being prepared. Any episcopal conference which was thinking of raising the contraception issue can think again: the ground has been preempted. ❏

9

John Paul's 'renewal' engulfs 'aggiornamento'

(November 16, 1979) A summit meeting of cardinals — an unprecedented event in modern times except on the death of a pope — took place Nov. 5-9. For juridical reasons, it was not called a "consistory." Instead it was simply known as a "meeting" or a "plenary assembly," and its rules were devised ad hoc. But it took the form of the pre-conclave congregations of last year: reports followed by questions and discussions.

Life was imitating literature, once again. In Morris West's *The Shoes of the Fisherman*, the Russian-born Pope Kiril summons the cardinals to Rome to assess his first year as pope. That is not quite what happened, and Vaticanologists who wrote that "the pope is submitting himself to the judgment of his electors" were wide of the mark.

John Paul II put it rather differently. "You elected me," he said in effect, "and now you have the task of sustaining me. You wanted a pastor and a bishop, and I have done my best to be that, and now you must help me with the administration."

But it all started rather badly on the evening of Nov. 5. There was the touch of farce which seems inseparable from Roman events. All day long it had been said that the pope's inaugural speech would not be released to the press. A strictly selected pool of 12 journalists was allowed into the synod hall at 5 p.m. to observe their eminences arrive, recite the *adsumus*, and then sit down. At that point the reporters departed.

By 8 o'clock that same evening the pope's speech was available, but only to the zealous who were still on the phone. The next day, a Vatican spokesman explained what had happened: "It was never intended to make the pope's speech available, but when the cardinals heard it, they urged the pope to publish it for the good of the church." I put this remark to the four French cardinals on Wednesday, and it was evidently the first they had heard of it. They just about managed to keep straight faces.

An Asian cardinal told me: "Those of us from the Third World find the secrecy very difficult. What can we say when our people at home ask us what we did in Rome? And anyway, we know that they are going to read all about it in the Western press."

By making the pope's speech available, however belatedly, the Vatican released more than it intended. For although the particular questions under discussion — finance, reform of the curia, the church and culture — may sound more enticing topics, John Paul's "state of the union" speech revealed the central strategy of the pontificate. And its ambivalence.

For there was a double movement in the speech. The pope praised the council even as he domesticated it. There can be no doubt that he committed himself sincerely — as he did on the day after his election — to the implementation of Vatican II as the central task of his pontificate: "a consistent putting into practice of the teaching and directives of the council is and continues to be the main task of the pontificate."

His rejection of Archbishop Marcel Lefebvre and all those who quite frankly regarded the council as a disaster is firm. And his commitment to the council is irreversible: "It is not possible to claim to make the church go back, so to speak, along the path of human history."

However, there is to be no unseemly rushing forward either. This is where the misunderstanding arises. In the United States and Western Europe, to be "for the council" does not mean what it means in Poland. In John Paul's interpretation of the council it was an end and not a starting point; it settled questions rather than opened them up; it changed the vocabulary, but it did not result in any substantial change; it poured old wine into new bottles. John Paul developed his interpretation of the council in three points.

The first concern, "the proper understanding and exercise of *freedom* in the church." It does not mean an anarchic free-for-all. It does not mean doing your own thing. "Very often," explained John Paul, "freedom of will and the freedom of the person are understood as the right to do anything, as the right not to accept any norm or any duty that involved commitment in the dimension of the whole of life, for example the duties following from the marriage promises or priestly ordination."

In Christ, the pope says, the first freedom is not "freedom from" but "freedom for." Freedom exists for service and we give to the Spirit.

The second theme was "solidarity" or "social love." During and since the council, the church has become aware of its interdependence more than ever before. But there are striking differences between churches. Some are rich and free, others are neither free nor rich. In a passage that could have been inspired by his U.S. trip, John Paul said that the navel-gazing crisis of introspection from which certain churches were suffering would be banished by helping the less fortunate churches: "Difficulties will be effectively overcome when (in a certain sense, taking the gaze off themselves) they begin to serve others in truth and charity."

The pope's final slogan was *renewal,* which he linked with interior conversion. Renewal thus defined has completely swallowed up Pope John XXIII's term of *aggiornamento,* or updating. Renewal is happening. There are trends in which John Paul detects "the authentic breath of the Spirit."

They include: "The reawakening of the need for prayer, for the sacramental life and especially for sharing in the Eucharist; the profound return to sacred scripture; the increase, at least in some cases, of vocations to the priesthood and religious life."

It sounds very much like the charismatic program — which is not surprising since the pope champions the movement in Poland. It does not leave much room for what he dismisses as "contrary proposals" which claim to be prompted by the council but are in fact aberrations. They remained unidentified. "Obedience to the teaching of the Second Vatican Council," says John Paul in conclusion, "is obedience to the Holy Spirit."

This, then, was the context of the assembly of cardinals. This was the "philosophy," as the pope said, that was to guide them. Within this framework, the particular questions they were invited to discuss might seem like an anticlimax, but in fact there is a close relationship between them and the "philosophy."

Cardinal Gabriel-Marie Garonne's paper on "The Church and Culture" was concerned with faith and modern society. Pius XI had founded the Pontifical Academy of Sciences at a time when the physical sciences seemed to threaten the faith. The main threat today comes from the human sciences; and the pope, while recognizing that this work is already going on in various institutions, hopes for "a more collegial approach" to these problems of anthropology.

Cardinal Agostino Casaroli's paper on the functioning of the Roman curia raised the question of overlapping competencies and wasteful duplication of effort. Thus the Special Committee on the Family could be integrated into the Council for the Laity.

Other, more radical proposals, were later aired, such as the fusing of the three secretariats — for Christian Unity, Non-Christian Religions and Non-Believers — which, if implemented, would mean the death of ecumenism. Fellow Christians who share in the same baptism and faith in Christ cannot be put on the same level as nonbelievers.

So that proposal ought to be a non-starter. But on the pretext of the need to make financial economies, the "post-conciliar" curia is certainly threatened. And Cardinal Jan Willebrands, who is both president of the Secretariat for Christian Unity and primate of the troubled Dutch church, is hardly in a very strong position to defend himself.

Money talks. Cardinal Egidio Vagnozzi's financial report was bleak and discouraging. The annual deficit has been running at $14 million and the deficit anticipated for 1980 is $18 million. Economic recession, European inflation and the dollar crisis were given as the main reason for this unhappy state of affairs.

Outside the meeting, Cardinal Alexandre Renard, archbishop of Lyons, volunteered the information that more than 1,000 dioceses in the church cannot support themselves. This suggests that the solution is to be found along the line of the "solidarity" mentioned by the pope. The rich churches will have to dig deeper into their pockets. There has been talk of imposing a "tax" on them.

The meeting was "for information" and a wide variety of views was expressed; there were no publishable "conclusions." The cardinals are in any case free to make written submissions on the questions under discussion.

Was it a worthwhile meeting? Cardinal Jean Guyot of Rennes, France, said that ever since he became a cardinal, their stock has been falling. Their real task was to elect a pope. Moreover, their numbers had doubled, which, he thought, had halved their influence (frowns from the other three French cardinals at this). But now they were being given serious work to do. It was a fine expression of collegiality in action.

That's the official view. ❏

10

Most-asked question in Rome: 'Who goes next?'

(December 28, 1979) It would not be true to say that there was a mood of glee in the Roman universities after Edward Schillebeeckx's hearing and Hans Küng's condemnation. The mood was rather one of deep apprehension. "Who is next?" and "Where is the pontificate heading?" were the questions earnestly discussed over coffee.

The feeling of gloom was particularly acute at the Jesuit Gregorian University, which houses Fr. Jean Galot. Last Saturday John Paul II went to the Gregorian and offered a gift-wrapped olive branch for Christmas. Galot was introduced to him after supper. "I think we've met before," said John Paul. Someone said, *sotto voce,* "Yes, of course, you've met. He's your Grand Inquisitor."

"There is a feeling," said one Gregorian professor, "that Galot has isolated himself from the way the Society of Jesus should work. He is altogether too mordant, too biting. He constantly questions the methods of theologians — unjustly. And his intervention on Vatican Radio was a disgrace."

"Jesuits who work in Rome," continued the necessarily anonymous source, "have a strong sense of the magisterium and a firm allegiance to the pope — perhaps stronger than in the U.S.A. But they also have an allegiance to correct principles of conduct vis-à-vis fellow theologians. Galot has not observed them."

"Galot's lectures on Christology," said a student from the Latin American College, "consist entirely in an attack on all theologians who have dared to ask questions about Chalcedon. His view is that since everything was settled 15 centuries ago, there is no point in going back on past history."

It is also fair to say that a distinction is usually made between Schillebeeckx and Küng. It is felt that Schillebeeckx has played the game according to the rules. Küng on the other hand has sometimes been deliberately provocative — publishing, for example, his correspondence with the Congregation for the Doctrine of the Faith. Some go further and suggest that some sort of statement on Küng was needed. Otherwise, "the whole idea of church could become so indefinite as to be emptied of all content." But nobody is dancing in the streets.

"This will be a thorny pontificate," said another Gregorian professor, "and a cause of deep suffering to theologians and intellectuals. It is true that they do not make up the whole church, but they are an important part of it, and there is no point in making them feel angry, hurt and bewildered."

"The pope," said another, "has tried pastorally to occupy what he thinks is the center ground in the church. He wanted to bring a sense of joy and unity. He has taken action to the left and to the right, and told them both that there are limits. But the limits have been rather hastily drawn. We will know just how things stand when, as is rumored, there is a reconciliation with (Archbishop Marcel) Lefebvre." ❏

11

Pope: Africans must adhere to Roman rites, rule

(May 16, 1980) Pope John Paul II packed his doctrinal message to Africans into the first days of his trip. The rest would be dancing and celebration. The adjectives — "exuberant, boisterous, vivacious" — soon would be exhausted.

But he gave his message to Zaire. It is the largest country he visited, and the one with the most Catholics — half the 29 million population — and the most bishops (66). As usual on these trips, the speech to the bishops was most decisive. John Paul stressed the limits of "Africanization."

"It covers," he said, "vast areas, many of which have not been properly explored." The Africans would have to learn to be patient, to bide their time. Poland, he pointed out, had taken 10 centuries to assimilate Christian faith and culture. It seemed a strange comparison in the equatorial heat, but it was meant to introduce the personal touch.

The dangers of Africanization were particularly apparent in worship. There should be a "substantial unity with the Roman rite." The people of Zaire are incapable of doing anything without dancing, so they dance the Gloria and the offertory procession.

Theology, said the pope, should not be merely a confrontation between the gospel message and the local culture: it could not, without grave loss, ignore the cultures in which it has been historically expressed (European cultures). There is only one gospel and one theology.

The same principle was applied to marriage customs. In an address to young couples in Kinshasa, capital of Zaire, John Paul went back to the first chapters of Genesis to show that monogamous marriage was a Semitic idea (not "European"). Africans were perfectly capable of it, and standards must not be lowered. Being a Christian means being converted.

It was a stern lecture, as though John Paul had come to Africa to retrieve a situation that was in danger of getting out of hand. Though he paid tribute to the values found in what he called "the African soul," the stress fell on the need to "purify and elevate" these African elements.

No Sr. Theresa Kane rose up to protest the pope's words. But Cardinal Joseph Malula, archbishop of Kinshasa, did put in a quiet word in his speech of welcome. It was a pity, he said, that the pope could not see a Mass in the Zaire rite.

The official explanation was that this Mass is at the "experimental stage," and if the pope were to be present at it, he would endow it with the stamp of his authority. But probably the real reason was that Cardinal Angelo Rossi, prefect of the Congregation of Propaganda, does not like it. He accompanied the pope throughout the trip.

Malula also regretted that John Paul would not meet the theology faculty in Kinshasa — an extraordinary omission in a five-day visit to Zaire. The omission was even more astonishing in that the pope addressed, or believed he was addressing, university students — though the government had recently closed down the university.

Malula's third gently expressed regret was that John Paul would not meet any of the catechists who are fully responsible for parishes in some areas. These are the married men he would like to ordain. When the priest is a rare visitor, he becomes a kind of "magical mystery man." And meanwhile the catechist does his work of community building — but without the strengthening of the sacraments. It was another problem Propaganda and the pope were reluctant to face.

It became quite clear that John Paul is happiest with the older, more romantic view of the missionary. He fixes his solar toupee firmly on his head, juts out his chin and leads a lonely life for Christ in an inhospitable climate. That was the reason for the visit to Kisangani, in Upper Zaire.

Kisangani is at the point where the Zaire river becomes navigable downstream. Here Sir Henry Stanley started his coastward journey. Here, in the civil war after independence in 1964, 38 missionaries lost their lives. No one has quite claimed they were martyrs, though one of them, Sr. Anwarite, may soon be beatified.

At Kisangani John Paul delivered his homily on the merits of rural life where one lived in harmony with the seasons. There is only one season in those parts, but many gospel themes strike home quite naturally as one sees the fishermen casting their nets in the river.

Also in Kisangani, the whole mood of the visit began to change. The heady lectures prepared in advance were passing over the heads of the pope's listeners, who did not have a good command of French. In Kisangani, John Paul evidently decided he might as well enjoy himself.

As he stepped off the plane, he beat time to the music, and eventually assayed a sideways shuffle with teenage girls dressed in papal white and gold. It was just enough to be able to say, "The pope danced." Everybody by now was in a good mood.

John Paul had behind him a political triumph in the six-hour visit to the People's Republic of Congo, a reputedly Marxist regime. It is a poor country, with hardly any resources, but it has a certain French panache. By going there, John Paul put it on the map, and consecrated a new phase of good relations between church and state. He read a lecture on their "distinct competencies." He is serious about "priests keeping out of politics" (as the Drinan case showed).

From here onward, the visits were shorter, and there was little time to develop any major new themes. John Paul was showing the flag — and Africa was responding. Most of Africa's visitors have come to exploit it in one way or another. John Paul really is, as he claimed on the plane out, "a pilgrim of hope." ❏

12

Is the pope committed to ecumenism?

(July 4, 1980) Pope John Paul II's pontificate has by now acquired a definite shape. Though, no doubt, surprises are still in store, it seems clear that it will be a pontificate in which Catholic identity is vigorously stressed, doctrinal orthodoxy is insisted upon, priests are called to order and nuns told to return to prayer and their habits. After a period of drift and confusion, order will be restored. The emphasis will fall on consolidation rather than experiment. This program has little place for ecumenism.

Yet John Paul's personal commitment to ecumenism is not in doubt. On the day after his election he pledged himself in the work of ecumenism without any hedging reservations: "We intend . . . to proceed along the way happily begun, by favoring those steps which serve to remove obstacles. Hopefully, then, thanks to common effort, we might finally arrive at full communion" (Oct. 17, 1978).

That is less jejune than it may sound. Not everyone in the Roman curia would accept that it was desirable to "proceed along the way happily begun"—a phrase that could be taken as approval of previous discussions. John Paul appeared to be forward-looking. He had no desire to turn back. And he has repeated this commitment to ecumenism in similar terms on many occasions. This fact keeps the Secretariat for Christian Unity in business.

But other facts are more disquieting. The first is the kind of schizophrenia that has been introduced into Catholic discourse. One set of statements is made in an ecumenical context, while quite different statements are made for internal consumption. The concept of "ministry," for example, so painfully hammered out by the Anglican/Roman Catholic International Commission, left no mark at all on the 1979 Holy Thursday "Letter to Priests." As far as the letter was concerned, the agreement might as well not have existed.

There is, then, this marked contrast between ecumenical language and internal language. It has nothing to do with sincerity or its absence; it has much to do with a lack of communication. Once again the old law of ecumenism is verified: only those personally involved in the dialogue process appear able to profit from the learning process it entails. Those not so informed remain unchanged.

John Paul knows the theory of dialogue. In his letter to the Presbyterian church (of Ireland), he notes that "dialogue has been well-described as a process of both making oneself understood and seeking to understand." But his own ecumenical encounters — crammed into the tight schedule of his visits to Ireland and the United States — were disappointing precisely because there was no time to "seek to understand." The pope talked, and everyone else had to listen.

This was particularly galling in Ireland, where the Presbyterians were risking unpopularity in their own communities by going to meet the pope at all. Unable to talk with him, they had to hand their prepared address to his secretary. It declared that "our ecumenical scene . . . is at a standstill, if not in retreat." They received a courteous reply — five months later.

At Trinity College, Washington, on Oct. 7, 1979 — the last memorable day of the U.S. trip — the speech to the ecumenical gathering emphasized difficulties: "Recognition must be given to the deep divisions which still exist over moral and ethical matters. The moral life and the life of faith are so deeply united that it is impossible to divide them." This could be read as a necessary plea for realism and warning against being stampeded into unity. But it could also be seen as its indefinite postponement.

Surprisingly little attention was paid to another passage in the Washington speech. Quoting what he had said previously at a general audience, John Paul stated that the problem of division within Christianity is "binding in a special way on the bishop of the ancient church of Rome, founded on the preaching and testimonies of the martyrdom of Ss. Peter and Paul."

Again there is a hermeneutical problem. By returning to Peter and Paul, John Paul was perhaps leaving room for a reinterpretation of the church's "Petrine ministry" (as he had hinted in his first address Oct. 17, 1978). On the other hand, he has regularly assumed the whole developed inheritance of the papacy (including Vatican I), and so the binding task laid upon the bishop of Rome could be that of bringing back others to the one true fold.

He has not yet said, as Paul VI did, "We ourselves recognize that our office is one of the obstacles to unity." He has not said it because he does not believe it. (Paul VI, incidentally, was not stating his own conviction but entering sympathetically into the minds of other Christians.)

In ecumenical questions, much depends on emphasis. Given a choice between stressing what is held in common and what divides, John Paul tends to favor the latter. A typical example occurs in the apostolic letter, *Catechesi Tradendae*. After reminding Catholics that ecumenism is a duty Vatican II imposed on them, and cautiously commending an ecumenical approach to catechesis, the text goes on: "But the communion of faith between Catholics and other Christians is not complete and perfect; in certain cases there are profound divergencies. Consequently this ecumenical collaboration is of its very nature limited; it must never mean a 'reduction' to a common minimum."

It is difficult to know what is being talked about here, and the text seems unlikely to fire anyone with enthusiasm for ecumenical catechesis. It is a feature of John Paul's style that, as he never gives examples, one cannot "cash in" his concepts. Are the ecumenical agreements that have already been reached, say with Anglicans and Lutherans, instances of "a reduction to a common minimum"?

The Anglican/Roman Catholic International Commission has all but completed its work. Its three agreed statements, together with the volume called *Elucidations* (jokingly referred to in the Secretariat for Unity as "Hallucinations"), will shortly be presented to the respective "authorities" for further action. But who are the "authorities"?

The Anglican answer is straightforward: the documents will be debated and reported upon by the 27 synods of the churches which make up the Anglican Communion. No one has so far stated who will be the corresponding "authority" on the Roman Catholic side. The idea was floated that perhaps a special Roman synod should be summoned, composed of bishops who had contact with Anglicans or were otherwise ecumenically competent. But after the experience of the special synod of the Dutch church and of the Ukrainian Catholic church, enthusiasm for this idea waned rapidly.

John Paul himself commented on this dialogue in his speech to the plenary assembly of the Secretariat for Christian Unity. He said the commission would complete its work next year, and added: "The Catholic church will then be able to pronounce officially and draw the consequences for the next stage." (Feb.8, 1980. The speech was in French, and the passage reads: "*L'Eglise Catholique pourra alors prononcer officiellement et en tirer les conséquences pour l'étape qui devra suivre.*") After meditating on this sentence since it was uttered, I still do not know what it means.

Does *"pourra"* mean it will pronounce, or merely that it will be in a position to — though it may not? Is the next *"étape"* a matter of more talking? ARCIC thought the time had come to move from talk to action. Does *"qui devra suivre"* mean that maybe it ought to follow but will not? (We are no better informed about precisely who will make this official pronouncement, or of those who will be consulted before it is made).

John Paul's belated reply to the Presbyterians asserts a principle which, though it had a local application to Ireland, is susceptible of wider application: "Inevitably such dialogue must first involve a small group of qualified representatives of either church but, once they arrive at consensus, it remains difficult to translate words into actions until the results of the dialogue have been communicated to the members of the churches at every level, often by a process which is itself a form of dialogue."

From one point of view, this is mere common sense. A dialogue "above the heads of the faithful" will be difficult to implement. The "experts" (as in ARCIC) reach agreements that the people in general will take time to assimilate; that could take a long time. On the other hand, where pressure comes from below (for example, for intercommunion in Holland), the appeal to the "basis" is rejected as a theological source.

But if ecumenical change can come neither from above ("the experts") nor from below (the *sensus fidelium*), it is difficult to see how any change can come about and how we can get out of the impasse. There seems to be an ecumenical logjam. And at this point recourse is had to the Holy Spirit.

All the remarks so far made apply exclusively to the dialogue with churches that issued from the Reformation. Concerning dialogue with the Orthodox, the tone changes significantly and there is no talk of perils and dangers. This dialogue with the Orthodox has, in the mind of John Paul II, a priority that is both chronological and logical.

In Istanbul he declared that unity between the Catholic and Orthodox churches "would be a fundamental and decisive step in the progress of the entire ecumenical movement. Our division has not been without influence on later divisions" (Nov. 30, 1979). Dialogue with the West is not rejected here, but it is relegated to the second place because dialogue with the Orthodox is more fundamental.

The theory behind this is far from the self-evident position that was elaborated by Fr. Yves-Marie Congar and others in the 1950s. If the schism between East and West had not occurred — it is conventionally if somewhat inaccurately dated 1054 — the Reformation would have been unnecessary. The Roman church would not have been able to impose its feudal and juridical pattern on the West. Belonging to one church would not have been incompatible with a wide variety of traditions and liturgies. This is all rather speculative.

But it is certainly a thought that is uppermost in John Paul's mind. He repeated it in his speech to the plenary assembly of the Secretariat for Christian Unity: "I am convinced that the rearticulation of the ancient traditions of East and West and the balanced exchange that would result from rediscovered full communion could be of the greatest importance for the healing of division born in the West in the 16th century" (Feb. 8, 1980).

Does this mean, therefore, that ecumenical dialogue in the West has to *wait* until full communion has been restored with the Orthodox churches (for which the symbolic date 2000 has been tentatively suggested)? That seems the clear implication of the statements. It would also explain the contrast between the ceaseless warnings issued in the Western context and the expressions of hope and confidence in the Holy Spirit that are reserved for the Orthodox.

Moreover, the dialogue with the Orthodox is presented as the best and most appropriate *method* for interchurch dealings. This is often put in the form of saying "the mistakes of the Council of Florence are not to be repeated." Its fundamental mistake was that it reached an agreement but could not make it stick.

To avoid this mistake in the upcoming dialogue, two basic principles are being observed: 1. church leaders — and not just theologians — are to be involved from the outset (Cardinal William Wakefield Baum is there rather than Gregory Baum); 2. there will be no hurry, so the people can be prepared pedagogically for what is going on.

These two principles reflect with great precision what John Paul said in his letter to the Presbyterians (quoted above). The critique of the method of the Council of Florence could be taken by the skeptical as an implicit critique of the method used in the ARCIC dialogues: they were too much confined to "experts" and they neglected what ordinary people thought. (I am not saying this judgment is true, but it seems implied.)

There are, of course, many reasons why John Paul should be more drawn to the East than to the West. He is a Slav. And the

Orthodox tradition does not present the same kind of *theological* challenge the churches of the Reformation might appear to present.

Among the Orthodox he finds confirmation for the positions he has taken up within the Roman church itself: his insistence on high Christology, sacramental doctrine, Mariological devotion, monasticism, resistance to "secularizing" trends, a "sacred" view of the priesthood and so on. Moreover, dialogue with the Orthodox can also serve the purposes of his more aggressive *Ostpolitik* (relationship with the East) and contribute to the vision of "wider Europe" sketched out in Gniezno, June 3, 1979.

Dialogue with the Orthodox will not be plain sailing, and there is no guarantee that this vision of unity will be realized. Craggy problems remain concerning the post-schism councils in the West, notably Vatican I. (Vatican II could probably be coped with.)

There is no question of insisting with the Orthodox on Vatican I's definition of papal primacy and infallibility. John Paul, speaking in the Orthodox Cathedral of St. George in Istanbul, Turkey, gave a very "Greek" view of his Petrine ministry which was modest in its claims and inoffensive in its presentation. (Hans Küng would have been able to agree with every word of it.)

"Peter," he explained, "as a brother among brothers, was entrusted with the task of confirming them in their faith." That did not suggest that the Congregation for the Doctrine of the Faith would soon be operating in Istanbul and places farther east.

Provided the schizophrenia mentioned above — one language on ecumenical occasions, another for home consumption — can be avoided, this way of stating the Petrine ministry could also help to resolve Western difficulties. For on these points Anglicans and Lutherans have similar objections to those of the Orthodox. In that case, the centrality of the dialogue with the Orthodox might turn out to have unexpected results.

I conclude, therefore, that John Paul is not anti-ecumenical nor even un-ecumenical, but that he is ecumenical in his own way. It may be a matter of astonishment that a pope can make so much difference to the life of the church, apparently without any consultation with anyone; indeed it should be a matter of astonishment.

Nothing could make it clearer that popes are not just interchangeable figures who give blessings from a distant window. It matters very much who is pope. Did the cardinals know what they were doing Oct. 16, 1978, when they surprised the waiting world by electing a Polish pope? Whether they did or not, they are still discovering further consequences of their action. ❏

13

Hints surface of papal role in Polish events

(September 19, 1980) Lech Walesa, the mustachioed leader of the free labor union in Gdansk, Poland's principal Baltic seaport, last week indicated he plans to go to Rome "to pay homage to the Holy Father." Sources here say Pope John Paul has extended an invitation to the labor leader.

The trip to Rome could merely be the conventional tribute of a pious Polish Catholic to the world's most famous Pole. But it could also be a recognition that John Paul has been more active in recent Polish events than was at first apparent.

Protocol demands that the pope should not interfere publicly in Polish affairs. But his heart is still there. "It is hard to leave Kraków behind," he said on leaving the city the last time June 10, 1979. The tears flowed abundantly.

It is some measure of how much Poland has changed in the past few weeks that Walesa, who has become a national hero, attended a mass this month celebrated by Cardinal Stefan Wyszynski in his private chapel and then gave the cardinal a progress report on the Free Labor Union and the likely response to it of Poland's new Communist Party leader, Stanislaw Kania.

The Catholic church channels between Poland and the Vatican have been kept open throughout the August strikes.

Pope John Paul has been exceptionally well informed about events in Poland because his Polish-language secretary, Fr. Stanislaw Dziwisz, has been "on holiday" in Poland throughout August. John Paul could hardly remain indifferent as a new Poland struggled to emerge.

It is possible to guess at the exact nature of his discreet involvement. On Aug. 26, Wyszynski's sermon at Czestochowa was, against all precedent, televised and repeatedly broadcast throughout the day by the Polish national network. The cardinal urged the workers to return to work and said that otherwise Russian intervention would follow. This both disappointed the striking workers and echoed the government's line.

It also caused displeasure in the Vatican (more precisely, at Castel Gandolfo, where the pope has been spending his summer vacations). We know for two reasons:

First, Vatican radio spent the next few days explaining to its listeners, especially Polish ones, that Wyszynski's sermon had been edited for television in such a way as to falsify its emphasis. Wyszynski had, it conceded, warned about the danger of Russian intervention; but he had also supported the justice of the strikers' cause, and this part of the sermon had been omitted from the televised version.

But the more decisive evidence of fresh instructions from the Vatican came Aug. 28, when the Polish bishops held their first plenary session since the crisis began. Their declaration was an enthusiastic endorsement of the workers' case: They stressed the right to free association, the right to information and the church's right to access to the media.

There was no mention of "the threat of Russian intervention." And it was twice said that Wyszynski's sermon had been transmitted "without his consent" and that "important passages were omitted from it" (though it was not said what they were).

Cardinal Karol Wojtyla and Wyszynski did not always agree in analyzing the Polish situation. This difference has now been emphasized: Wyszynski continues to be more cautious and diplomatic, ready to back the government in exchange for concessions; Wojtyla, endowed with the prestige of the papacy, is more adventurous, risk-taking, destabilizing and prepared to call the Russian bluff.

The question comes down to who rules Poland. No doubt the answer is Kania and the Politburo. But John Paul's interventions have reminded them that they rule by courtesy of the church. ❏

14

Synod on family concentrates on marriage and sex

(October 17, 1980) At the halfway point, the synod on the family has posed more problems than solutions. Speeches have largely centered on the questions of marriage and sexuality. And the outcome of the gathering remains unpredictable.

During the first week there were 162 speeches plus a number of written submissions. Week two began with three speeches from the hitherto silent "auditors" — including Mother Teresa from Calcutta, India, who spoke without notes. Then all withdrew into their language-based discussion groups.

What are they discussing? On Oct. 6, Cardinal Joseph Ratzinger of Munich, Germany, offered a 45-minute summary of the previous week's 162 speeches. It was like pouring a quart into a pint pot. His report was accepted as a fair summation. He was applauded for his efforts.

But I prefer to present first my own analysis of the speeches. It will be less bland and more conflictual than Ratzinger's account, but, I believe, no less faithful to what happened.

Five major themes have so far emerged. They correspond, roughly, to the synod members' geographical origins. The synod is a partly elected, partly nominated body. Of its members, 262 were elected by their episcopal conferences. Ten are major religious superiors (all male) elected by the other generals.

Then come 20 curial cardinals, and the 24 members named by Pope John Paul II (including Cardinal Terence J. Cooke of New York). One can usually tell from reading a speech whether it comes from an elected member or from a nominated or curial member.

Nearly all the elected members spoke for (and perhaps to) their constituencies. One African bishop put it picturesquely: "I know you have heard all this before, but if I don't say it again, it will be difficult for me to go back home."

The nonelected members, having no constituency, speak in the name of God or authority or themselves. Thus Cardinal Pericle Felici in effect replied to Archbishop John J. Quinn's remarks on dissent from *Humanae Vitae* by saying the discussion was closed: "There is no need to give credence to statistics because statistics don't mean anything."

No elected member would have said that. They were characterized by a common factor: "pastoral realism." The wool having been removed from their eyes, they did not propose to pull wool over anyone else's. They spoke painful truths.

What they said varied. Top of the list, for a statistical analysis, came the African bishops' insistence that their traditional or "customary" marriage should be taken seriously and, said some, raised to the dignity of a sacrament. They resent the imposition of Western canon law and Western "nuclear family" ideals on their people.

It was not always easy to follow what they meant. The main elements of customary marriage appear to be these: marriage is not a relationship between two individuals who "fall in love" but between two families; it does not take place at a given moment, when the vows are exchanged, but unfolds progressively; it is finally sealed after the birth of the first child.

They all denounced polygamy, but pleaded that the wives of a convert polygamist could not be thrown out, for then they would be outcasts, with no role and no place in society. No one challenged the Africans, because no one knew enough about their situation to do so. But what they said seemed to be in flat contradiction with John Paul's statements during his Africa trip earlier this year. This is another example of an officially "resolved" question that has refused to go away.

The same can be said of artificial contraception. Few speeches were made on this theme, but they came from weighty sources: the United States, Canada, Britain, France, Belgium. Here "pastoral realism" consisted in noting that dissent often came from people who were otherwise dedicated Catholics.

And it must have been disappointing for the curia to observe how this "Western" judgment was so frequently backed up by people from the Third World, especially from Asia. It was important that the bishop from Bangladesh should admit that nation had a "population problem" which defeated all progress toward development. The moment the shantytown dwellers are rehoused, another shantytown springs up alongside the abolished one.

The Latin Americans had a completely different approach. Some claimed the "population explosion" was a myth the First World dreamed up to oppress them. The secretary general of CELAM, the Latin American episcopal conference, Archbishop Alfonso Lopez Trujillo, declared that "exaggerations about overpopulation and the specter of hunger" should be dismissed. But he was a papal nominee.

The Brazilians showed rather more subtlety. Cardinal Aloísio Lorscheider of Fortaleza opposed romanticization of the family. The gospel, he noted, quoting Matthew 10:35-37, has "hard sayings" about the family. And in the Acts of the Apostles, what counts is the community of the disciples, not families.

His cousin, Bishop José Ivo Lorscheiter of Santa Maria, also denounced "utopian" exploitations of the family which reduced it to a cozy private nest without social commitment. He said recent studies showed that family, school and church influenced attitudes only up to 25 percent, the rest being accounted for by the surrounding "culture."

It was futile, he argued, to try to evangelize the family without at the same time evangelizing the "culture." Someone close to the Brazilian bishops assured me, in all seriousness, that they have been reading the Italian Marxist Antonio Gramsci. He held that Lenin's revolution failed in the Soviet Union because an elite imposed it and because it was not "culturally prepared." The "cultural preparation" seems to interest them more than the family as such.

The fourth synodal theme to emerge concerned pastoral care of the divorced and remarried. Here there was no geographical limitation. The cry for compassion went out from England, Canada, Thailand and from parts of Africa.

Pastoral experience suggests that second marriages are often more stable and successful than unhappy first ones. Does this mean, asked Archbishop Henri Legare of Grouard-McLennan, Canada, that we need to review the conditions for the validity of marriage? Impulse marriages hardly seem free. The church's doctrine of "no sex before marriage" impels some into marriages they later regret.

The problem of the admission of the divorced and remarried to the sacraments prompted one of the few genuine debates the first week. Bishop John W. Gran of Oslo, Norway, said such couples should not be "ostracized." Legare called for "a pastoral plan of mercy." The Dominican master general, Fr. Vincent de Couesnongle, suggested that "too many couples believe that they are condemned by the church because they find it difficult to follow its teachings about sexuality." God's plan, he explained, is a plan of love, and it excludes guilt feelings.

But this "compassionate" approach was rejected by Malta and, with great virulence, by Argentina. It seemed like the "thin end of the wedge." The auxiliary bishop of Azul, Argentina, Emilio Bianachi de Carcarmo, said that "to propose hasty solutions for these sad cases would weaken respect for the magisterium, discourage those who wish to fulfill God's law, and confuse the situation."

One final synod theme deserved a mention, even though only one synodal father addressed it directly. Cardinal Jan Willebrands of Utrecht, Holland, spoke as president of the Secretariat for Christian Unity.

He said "mixed marriages," which he preferred to call "interchurch marriages," needed special attention. Because both parties are baptized, they undoubtedly confer the sacrament of matrimony on each other. It seems then anomalous that they should not be allowed to go to communion together.

Willebrands is no firebrand. As usual he was cautious and probing and soundly theological. Assuming that the non-Catholic partner shares in the eucharistic faith of the church (and the Episcopalian and Lutheran agreements have shown this common faith exists), most conditions of the 1972 instruction on intercommunion have been fulfilled.

One condition is that a genuine "need should exist." This is described as follows: "A need for an increase in spiritual life and a need for deeper involvement in the mystery of the church and its unity" (4,2). Such a need, he held, was found in many interchurch marriages. He called for further study of this question.

So far, then, the synod has produced more problems than solutions. The curia strategy will be to exploit the variety of views expressed to suggest that chaotic incoherence can be the only result of listening to them. This will give John Paul a dilemma.

On the one hand, he has frequently said he accepts the principle of collegiality and that the synod is an expression of it. But on the other hand, he cannot be greatly gratified at the various challenges to his authority that have been expressed. The synod has been free so far.

Will it remain free to the end?

Here the contraception issue will act as a litmus-paper test. The U.S. bishops seem to want a no-conclusion synod with a subsequent broadly based commission to reexamine the question.

Others have proposed a "pastoral solution" which buys time: Marriage is a vocation, and few realize their vocation perfectly from the outset. There is need for a growth in maturity.

What seems to have been averted is any kind of panacea solution along the lines of the Billings method of contraception. The synod is reluctant to canonize a disputed scientific method even though most of its lay advisers are connected with natural family planning policies.

The bishop of Breda, Holland, Hubert Ernst, has proposed an ingenious way out, that, considering its source, is unlikely to be accepted. The church's "social doctrine," he pointed out, confines itself to general principles and leaves their application to the individual conscience. Why should there be such a contrast between the vagueness of social doctrine and the precision of the teaching on sexual ethics? Could not the church state the principles of sexual ethics, and let people work out the implications for themselves?

This idea has been echoed, though discreetly, in a number of French interventions. The church is concerned with values rather than rules. The trouble with *Humanae Vitae* is that people cannot see the splendid values it asserts because of the rules it lays down. Putting the two together again has become problematic.

In his official report, intended as guidelines for the discussion groups, Ratzinger made much the same points. But he added a thought about theological method that goes to the heart of the question. On its resolution depends the synod outcome.

He said two theological methods were at work in the synod speeches. Some fathers stressed that mere repetition was not enough, that the experience of the married was an important theological source, that the "sense of the faithful" and psychological and sociological insights were the basis of the reflection of theologians and the teaching of the magisterium. We may call this (though he did not) an "ascending method."

The other method starts from a clear and unambiguous proclamation of church doctrine. It is skeptical of the methods of the human sciences, which can in no way dictate to it. It regards the gospel, as interpreted by the magisterium, as the unique remedy for the world's ills and Christians' sins. We can call this (though again he did not) the "descending method."

At a press conference Oct. 7, Cardinal Joseph Cordeiro of Karachi, Pakistan, and Archbishop Dermot Ryan of Dublin, Ireland, tied themselves into intricate knots as they attempted to explain how these two different approaches could be harmonized and reconciled. There was much talk of "building bridges."

Meanwhile John Paul II has been at every session, except once when he was at the general audience. He has heard many of his favorite theses challenged. He cannot be enjoying himself. On Oct. 12, he will get a chance to recoup: with all the synod bishops, he will celebrate a mass for families in St. Peter's Square. It will be a great rally, a demonstration of the "silent faithful," a pro-life display.

Perhaps the most important part of Ratzinger's report was his final sentence: "It will be the task of the discussion groups to decide the concrete goals toward which this synod must aim." The working papers prepared in advance are not forgotten: the future of the synod lies with its members. ❏

15

John Paul: Is the style the man?

(October 17, 1980) Most commentators on Pope John Paul II discuss, properly, the content of what he has to say. I would like to concentrate, for a change, on the literary style of his homilies and speeches, especially during his visit to Brazil. This is based on the conviction that "the style is the man."

A preliminary difficulty is that the pope's speeches are written in Polish. On this occasion they were translated into Portuguese, then into Italian, and finally they made their laborious way into some sort of English. Few poets could survive such a linguistic mauling. Yet it is surprising how much of John Paul's characteristic style comes through.

One feature of his rhetoric is the way he interweaves human experience and its theological interpretation. His inaugural sermon at the Brazilian Eucharistic Congress was a good example. Its theme, "Where are you going?" was an invitation to consider the concrete problems of "inner emigration" within Brazil in the context of the whole meaning of life.

In his homily John Paul switched from level to level. The painful realities of emigration in Brazil were faced, the pastoral problems it led to were discussed, but the whole was counterpointed with the words of St. John's gospel, "To whom shall we go? You have the words of eternal life."

In this way the emigrant becomes the type of the human pilgrimage generally. And the homily ended with a prose poem: "Harassed by the passage of time, wandering along the streets of the world, journeying in the shadow of the provisional, in search of the true peace and joy for which our hearts are hungry." In the Eucharist, Christ meets the pilgrim/emigrant, John Paul concluded.

This is an instance of what might be called "catechetical" style. At Pôrto Alegre on July 5, his whole homily was devoted to the nature of catechetics. Christianity is not just a "doctrine" but also a "message": One is not simply propounding ideas, but evoking a response.

Furthermore, the message "is not addressed to some abstract, imaginary hearers but to particular people living at a particular time, with their hopes and their dramas." John Paul was well-briefed about Brazil — the bishops had done their lobbying well — and this enabled him to obey his own principles. People love to hear themselves talked about with a show of understanding.

But not all the homilies in Brazil were written in this catechetical style. Some of them were mini-treatises on urgent social problems, sketches for a future social encyclical. And here the style becomes grave and expository. The old professor takes over.

The main feature of John Paul's expository style is clarity and authority. His yes is a yes and his no is a no. He does not appear to know doubt or hesitancy. He lectures the "world." He told a gathering in El Salvador: "The church, founded by Christ, shows contemporary man the way he must go to build up the earthly city, which, despite its imperfections, foreshadows the heavenly city." It would be appropriate to call this stylistic characteristic "magisterial."

John Paul speaks a great deal. Anyone who talks so much inevitably falls back on the same rhetorical devices. I'll list some of them, all part of the classical repertoire.

1. What used to be called *captatio benevolentiae*, getting people on your side. It often takes the form: "I could not possibly come to Brazil without having a meeting with the people of X or Y." The people of X or Y then cheer wildly.

2. This is a variant of No. 1 and goes like this: "I would like to greet you all personally/to shake hands with you all/to enter every

Brazilian home/to sit down with every family/to embrace every leper — but unfortunately, as you well realize, this is impossible."

3. This is much more profound. It is an appeal to John Paul's personal experience. It alludes to the autobiography that — presumably — will never now be written. There were two classic instances in Brazil.

He said to young people in Belo Horizonte that in his youth he had shared their desire to transform radically unjust social structures. With them he had felt it was impossible to be happy while vast numbers of their fellow citizens were in misery. "As a young man," he told them, "I expressed these ideas in poetry and literature."

Then came the war. These ideas were mocked and trampled on. They seemed to have been swept away in the whirlwind of war. "One day," went on John Paul, "I brought these ideals to Christ, and understood that he alone could reveal to me their true content and value." This is as close as we are likely to come to an account of the vocation of John Paul II. It was born in the crisis of war.

Another wartime memory was evoked in Fortaleza, in the introduction to the Eucharistic Congress: "During the harsh and terrible war in Poland I saw young people leave without hope of returning, parents snatched from their homes without knowing whether they would ever see their loved ones again. At the moment of parting, there would be a gesture or a photograph or object would pass from hand to hand in order to prolong presence even in absence. Such symbols are the best human love can do."

The purpose of this passage was not directly autobiographical: it was to contrast human love with divine love, which, in the Eucharist, is a permanent and effective symbol of real "presence in absence." But it gains in weight thanks to the autobiographical content. This is a man speaking, not a manual.

No. 4 is a variant of the personal appeal. It was used in Rio de Janeiro in the homily on the family. "May I confide in you?" asked John Paul. This is an irresistible device, calculated to rouse any slumbering listener. The fact that radio and television made this less than an intimate confession was irrelevant. Please, Holy Father, please do go on.

The confidence was about the first person who had told him about Brazil. The anonymous individual had informed him that Brazil, despite its vast problems, had brought together a great diversity of races in a wonderful way, so much so that he could say that "Brazil is one great family."

No. 5 is the apostrophe. This is reserved for the conclusion of homilies. A good example occurred at Belem. John Paul turned toward the statue of Our Lady and addressed the Mother of God. "Mary, you are the second Eve . . ." There was transition from preaching to praying.

6. Here the rhetorical device also contains a psychological ploy. It consists in a quotation from the very person or persons whom he is addressing. It is most commonly used with bishops who feel gratified, flattered and — it must be admitted — hoist with their own petard.

In Brazil, John Paul used this device in his address to President Joao Figueiredo. If reforms are to be realized, then mentalities have to be changed, he told the president, adding: "always enlightened by 'the certainty that man is at the center of our concerns and responsibilities,' as you wrote to me recently."

It was a shrewd move. The president could hardly object to having his own words quoted back at him. But now he was being forced to consider the further implications of what may have been no more than a rhetorical flourish. Since the centrality of a man (the human person) was the theme of the entire visit, it was a perfectly fair procedure.

John Paul's rhetorical style derives from Cicero and Bossuet — and, no doubt, Piotr Skarga, the 18th century Polish preacher. It is a style that has largely vanished from the Anglo-Saxon world where television demands a different kind of intimacy and "I'd just like to say a few words" is the only form of public discourse left. But it seems to work in Latin countries. ❑

16

Pope foresees growing battle between good and evil

(January 9, 1981) As Pope John Paul peers into the future, he sees not the next decade but the next 20 years. The year 2000 fascinates him like the eye of the basilisk. What is going to happen in this period is an intensification of the age-old struggle between good and evil. Two women stand guard over the whole sweep of history: the woman in the Book of Genesis who will "crush the head of the serpent" and the woman of the Apocalypse.

This cosmic, dramatic view of the world affects all John Paul's attitudes. The priest is in the front line of the battle. He resembles the Abbé Donissan in Georges Bernanos' first novel, *Sous le Soleil de Satan*. He is a spiritual athlete, the hero of God, the champion who struggles single-handedly with the evil one. Hence the primary virtue of the priest is courage. This is why the norms on laicization were changed: deserters have no rights.

If the priest is seen in these dramatic terms, so also is his adversary, the "atheist." In one of his speeches John Paul deplored the way some theologians have tried to present the atheist as "an unconscious believer" and so had transformed a "profound drama" into a superficial misunderstanding. He positively relishes his drama.

It would be no use trying to point out that most "atheists" do not have the energy to be Luciferian or Nietzschean rebels. They are more often puzzled persons trying to cope than stealers of fire from the gods. But John Paul does not accept that.

In his picture of the world, there is black and white, but the existence of gray areas is not recognized. Or else it is identified with compromise, weakness, surrender to the world. Instead, the watchwords are defiance, challenge, "they shall not pass."

The marathon papal journeys stretch human endurance to the limit and so become a display of heroism in action. John Paul conceded the truth of the charge that he was traveling too much, "from a human point of view." "But," he continued, "it is providence that guides me and sometimes it suggests that we do certain things to excess." It is difficult to argue with providence.

The question for the next decade will be how long John Paul can keep it up and whether the rest of the church will want or be able to keep pace with him. For it is not always clear what the precise effect of the apocalyptic vision will be.

Will it repopulate the seminaries, for example? For those not attuned to the same pitch of heroism, it may be discouraging to hear the idea of temporary vocation being denounced: if the consequences of being mistaken are so catastrophic, and if all escape routes are blocked off, unheroic souls may prefer not to take the risk. And if the rhetoric of heroism may appeal to those in their 20s, there can be a rude awakening in middle age. An insistent little voice keeps on saying that priesthood should be measured not by the level of heroism but by the quality of service.

There have been one or two signs that the church, while being prepared to admire and applaud the exciting pontiff, is not always ready to follow him unquestioningly.

For example, in Chicago on Oct. 5, 1979, John Paul told the U.S. bishops what the line was on contraception and other disputed moral questions. Yet a year later, the U.S. bishops arrived at the synod with evidence to show that most U.S. Catholics did not accept the ban on contraception.

There was a genuine misunderstanding here. What, to the Angle-Saxon mind, could be more sensible than to give evidence based on questionnaires and polls? But in the heroic view this evidence is useless: it merely shows how far the rot has set in, and the urgency of decisive counteraction.

The Africans fell into the same misunderstanding. Although John Paul told them clearly enough in June that no concession would be made on "customary marriage," six months later they arrived at the synod and insisted on discussing this taboo topic as though he had never spoken.

These are two instances of "inoperative authority." But they also illustrate a language gap. It is as though in the stage foreground people come and go, discussing for the thousandth time birth control or women's ordinations. Meanwhile in the background, for those who have eyes to see, the real drama is being played out.

In Germany, John Paul told religious that prayer was "opening a breach to the invisible." Through the gap he sees clearly that "the history of mankind, and with it the history of the world . . . will be subject to rule by the word and the anti-word, the gospel and the anti-gospel." ❏

Part II

The Middle Years

17

Populism is guide for Polish pope as pontificate matures

(May 22, 1981) This is not, fortunately, an obituary, but an interim report. We do not yet know how long Pope John Paul's convalescence will take, but we can expect a pause in the frantic activity that has marked the pontificate so far. And two and a half years is certainly long enough to draw up a provisional assessment.

The most important fact about John Paul, despite his European culture and grasp of languages, is that he is Polish. This means he has a populist concept of the church. The leaders of the church act as the tribune of the people. They put into words the soul of the nation.

Hence the need for simplifying slogans. Hence the mass rallies he has conducted around the world. Hence the mistrust of those who "break ranks" or ask too many disturbing questions. John Paul's aim has been, to quote his own phrase, "to bring the joy of faith to a troubled world." He does not seem to know the meaning of the word doubt. It is not in his Polish lexicon.

This populist approach to some extent commends him in Latin America despite differences about "liberation theology." For as the final message of the 1979 Latin American bishops' meeting in Puebla, Mexico, makes clear, the Latin American bishops also speak in the name of their oppressed peoples — and there is no one else to speak for them.

It has been less successful in the United States and in Europe, where pluralism and democracy have accustomed people not to regard their opponents as misguided or insincere, and where "dissent" is not necessarily regarded as treason. Though he theorized about it in his philosophical work, John Paul seems to lack a concept of "loyal opposition."

Within the church his policies have all been based on the premise that things got badly out of hand during the post-conciliar period. Anarchy reigned. Discipline was lost. There was a crisis of priestly, religious and simple Catholic identity. He made it his aim to resolve this triple crisis by speaking out clearly on all disputed issues.

Priests were to be spiritual guides, not social activists. Religious were to return to their prayers and their habits. Theologians were painfully — in some cases — reminded of their primary duty of loyalty to the magisterium.

It would be wrong to see all these moves — and many others in the same vein — merely as an expression of "Polish" conservatism and clericalism. In John Paul's eyes they are a condition of speaking effectively to the world. If the bans on· artificial contraception, divorce and abortion were vigorously reaffirmed, this was first because they belong to the "law of God" and second because a divided church can offer only a muted message.

In an age of increasing tension and lackluster politicians, John Paul's international importance has been greatly enhanced. He is a beacon of sanity and good sense. He has spoken out on the rights of humans and the rights of small nations (here again Poland is his exemplar). He has carried his message to the United Nations in New York, to UNESCO in Paris and to Hiroshima in Japan. He has said yes to peace and detente, no to nuclear weapons.

He is out of tune with the prevailing mood among world leaders. This makes him — and through him the church — more than ever the lucid conscience of the nations. It is ironical that he should fall victim to the violence he has so steadfastly denounced. ❏

18

Bullets pare down papacy to 'Praised be Jesus Christ'

(May 29, 1981) "Praised be Jesus Christ" were the first words Pope John Paul II spoke from the loggia of St. Peter's Oct. 16, 1978, the day of his surprise election. And "Praised be Jesus Christ" were his first words, broadcast over the square May 17.

Then, with difficulty and in evident pain, he read out six sentences that will never be forgotten by those who hear them: "Dear brothers and sisters, I know that in these days, and especially in this moment of the *Regina Coeli*, you are united with me. I thank you for your prayers, and I bless you all. I am particularly close to the two people injured at the same time as me. I pray for the brother who attacked me, whom I have sincerely forgiven. United with Christ, the priest and victim, I offer my sufferings for the church and the world. To you, Mary, I say again: *"Totus tuus ego sum*; I am entirely yours."

After reciting the *Regina Coeli*, three Glory Be's, the prayer for the dead, and giving his blessing, he concluded with "Praised be Jesus Christ." It was as though the whole pontificate, thanks to the bullets of Mehmet Ali Agca, had suddenly been simplified, pared down to its essentials of prayer and praise.

The vast crowds, the chanted slogans, the great religious spectaculars that had marked the first phase of his papal ministry, were now over for the foreseeable future. But if the essence of the Petrine ministry is to be like Peter himself, a witness to the passion and resurrection of the Lord, then a stricken pope can do that better than a vigorous, globetrotting, superstar pope.

Like Peter himself. There has always been a contrast between St. Peter's Basilica and the reason it is there. It is a swaggering, Counter-Reformation statement about papal privileges, a defiant challenge to the Reformation notion that one could be faithful to apostolic doctrine without the intermediary of the pope. "Thou art Peter, and upon this rock I will build my church." The text is picked out in letters of gold. It has become an assertion about political power and doctrinal authority.

Move outside onto the square, and the same message is repeated even more exuberantly. One hundred forty windswept saints gesticulate and orate with total confidence. Doubt never afflicted them. But in the middle of the square stands an obelisk. It used to be the centerpiece of the circus of Caius and Nero, a few hundred yards to the left, between the Gianiculum and Vatican hills.

If the obelisk could speak, it could tell us what happened that chilly Oct. 13, A.D. 64 , when Peter of Galilee was crucified as the high point of entertainment. Nero was using the games to make Christians scapegoats for the fire that had devastated the city the previous July.

So the whole triumphant edifice of St. Peter's is built on a failure. There would be nothing here, or only expensive apartments, unless Peter's body had been reverently laid in a rock crevice, covered over and the spot marked.

But — apart from unrepented sin — there is no Christian failure. Or rather, it has a different coefficient. The pattern of Christ's life suggests that his passion, which was a form of defeat, was the pathway to the resurrection, which was his victory. That pattern was mirrored in the life of Peter. It has now touched John Paul.

He was prepared for it. Commentators reached for their clichés. They talked of "outrage," "indignation" and "dastardly crime" — and got it all wrong. They should have attended to John Paul's word. Since Easter Sunday his catechesis has been largely about the Good Shepherd who provides "the pattern for the ministry" and who is ready "to lay down his life for his flock."

John Paul, from his early philosophical studies, has always known that words and prayer itself are a form of commitment. They catch up with you sooner or later. They have to be "cashed." Sunday, May 17, John Paul's words reached a level of "authenticity" (to use another of his philosophical concepts) never before so limpidly attained.

The pontificate that had been frantic in pace and prodigal in words, suddenly entered a new dimension. There was pause for reflection, a moment of discernment.

But history does not stand still. On Monday, May 18, his 61st birthday, John Paul was inundated with gifts and good wishes from all over the world. There were some touching letters from the 20 children who were also patients in the Gemelli hospital. They had saved their candy money to buy him a present.

At 1:50 p.m., the doctors brought him the best gift of all. He was moved from the artificially lit intensive care unit on the third floor to a room on the 10th floor. From there he could glimpse the dome of St. Peter's. But later that day he received a most unwelcome present.

Italians had been voting in their five referendums. On each point, they opted for the status quo, which meant the relatively liberal law permitting abortion remains in force. The pro-life movement proposal, which would have restricted abortion to cases involving danger to the life or physical health of the mother, was massively rejected with 67.9 percent voting against it.

And in so doing they were going against the explicit orders ("advice" would be too weak a term) of the Italian bishops and John Paul himself. The bishops had said a "yes" vote was "gravely binding on the Christian conscience." John Paul, only the Sunday before Ali Agca's attack, had addressed a mass rally in St. Peter's Square and said, "This is a sacred cause." The opposition, he declared, had sunk into "moral insensibility and spiritual death."

If that is so, 67.9 percent of Italian citizens have blunted consciences and are spiritually moribund. They have snubbed the pope in the cruelest possible way, precisely when they might be expected to have sympathy for his feelings. The referendum result has demonstrated two things, which have an application far beyond Italy.

The first is that John Paul's immense popularity, his crowd-pulling appeal, does not mean people are listening to what he says, still less obeying him. *They like the singer, but not the song.*

The second lesson is that John Paul, when he recovers, will have to revise his "image" of Italy. He has so far thought of it as a Catholic country, and recalled it to its Catholic traditions. But the referendum result suggests this image is a mirage. Italy is not Poland.

It is a more secularized and pluralistic country than John Paul had imagined. And the referendum confirmed a continuing trend. In 1974, 55.8 percent defied episcopal orders and voted in favor of divorce. Now 67.9 percent have opted for legalized abortion.

Moreover, the Italians have shown themselves to be sophisticated politically. They can, and want, to distinguish between church and state, between morality and legality. They can conduct an open, democratic debate on moral issues without rending the nation apart.

The pro-life movement does not accept this. Its position is that it may have lost a battle, but it intends to go on fighting the war. The disquieting fact is that much of its support has come from rent-a-crowd groups who are intensely right wing religiously and politically.

Adriana Zarri, 62, the first woman to be admitted to the Italian Theological Association, has studied *Communione e Liberazione*, which has supplied many young recruits for the pro-life movement. She finds them "fanatical and neurotic."

"These people don't want to listen to arguments," she says, "their cultural level is low, and they merely repeat slogans. In their insecurity they cling to their leader . . . it has an atmosphere of fascism."

It is difficult to describe the reaction of the Roman curia to the referendum humiliation — difficult because no one is talking in public. Privately there are a few murmurs of "We told you so." Pope John Paul, the theory goes, does not know the Italian scene, and should not have committed himself so fully, thus running the risk of a rebuff.

The Christian Democrats, who know the score, were more discreet, refused to turn the campaign into a crusade, talked about the rights of conscience, and so lived to fight another day. There are elections in Rome and elsewhere June 21.

But such Machiavellian considerations would never count with John Paul, and the curia knows it. He likes his "yes" to be a "yes" and his "no," a firm "no." The Christian Democrats, of whom he does not have a high opinion anyway, have let him down.

They are not the only ones. There could be trouble brewing for the numerous priests and theologians who are on record as saying Catholics could, and in some cases should, vote in favor of the current abortion law. (This did not mean they favored abortion. They opposed it, but the argument was about law, not morality.)

John Paul's absence from the Vatican will not otherwise make much difference to the Roman curia. Business will be as usual. On all major points of policy, the pope has laid down the basic principles, and all the curia has to do is to carry them out. The impetus already given to the pontificate will see them through the next few months — at least as far as mid-July when the vacation begins.

The routine will continue. Anyone seeking an annulment — of a marriage or/and ordination, which is now being treated like marriage — will have the usual lengthy waiting time. The Congregation for the Doctrine of the Faith will continue to investigate the works of theologians deemed harmful to the ordinary faithful. (Dominican Fr. Edward Schillebeeckx has just got out of the wood for his *Christology*. He is likely to be thrust back there now that his book on ministry is out in English.)

The Secretariat for Christian Unity will continue to prepare hopeful papers on ecumenical questions, deeply regretting that the meeting with World Council of Churches officials in Geneva cannot now take place. And the so-called "ecumenical experts" of the CDF will continue to "shadow" their work, and find it wanting. No change there.

At the Congregation for the Causes of Saints, Cardinal Pietro Pallazzini will urge his men (yes, males) to work even harder for the beatification of Msgr. Escriva de Belaguer, founder of Opus Dei. To cheer the recuperating pope, he will want to speed the reports on Sr. Faustyna, the Polish nun who died in 1933 after visions in which she was told to encourage the cult of the divine mercy. (*Dives in Misericordia*, John Paul's second encyclical, may originate here.)

One difference the pope's absence will make is that those who invariably claim to be acting in his name will sound rather implausible. Even at the peak of physical fitness, John Paul could not supervise everything. He certainly cannot do so now.

That will make life particularly difficult for the Congregation for Bishops, headed by Cardinal Sebastiano Baggio. Though its task is merely to recommend candidates to the pope, who alone appoints them, it has great influence, as it works in liaison with the local papal representatives. But it does not have the last word. That is reserved to the pope personally. There is no system of delegation.

And there's the rub. The papacy is the last elective life monarchy in the world. There is no deputy-or-vice-pope, no one who is "a heartbeat away from the papacy."

But someone has to look after the shop. The cardinal secretary of state, Agostino Casaroli, a small, dapper, industrious and humorous diplomat, will have to hold the tangled threads together. He already presides at the monthly meetings of department heads. He, together with Archbishop Giovanni Coppa, oversees the team of Polish writers who have hitherto helped the pope in his enormous literary output. They are said to write effortlessly in his style.

And Casaroli will have to see to the daily dispatch of telegrams and telex messages to and from the world's trouble spots — from Lebanon to El Salvador, from Northern Ireland to, with some trepidation, Poland. A man of vast experience, he will play for safety, knowing the mind of the pope, and unwilling to take personal initiatives.

But it can't go on forever. Four months is the maximum time the pope's absence would not be noticed. By then the sub-empires would have been built. As this is a highly personalized papacy, which relies on John Paul's personal appearances, he cannot be away too long without the impetus being lost.

Meanwhile, the attack and its emotional impact will muffle the criticisms that were beginning to be heard about the style and substance of this pontificate. On June 4, during the visit to Switzerland, now obviously canceled, the theological students of the Catholic University of Fribourg had planned a demonstration. Their protest was to have been about the neglect of human rights within the church and the refusal to ordain women and married men. Cardinal Michele Pellegrino talked on similar themes only a month ago.

But now, out of sensitivity for the feelings of the patient, these things cannot be said. Yet they will not go away. The temptation to make silence and sympathy a loyalty test will be great.

The other temptation will be to use a rhetoric of indignation that slides to the edge of orthodoxy. Cardinal Ugo Poletti, who looks after the Rome diocese on the pope's behalf, said at a meeting in St. Peter's Square: "We make a prayer of reparation for this insane act which, directed against the sacred person of the pope, is directed against the God whom he represents, and the humanity which he loves as a father."

The Vatican newspaper, *L'Osservatore Romano*, has been writing in the same exalted vein. Its deputy editor, Fr. Virgilio Levi, assured its readers John Paul was saved from death because he was "protected by Our Lady of Fatima. This is not the product of pious imagination," he gravely added. In that case, he must have access to sources not made available in the Vatican press office.

The office has been totally transformed by the shooting. It has lost control of the papal news operations. Its monopoly has been broken. With the operating team at the Gemelli hospital talking to all and sundry and Digos, the security police, always willing to spin a conspiracy theory, the action has moved elsewhere. That is not necessarily better, but it is different.

I will end where I began with that extraordinary Sunday, May 17, when the bells rang out across St. Peter's Square. Despite everyone's awareness of the pope's sufferings, it was a joyful occasion. There came to mind what John Paul had said in Harlem: "We are the Easter people, and alleluia is our song. If we do not proclaim that, the very stones will cry out." That is the heart of the Petrine ministry. All the rest is Vaticanology. ❑

19

Labor encyclical: Worker, not capital, key to moral order

(September 25, 1981) Pope John Paul, eager to forestall interpretations of his third encyclical that would reduce it to a commentary on recent events in Poland, explains that the original intention had been to publish it May 15, the 90th anniversary of Leo XIII's encyclical *Rerum Novarum.*

"But," the pope confides, "it is only after my stay in hospital that I have been able to revise it definitively" (27). Since the assassination attempt was May 13, John Paul is saying that, in top form, he could "definitively revise" an encyclical in a single day.

The purpose of *Laborem Exercens* — the title does not come trippingly off the tongue — is, in the pope's own words, "to highlight — perhaps more than has been done before — the fact that human work is a key, probably the *essential key*, to the whole social question, if we try to see that question really from the point of view of man's good" (3).

Encyclicals have not usually used the language of "perhaps" and "probably." They have laid down the law without hesitation. One should not conclude that *Laborem Exercens* is a tentative document, but it is more like a position paper for discussion than an authoritative statement.

Its starting point is the Book of Genesis, where Adam is told to "subdue the earth." In this way he becomes a cocreator and realizes the image of God in himself. It may seem a far cry from this doctrine to the world of automation and microchip, and John Paul is aware of the distance to be traveled. But he insists the ancient doctrine is still relevant.

The fact that John Paul makes the Book of Genesis his starting point is interesting for two reasons. First, because he wishes to say Christian "social doctrine" did not start in 1891 with Leo XIII's encyclical. Second, because this "social morality," as he also calls it, is based not on some natural law theory but on revelation.

The Book of Genesis provides the criterion or yardstick by which we can judge all work. Does it consist in making things which are of use to human persons and which build community? And next: is it the sort of activity in which the human person can find fulfillment and the satisfaction of his or her deepest desires?

The Greeks thought certain work was suitable only for slaves and therefore beneath the dignity of "free men" (from which we get the concept of the "liberal professions"). But, says John Paul, this distinction is broken down in the gospels. They show Jesus "devoted most of his life on earth to manual work at the carpenter's bench" (6). This suggests that who is working is as important as what he or she is doing.

John Paul stresses the great diversity of human work, which makes generalization difficult. Anyway, "work" has never described a single activity. He sees "new forms of work appearing, while others disappear" (8). He thinks "toil" is a feature of much work, but it is a "good thing for man — a good thing for his humanity — because through work man *not only transforms nature*, adapting it to his own needs, but he also achieves *fulfillment* as a human being" (9).

Half of humanity, already irritated by use of the term *man* for humanity, would not be impressed by the fact that the detailed list of toilers in Section 9 concludes with "women who, sometimes without recognition on the part of society and even of their own families, bear the daily burden and responsibility for their homes and the upbringing of their children."

John Paul sees homemaking as a mother's "primary mission," and therefore home is the place where she should be. "Having to abandon these tasks," he goes on, "in order to take up paid work outside the home is wrong from the point of view of the good of society and of the family" (19).

And if the mother is the homemaker, the husband is seen as the breadwinner. That is why the suggestion of a "family wage" is included in the discussion of the "just wage" (19). The family is defined as "a community made possible by work" and also as a "school of work" (10). The sense that one is "working for others," he suggests, can be the way in which monotonous work, even the most alienating, can be rescued from meaninglessness (6).

Part 3 of the encyclical, subtitled "The conflict between labor and capital in the present phase of history," plants several sticks of dynamite. For here John Paul descends from the stratosphere of principles and starts to draw some conclusions from what he calls a "postulate" (15) or fundamental axiom: that is, "the priority of labor over capital."

What does this axiom mean? In the first place it leads to a severe judgment on "unrestrained capitalism," on all who think the free play of market forces alone is the best way to organize the economy. John Paul justifies his preference for labor over capital on the ground that labor (work) creates value by transforming natural resources, while capital is a mere instrument that sets the process of work in motion. In opting for labor rather than capital, John Paul is preferring persons to things.

He then does his professorial best to spell out what he means. He thinks the opposition between labor and capital should be broken down. The worker at his workbench has a double inheritance: on the one hand he or she is taking natural resources and turning them into something of service to humanity; on the other hand he or she needs a set of expensive instruments, tools or machines, all of which require capital. Conclusion: labor and capital should work harmoniously together.

But in practice they do not. They have been antagonistic, and theories have been developed to legitimate and exult this antagonism. They are known as "capitalism" and "communism." In common, they reduce the human person to *homo oeconomicus*. He or she becomes a mere pawn in their projects, an instrument in their impersonal schemes. At this point John Paul declares a plague on both these ideological houses.

The question then becomes: how can one devise a method of organizing human work which replaces the antagonism of labor and capital with their cooperation? One only has to ask this question to see it answered. If cooperation is to be the norm, then "proposals for joint ownership of the means of work-sharing by the workers in the management and/or profit of businesses, so-called shareholding by labor, etc." (14) are the way forward.

The trouble is that copartnership and other forms of worker participation are hardly off the drawing board. John Paul himself wonders whether "these various proposals can or cannot be applied concretely" (14). He must know that Yugoslavia is about the only country which (in theory) has attempted a form of self-management on a systematic basis. And it is interesting that the Polish union Solidarity should have proposed something similar at its first-ever congress in Gdansk earlier this month.

Better to denounce systems which forget about "man," John Paul coins a new word: *economism*. "Economism" apparently refers to any system of economic organization that reduces the worker to an instrument, deprives him or her of intelligent choices about his or her work, and in effect makes him or her a wage slave. This can happen under capitalism or communism.

John Paul deplores what he calls "rigid capitalism" (14). For "rigid" read inflexible. Leo XIII, he points out, asserted the right to private property, but he did not say this right was "absolute and untouchable" (14). The right to private property is enough to reject the Marxist solution of "collectivization," but it does not mean "anything goes." It has to be set in the context of the "common use" of all the world's goods. (This was the principle that justified Robin Hood who "robbed the rich to feed the poor." If I am dying of hunger, I can steal apples from the orchard of the rich man.)

If Section 3 seeks to establish a truce in the class war, the next section, called "the rights of workers," is an attempt to work out a universal bill of rights for workers everywhere. No one can complain that it is imprecise or not specific.

It asserts the right to work, to a just wage, to paid holidays, to pension schemes and insurance, to strike (but not indiscriminately and only as a last resort). Then there are rights for specific groups: the right of the disabled to professional training and work, and the right of immigrants to be treated — and rewarded — in the same way as other workers.

The most withering condemnation in the encyclical is here. Multinational or transnational companies are said to "fix the highest possible prices for their products, while trying at the same time to fix the lowest possible prices for raw materials or semi-manufactured goods" (17). This practice not only increases the division between the haves and have-nots, but it also has a catastrophic effect on working conditions in Third World countries.

John Paul is similarly blunt about unemployment, saying "it is in all cases an evil and, when it reaches a certain level, can become a real social disaster" (18). Its demoralizing effects on the young are noted. It could well be thought that unemployment, in the United States and in Britain, has already reached the level at which it has become "a real social disaster." Are we therefore morally obliged to attack the "monetarist" policies which have led to mass unemployment?

The most baffling passage concerns labor or trade unions. Inevitably it will be read in the light of the experience of Poland's Solidarity. Obviously the "right of association" is defended, as it was by Leo XIII in 1891, and it is the basis of unemployment existence as a free union in a country that previously only had party-controlled unions.

But what are unions for? John Paul's answer is that "their task is to defend existential interests of workers in all sectors in which their rights are concerned" (20). They are in the business welfare. The do not exist to reflect class divisions, and even if at times they are inevitably involved in "struggle," this is motivated by a quest for social justice, "not for the sake of struggle or in order to eliminate the opponent" (20). This sounds like pragmatic advice for Solidarity.

If taken seriously elsewhere, it would mean the end of the British Labor Party and many other Western political parties that depend upon union support. A sensible and arguable case can be made for saying unions should be independent of political parties. But it is more difficult to present this as a major tenet of "Catholic social doctrine."

And this is the difficulty with *Laborem Exercens* taken as a whole. It is a deliberate attempt to breathe some new life into Catholic social doctrine. In the post-conciliar period, it was frequently said Catholic social doctrine — as expounded in the encyclicals of Leo XIII and Pius XI — was moribund.

This doctrine worked on too high a level of generality. No one paid any attention to it. The only politicians who claimed to be implementing it were the Fascist dictators, Francisco Franco of Spain and Antonio Oliveira Salazar of Portugal.

And Pope Paul VI acknowledged the demise of Catholic social doctrine. In *Octogesima Adveniens* (which, like this encyclical, was also in commemoration of *Rerum Novarum*), Paul VI admitted: "In view of the varied situations in the world, it is difficult to give one teaching to cover them all or to offer a solution which has universal value. This is not our intention or even our mission."

So the buck was passed to the local churches, which tried, in their various ways, to "discern the signs of the times." The theology of liberation was one attempt to fill the vacuum and to show the continuing relevance of Christian faith to political and social life.

John Paul does not accept Paul VI's pessimistic diagnosis. He believes Catholic social doctrine can be revived, and that it is possible to sketch a blueprint for a renewed human society. Ignoring the frontiers of capitalism and communism, he tries to say what would happen ideally if the human persona were placed at the center of all our thinking about work. The answer is — with all the ambiguity of the term — utopia. ❏

20

The Roman pope is still a Pole

(October 16, 1981) Any assessment of the first three years of Pope John Paul's pontificate has to reckon with "the Polish factor." Apart from two years of study in Rome (1946-48), he spent his first 58 years in Poland. Even when, as bishop and cardinal, he began to travel, his first call was always on Polish communities in exile. Despite his mastery of an astonishing number of languages — and his cheerful readiness to tackle new ones — he is in no sense "cosmopolitan" and remains defiantly Polish. So far, so obvious.

The difficulty lies in saying how this Polishness affects his pontificate. The temptation is to equate Polishness and conservatism (in church matters) and leave it at that. But being Polish is not just a blinkered limitation; it provides a different perspective on the world from which we can all learn something.

Certainly Polish national consciousness is highly developed, so much so that a character in Kazimierz Brandys' novel, *A Question of Identity*, remarks that many of his compatriots behave "as if the individual in Poland had no psychology of his own, as if there were only a national psychology." That is nonsense, of course. There must be no question of reducing Karol Wojtyla to a specimen Pole. But anyone who wishes to understand him must start here.

John Paul has made this easier by talking about his past. He has evoked memories that explain his current attitudes. I want to describe some of those experiences here: they are material toward the intellectual autobiography he will probably never now write.

The first experience was that of defeat, in 1939, and the Nazi occupation which followed. It changed his life. It turned the poetry-writing, would-be actor into an intellectual priest of steely determination. In Brazil John Paul traced the start of his vocation to this wartime experience. The horrors he witnessed convinced him that only *spiritual* remedies could overcome them.

So whenever John Paul echoes the language of Jacques Maritain and talks about "the primacy of the spiritual" (to the annoyance or despair of liberation theologians), he is referring to this fundamental experience.

Another aspect of his wartime experience moved him deeply: the closeness of Auschwitz. It is only 17 miles from Wadowice, where he was born and brought up, and only 238 miles from Kraków. It is not unfair to say John Paul is haunted by the thought of Auschwitz (which he always calls, properly, by its Polish name, O´swięcim). He has referred to it as "this Golgotha of the modern world."

This helps to explain the "apocalyptic" strain in the thinking of John Paul. For Auschwitz represented evil on a gigantic, almost cosmic scale. Civilization is a thin veneer, easily set aside. Auschwitz was — a favorite Slav theme — a continuation of the passion of Christ. Yet only if this suffering is accepted can it be transformed, and only then can the reality of the resurrection be glimpsed.

This was not a theory, any more than heaped ashes of Auschwitz were a theory. For it had been embodied in the story of Fr. Maximilian Kolbe, the 47-year-old Franciscan who sacrificed his life to save a married man.

There is good reason for thinking most people have their "picture" of the world settled by about age 25. In John Paul's case the sense of life as an all-encompassing, life-or-death struggle between good and evil was summed up in Auschwitz. And this fundamental experience relativizes other questions. It makes it difficult for him to take seriously what we may call "the liberal agenda" for the church. Talk about birth control and women's ordination seems like irrelevant noises offstage if the center of the stage is occupied by the vast cosmic drama.

Auschwitz also contributed to his "model" of the priest: for Kolbe, the single-minded champion, "laid down his life for his flock." In the Sundays before the shooting, John Paul meditated on these texts about the Good Shepherd, whom he came so close to emulating himself.

* * *

Many other factors helped shape John Paul's concept of the priest. One can get a good idea of the Polish background in this matter from an article written by Fr. Adam Boniecki, from the Kraków diocese, who is now in Rome as editor of the Polish version of *L'Osservatore Romano*. Boniecki makes three points about the priest in Poland that throw light on our theme.

The first is that priests do not quarrel with their bishops and bishops do not quarrel with one another. "There is not, and cannot be," he writes, "any contestation in the Polish church." This idyll does not come about because Polish priests are more virtuous than others. It is a product of the embattled state of the church. The church is in a "to be or not to be" situation, and therefore any hint of dissent will be self-censored by the potential dissident if not suppressed by the bishop.

It would be interesting to know whether Solidarity has had any effects on church life and whether assistant pastors are banding together to discuss their lot. I doubt it. The exhortations to justice and democracy are addressed to the state or the Communist Party, and are not seen as applying to the internal life of the church. In all John Paul's vast output, there has been no praise for diocesan or national councils of priests. They have been mentioned only in the conclusion to the Dutch synod, where it was discouragingly said they should not resemble labor unions.

The emphasis on uniformity helps to explain John Paul's distaste, indeed incomprehension, when faced by "dissident" priests or theologians (and *a fortiori* dissident sisters or laypeople). He turns sadly away — or takes decisive action. He is insensitive to the argument that a totally united hierarchy is an incredible myth that can only be purchased at the price of suppressing differences. He told the German bishops at Fulda it was nonsense to suppose that making public their divisions would make them more credible. Unity is all.

So Polish priests are docile and obedient. Or if they are not, they depart on tiptoe. Boniecki reports that one priest friend of his preferred to resign from the priesthood because he could not, in conscience, impose the strict teaching of *Humanae Vitae* on his inadequately housed people. How many priests in the West have done the same?

The third relevant point Boniecki makes about Polish priests had better be given in his own words: "For other colleagues, the decisive problem was celibacy. Public opinion treats very badly a priest who leaves the ministry. It favors clerical celibacy. Nobody proclaims publicly a departure. It is rather concealed as though it were something shameful."

This is exactly the thinking that lay behind the latest "Norms for Laicization" (Oct. 27, 1980). The request for laicization is a disgrace and a confession of failure. The procedure has now been made as difficult as possible. And above all there can be no question of these undesirables exercising any future role in the church.

Cardinal Franjo Seper's letter accompanying the new norms said "the widespread diffusion of this phenomenon (that is, laicization) has inflicted a painful blow on the church." One would like to know the evidence for this statement; there is only a "painful blow" if one starts from the presuppositions noted above.

So John Paul's model priest is male, celibate, committed for life, dressed in clerical black, docile, prayerful, if need be heroic, holy and apolitical. His Holy Thursday 1979 letter spelled it out. Some apologists were so dumbfounded by it that they invented the fantastic tale that the conclave had drawn up some such document and imposed it on a reluctant pope.

But style and content proved it was his own work. What is more, he subsequently defended his letter against various rather imprecise attacks. "Here and there," he said when speaking to Polish priests at Czestochowa, "it has been suggested that the pope was trying to impose the Polish model of the priesthood on the whole world."

These anonymous critics, however, were brushed aside with the remark: "But these were isolated voices looking for something that was not there." Then John Paul conceded the whole case in his next paragraph: "I left Poland in the deep conviction that it was only with this vision of the priesthood that the church would survive."

* * *

The notion that Polish priests are apolitical may seem fanciful or absurd. At least on the top level of the hierarchy, they are up to their necks in politics. Cardinal Stefan Wyszynski did not need the ancient tradition of the primate being the inter-rex, the regent who governed in the absence of a king, to make constant political judgments. A stream of advice, exhortation and condemnations flowed from his vigorous pen. His successor, Archbishop Józef Glemp, has already started to behave the same way. Wojtyla was just as heavily involved.

Why, then, this paradoxical insistence that "priests should keep out of politics" when manifestly prelates do not? The answer is partly a semantic point. Until Solidarity turned the place upside down, political life in Poland meant the life of the Communist Party (or the United Workers' Party as it was ironically known). The party was the only manifestation of political activity that had government approval. So keeping out of politics was merely another way of keeping out of activities sponsored by the Communist Party.

Since this banal principle was of limited usefulness outside the specific Polish situation, when transferred to other countries (for example, Brazil, Nicaragua or the United States) it became an exhortation to stay out of *party* politics. And the rationale changed: now it was alleged that a priest should not be active in a political party because, as the sign of unity, he should not take stands on issues that are likely to prove divisive among his people. Fr. Robert Drinan cannot be a Democratic congressman because this will upset Catholic Republicans.

However, keeping out of politics or even party politics still leaves plenty of scope for other and perhaps more important forms of political commitment. John Paul's commitment could be most clearly seen during his visit to his homeland in June 1979. He exercised four interrelated "roles," all thoroughly political.

In the first place he appeared as the advocate of counterculture, an alternative society, based on the long intertwining of church and nation in Polish history. Edward Gierek, not yet disgraced and dismissed, spoke routinely of the achievement of 35 years of socialism. John Paul in reply pointedly ignored this and talked instead of the more than 1,000-year-old tradition of Poland. With that malicious wit of which he is capable, he congratulated Gierek on rebuilding the royal palace in Warsaw, "as a symbol of Polish sovereignty."

Second, John Paul in Poland acted as a kind of "tribune of the people." A bishop or a cardinal grows in authority in Poland (and no doubt elsewhere) if he can put into words what people are feeling but dare not say. In Victory Square, Warsaw, June 2, 1979, his sermon was interrupted for more than 10 minutes when he said: "Christ cannot be kept out of the history of man in any part of the globe. The exclusion of Christ from human history is an act against man."

At this there were chants of "We want God!" "We want God!" just like a football crowd. It was an extraordinary moment in the capital of a Communist country where atheism is officially inculcated from the nursery school to the university. Yet John Paul had done nothing very difficult. He had simply articulated what most Poles believe.

And the earth had not opened to swallow him up. At this moment — I believe — Solidarity became possible and likely. The pope had shown the Poles that the regime's bluff could be called, that perfect order could be kept without force and that the gap between rhetoric and reality could be closed. In this sense the papal visit to Poland was "destabilizing," and it was meant to be.

Yet John Paul did not behave as a demagogue, who merely flatters people by telling them what they want to know. As "tribune of the people," he also behaved responsibly. He incited no one to rebellion. But in exchange for this "moderation," he hoped the church would be able to secure better conditions for itself in negotiations with the state. Here John Paul appears as a "realist" with a keen sense of the "possible."

This was the tone he struck in his address to the Polish bishops at Czestochowa: "We are aware that this dialogue cannot be easy, because it takes place between two concepts of the world that are diametrically opposed. But it must be made possible and effective since the good of individuals and nations demand it" (June 5, 1979).

The context makes it plain that the "dialogue" envisaged is not a process in which the church expects to learn anything. It is rather a negotiation from a position of strength in order to gain certain rights. In return the church will not seek to overthrow the government. But that is a modest enough concession, and does not reveal any great enthusiasm for the "building of socialism." But that, in the nature of the case, is ruled out, because "the two concepts of the world are diametrically opposed."

So there will be a long and unyielding war of attrition, unless the link between "socialism" and the ideology which underpins it is weakened or dissolved. On a humbler and more day-to-day level, pragmatic considerations ("the good of individuals and the nation") can lead to cooperation. Here the pope's role is that of the tough, patient, wary negotiator who is sure to drive a hard bargain.

The fourth role, finally, is that of prophet or visionary. At the tomb of St. Adalbert, the Czech who in the 10th century had gone to convert the Baltic peoples at the invitation of King Bodeslaw the Brave, John Paul prayed for all Slavs everywhere. He wondered whether God had not chosen him, the first Polish pope, to bring a special Slav witness to the world. "Is not the Holy Spirit disposed" he asked, "to see that this Polish pope, this Slav pope, should at this very moment reveal the spiritual unity of Christian Europe?" (Gniezno, June 3, 1979)

In that setting it was an astonishing claim. The Slav peoples, without exception, are within the Soviet "sphere of influence" — but only by a temporary aberration of history, John Paul seemed to be saying. Does he therefore believe "the spiritual unity of Christian Europe," expressed inchoately in and through the church, can and should be matched by political unity? I think he does, though in God's mysterious ways.

This is another instance of the primacy of the spiritual that means so much to him. First think the right thoughts and change will follow. He consciously and deliberately inverts the Marxist theory of "dialectical materialism," which alleges that intellectual changes follow upon material changes. To talk of "the spiritual unity of Christian Europe" is a challenge to ignore frontiers on the map and to think of those "frontiers of the mind" of which Karol Wojtyla spoke in the last article written before he became pope.

His parents, he noted, had the passport of a foreign state (the Austro-Hungarian empire) while belonging to the Polish nation. This distinction between state and nation comes easily and spontaneously to him. For in the 19th century, during the partition of Poland, the Polish state had ceased to exist while the "nation" survived, its sense of identity maintained by the combination of church, culture and language.

This explains why John Paul is skeptical of states and enamored of nations. It is because, in the Polish experience, the "state" has so often been a tyranny or at least an imposition; and in preferring the "nation," John Paul is also making an appeal to the "people" over the heads of the state rulers. The roots of his instinctive "populism" lie here. The crowds that gather to hear him are voting with their feet, implicitly taking part in an informal plebiscite.

In his speech to UNESCO in Paris June 2, 1980 (almost exactly one year after his "spiritual unity" address), John Paul exhorted the whole world to protect and cherish the nation as the "apple of your eyes." Knowing that for some of his listeners the idea of "nation" has been tarnished because of its association with "nationalism," he directly appealed to his Polish experiences as the source and vindication of his theory of the nation.

He said: "The nation is the community that has a history which surpasses the history of the individual or the family. . . . In everything I am now saying, my words come from a particular experience, and are a *special witness*. I am the son of a nation that has undergone many experiences in history, a nation that has been condemned to death by its neighbors several times, and yet which has remained itself. It preserved its identity, and despite partitions and countless occupations, it preserved its national sovereignty, not by relying on physical strength but solely by *relying on culture*" (italics in the original French text).

Polish novelist Brandys has an illuminating comment which fills out this rather abstract statement and goes some way toward explaining the peculiar intensity of the national consciousness: Poland is a country that "for 200 years has been compelled to adopt the reflex of self-defense, a country which has only survived by means of prayers, of secret universities and of banned books; a country which, at a time when Western societies were achieving their unity, had only one goal: to survive."

In John Paul's vision of the world, the Polish experience is in some sense exemplary. And the political consequence of stressing the nation in this way is that it provides grounds for denouncing "interference in the internal affairs of another country." So in Poland he denounced imperialism, whether military, economic or political, and everyone assumed he was referring to the "friendly neighbor to the East." But the same remark was repeated in Africa where it was an exhortation to the superpowers to stay out of the continent, and it has been used in connection with Lebanon as a polite way of urging the Syrians to go home. This attitude also makes him sympathetic toward the Palestinians, another "people" without a "state."

But there are difficulties about making Poland an exemplary nation. The particular fusion of culture and Catholicism is found nowhere else. True, John Paul tried to rekindle it in France, which is why he concluded his Le Bourget sermon with the anachronistic apostrophe: "France, eldest daughter of the church, are you faithful to your baptismal promises?" In Brazil, too, he linked the birth of the nation with the first Mass said there on the feast of the Holy Cross, 1500 (which led the Indians to point out that they were there long before the Portuguese arrived). Again in the Philippines he said Mass in Cebu City, where Ferdinand Magellan planted a cross in 1521.

Germany, however, presented a more difficult problem than these ostensibly Catholic countries. For Lutheranism is the main determinant of its culture and tradition. John Paul solved this by setting up an "image" of Germany in which only its Catholic past had a place. His Germany was peopled by Boniface, a Cornish monk who evangelized the place, St. Albert the Great, teacher of Thomas Aquinas, a few medieval mystics and then with a great leap of the pontifical seven-league boots, on to the 19th century and Bishop Wilhelm von Ketteler, the workers' friend and inspirer of Leo XIII, and so on to the heroic anti-Nazis who perished in concentration camps.

When he visits Great Britain next summer — it looks as though this is still on — John Paul will be faced with an even more difficult problem of fitting together the nation and the state. For the one state is made up of four identifiable nations — England, Scotland, Wales and Northern Ireland — and if he pursues the "sovereignty of the nation" theme, he may well find himself endorsing Welsh and Scottish separatism and possibly even the Irish Republican Army.

Another problem is that English national consciousness was largely fashioned by the Reformation. I expect John Paul will solve this problem in the way he solved the German problem: by inventing an "image" of England in which its heroes are Augustine of Canterbury, King Edward the Confessor, St. Thomas à Becket (parallel with St. Stanislaw of Kraków), St. Thomas More ("died for the papacy"), John Henry Newman ("saw the light") and the late Cardinal John Carmel Heenan ("the model of a priest today").

The visit to Japan was interesting in that it was the only one so far where it would be difficult to claim Catholicism had made a notable contribution to shaping national consciousness. But even in these discouraging circumstances, John Paul showed that the martyrs of Nagasaki were important in Japanese history. For the rest he was obliged to fall back on the "natural virtues" in the Japanese tradition.

All John Paul's visits, then, have been essentially to *peoples* and to *nations*. Not only does he understand the nation on the analogy of Poland, but he has tried to assign nations some place in the scheme of divine providence. So Brazil becomes an instance of harmony among different races, and the Philippines has the missionary task of opening the Far East. It proves more difficult to assign a mission to secularized Europe and to the United States as superpower.

But during the U.S. trip John Paul brought out the *vocation* of the country to feed and serve the world's poor; and he saw the United States as a new nation arising from many nations — *e pluribus unum*, as he quoted in Grant Park.

It is fair to conclude that all John Paul's thinking and attitudes are conditioned by the fact that he is Polish. This is simply a cultural fact, onto which hasty labels should not be clapped. There are truths which the Polish perspective makes it difficult for him to appreciate, as there are others he can perceive more easily. He takes seriously, I believe, the title of a book written in 1940, *Poland, the Key to Europe*, written by L.S. Buell. On the frontier between East and West, Catholic and Orthodox, Slav by race and Latin by tradition, Poland could exercise a reconciling function.

One of John Paul's most significant acts was to make the two brothers, Ss. Cyril and Methodius, coequal patrons of Europe, along with St. Benedict, who had been assigned this office in 1964. Cyril and Methodius set out from Constantinople in the 10th century to convert the Slav peoples of the Balkans. They even reached the southern part of Poland.

"They were the true apostles of the Slav Peoples," said John Paul: "In translating the liturgy into Old Slavonic, they not only made a great contribution to evangelization but also to the culture of the Slav people, and indeed provided its foundation."

So by making the brothers patrons of Europe, John Paul was issuing another reminder of the "wider Europe" he had proclaimed at Gniezno. Like Charles de Gaulle, another who thought in terms of *l'Europe des nations*, he sees Europe as stretching from the Atlantic to the Urals. He does not take kindly to the European Community, partly because it contains the most dangerously secularized Catholics in the world (in Holland, West Germany and France) and partly because it has usurped the adjective "European," which properly belongs to the whole continent.

Cyril and Methodius become a compensation for the injustices of history, which has slighted the East, and Poland in particular, at the expense of the West. John Paul thinks it is his providential mission to put that imbalance right. ❏

21

Burgeoning papal literary industry

(November 6, 1981) John Paul II had his doubts about the wisdom of translating and republishing his 1972 book, *Sources of Renewal*. His doubts did him credit. For the book was written at speed and had a limited purpose: to provide a "working paper" for the Kraków diocesan synod which was to start 10 years after the first session of Vatican II. Since at that date no edition of the documents of Vatican II was available in Poland, most of the book — one-third on a rough estimate — consists of lengthy quotations from the council documents. So the book is not really for us at all.

Even so, it would be helpful if it allowed us to glimpse how Cardinal Karol Wojtyla interpreted the council and discover which of its insights seemed the most important to him. But it does not really do that, because for the most part the author merely provides linking passages that carry him safely to the next quotation.

Lest this judgment seem unduly harsh, consider a comment from Halina Bortnowska, a theologian and pastoral worker from Nowa Huta near Kraków, who was entrusted by John Paul himself with the task of producing a more readable and accessible version of *Sources of Renewal*. This has now appeared in Italian with the title *The Enrichment of Faith* (*L'Arricchimento della Fede*). It has been published by the Vatican Press.

Bortnowska says in her introduction: "It (*Sources of Renewal*) was a first and provisional sketch. The author hides behind numerous quotations from the council. Often he does not give his own thought, but rather suggests: Read this text in the light of that other text. . . . The council texts and they alone occupy the stage, and there is no appeal to post-conciliar discussions or even conciliar discussions. One has an impression of great abstractness and remoteness from the world of people in search of a direction for their life."

Love and Responsibility is an altogether more important book which introduces the interested reader to Wojtyla's characteristic philosophical style. It is based on lectures given in the Catholic University of Lublin in 1958-59.

The book can be considered as a treatise on the nature of love. It differs from most previous theological presentations of the topic in that it takes seriously, and attempts to integrate, "the sexual urge." To that extent, it may be called post-Freudian. And it foreshadowed the Wednesday audiences which — until interrupted by Mehemet Ali Agca's bullets — also dealt with themes such as "shame" and the possibility of "raping one's wife."

Wojtyla's starting point is a distinction between "using" and "loving." To "use" someone is to reduce him or her to a means to an end. But "anyone who treats a person as the means to an end does violence to the very essence of the other." The alternative to "using" is "loving," which comes about when "two different people consciously choose a common aim."

The ramifications of this simple principle are considerable, and they extend far beyond the man-woman relationship, which is what he chiefly has in view. The consequences of this doctrine for industrial work are noted (thus anticipating *Laborem Exercens*).

Further, this discussion explains why John Paul uses the words *consumer* and *consumerism* in such an odd way. For those affected by Ralph Nader, consumerism means being a wise and discriminating consumer. It is a good thing. But John Paul is thinking of the Latin root, *consumere* which means to "use" or "use up," to exploit.

This is linked with his denunciation of utilitarianism in which, as he sees it, others are reduced to their "usefulness" to me. This leads to his simultaneous attacks on capitalism and communism, because both are different forms of utilitarianism. Only when the concept of "good" is introduced can morality begin.

Anyone who wishes to understand how John Paul's mind works might start here. The task is made easier in that H.T. Willetts' splendid translation avoids gobbledegook.

But something else has to be said. *Love and Responsibility* has two prefaces by the author, one written in 1960 and the other in 1980. In 1960, Bishop Wojtyla replies to the argument that "only those who live a conjugal life can pronounce on the subject of marriage" and, more intriguingly, "only those who have experienced it can pronounce on love between man and woman." His reply is to concede a lack of "firsthand" knowledge, but to assert a superior and much "wider" knowledge derived from "pastoral experience." By 1980 he has become even more confident about the rightness of his method and the soundness of his doctrine. For the book has gone on being written, he says, in the lives of those who put it into practice.

So we find the astonishing claim: "This work is open to every echo of experience, from whatever quarter it comes, and it is at the same time an appeal to all to let experience, their own experience, make itself heard, to its full extent: in all its breadth and in all its depth. . . . *Love and Responsibility*, with this sort of methodological basis, fears nothing and can fear nothing which can be legitimized by experience. Experience does not have to be afraid of experience. Truth can only gain from such a confrontation."

It is difficult to resist this torrent of rhetoric — certainly one of the boldest appeals to theological empiricism one would be able to find in papal literature. One tends to forget that he is nevertheless talking about *other people's* experience.

Not everyone's experience coincides with the "ideal" experience described by the author, namely, that the use of artificial birth control involves treating the other partner as an object, "using" him or her, and so the doctrine of *Humanae Vitae* is both anticipated and confirmed by personalistic reflection. And how can one seriously claim to be trusting experience when as soon as someone produces hard evidence (as Archbishop John J. Quinn did at the last synod), it is dismissed as mere sociological head-counting. *Whose* experience is being talked about?

John Paul's account of the aftermath of *Humanae Vitae* is revealing. He distinguishes two phases. In phase one there was "a rather chaotic search for arguments and counterarguments as each side sought to win over supporters." But that is now all over. In phase two the debate has moved to "a stage of self-examination of a methodologically profounder kind."

Because he believes we are in this second phase, John Paul is convinced the hour of *Love and Responsibility* has struck. It is now more relevant than ever. After all, it is "a work untouched by the atmosphere of animosity, of polemic and counter-polemic, a work the spirit of which is determined by its sole concern: to ensure a hearing for all the truths that experience can furnish on the subject of love worthy of the human person."

It is all very well to evoke this atmosphere of tranquillity. But the "tranquillity" was more apparent than real, and it came about only because one side in the debate was not allowed to speak. Is it anyway conceivable that a Polish bishop in 1960 would have reached any conclusion other than the one taught by the church at that date? And if somehow he had reached the contrary conclusion in the light of experience, would he have published a book to say so?

The answer to both questions is a resounding "no." Moreover, his absence from the debate of the 1960s and 1970s means he appears not to have considered all the difficulties of his own positions. The central assertion in the personalist case in favor of the traditional view of contraception is this: "When the idea that 'I may become a father/I may become a mother' is totally rejected in the mind and will of husband and wife, nothing is left of the marital relationship, objectively speaking, except mere sexual enjoyment. One person becomes an object of use for another person."

The difficulties of this argument are too obvious and too numerous to need spelling out. But perhaps the most important feature of *Love and Responsibility* is that it abandons the old separable function-based natural law theory (the tongue is *for* telling the truth, the sexual organs are *for* procreation) and tries to apply the criterion of the fulfillment of the human persons involved, their growth in humanity. This is a crucial shift, and if taken with the "appeal to experience" noted above, could lead to conclusions that might surprise us all.

George Huntston Williams, in *The Mind of John Paul II*, remarks that *Love and Responsibility* makes most sense if one sees it in context. It concentrates on the "vocational problems of young Catholics" as they face the choice: marriage, priesthood or religious life. This is helpful. Williams' book is not so much a biography as an account of the setting — cultural, political, intellectual, theological — from which Wojtyla emerged.

Williams is well-equipped for this task. A Protestant theologian and the historian of post-Reformation Poland, he spent a semester in Lublin in 1952 where he was an academic colleague of Wojtyla; he has an interest in Spanish mysticism and "continental" philosophy — required for dealing with the pope's two theses on John of the Cross and Max Scheler; and finally he was "alternate" observer at Vatican II, where he met and talked with the youthful archbishop of Kraków.

He throws a flood of light on so many things John Paul takes for granted but which we have to learn about. He explains the importance of Polish "Messianism," which flourished in the romantic period when Poland was carved up among three of its neighbors. This led to a special sense of destiny, and the feeling that Poland would play an important role in salvation history.

He has been to the shrine of Kalwaria, and this gives him an interpretative key to understanding some of the poems of the young Wojtyla. He points out the decisive role played by Cardinal Adam Sapieha, who gave him his rather "martial" concept of priesthood. He introduces us to the Mariavites, excommunicated in 1906, whose priests and nuns were married to each other, and both distributed the Eucharist as equals. Could this atavistic memory have been revived when Sr. Theresa Kane made her modest proposal on that famous occasion?

Nor does he flag when it comes to the intellectual background. Max Scheler — whom Wojtyla studied in order to refute — was a more bizarre figure than he has so far been presented. For example, during the First World War he retired to the Black Forest where he wrote propaganda pamphlets alleging that the Central Powers (Germany and Austria-Hungary) were waging a war for Christian civilization against the Protestant English, who were notoriously a "nation of shopkeepers," interested only in profit; against the godless French, who had thrown out the monks and sisters and disestablished the church in 1904; and against the autocratic czars of Russia, who were flattered and fawned upon by a subservient Orthodox clergy. Wojtyla's father would have been subjected to this kind of guff.

I'm not saying that young Wojtyla inherited such attitudes. But there was perhaps a certain residue. Eventually the Americans, those frantic "consumers," take over from the declining English the mantle of utilitarianism (equals making a fast buck). Even if none of this is true, it makes the point that the image Wojtyla has of us — the "West," the "free world" — does not necessarily coincide with our image of ourselves. This explains the ambivalence of his U.S. trip in 1979.

Williams is constantly illuminating on everything to do with the background to John Paul. He is less good — and in fact is positively shaky — when it comes to the pontificate. But that does not matter. He has already made a notable and permanently valuable contribution to Wojtyla studies.

His attitude throughout is one of respectful admiration for this talented and courageous man. This is proper in a book written from an ecumenical standpoint. But along with this general goodwill — which is a condition of understanding — Williams makes one or two remarks which, if followed up, would prove devastating.

He notes, for example, that the Polish church has come to resemble the Polish Communist Party: "Nothing so much resembles a convexity as a concavity. The urge for moral and theological uniformity is very strong in the sovereign pontiff. . . . No loyal opposition is tolerated in communism." But this promising line of inquiry is not pursued.

Another significant hint, which could be taken as a comment in advance on the Schillebeeckx-Küng affair, is equally damaging. Discussing Wojtyla's 1971 address to the Polish Theological Association, he writes: "He seemed obsessed with the magisterium, without entering into details about specific current theological problems, seemingly content to handle sacred truth, as it were, bureaucratically." I have read the address Williams refers to. Its oddest feature is that, although he denounces various vague errors, he also says none of them existed in Poland.

Now we come to a series of works which do not deal exclusively with John Paul, but in which he makes an appearance. First, though, one in which he does not appear. J. Derek Holmes' *The Papacy in the Modern World, 1914-1978* disappointingly stops with John Paul II's election.

The reason for this self-denying ordinance is explained by the author in his preface: "The dangers of commenting on the recent past are well-known. The lack of much original material coupled with the need to see events from a more distant perspective creates obvious pitfalls." There speaks the professional historian, with the comfort of chair and tenure.

Journalists cannot afford to wait for that "more distant perspective." They rush in where historians fear to tread. John Paul has largely been left in the hands of the journalists. In some ways this is a pity. It is high time that study of the Vatican was placed on at least as serious an academic level as the study of the Kremlin.

If that day ever dawned, then Redemptorist Fr. Francis X. Murphy would be leading contender for the Cardinal Augustin Bea chair of 20th century papal history. For his book, *The Papacy Today*, is not about the papacy today but about the popes of the 20th century on whom he is well-informed (though I wish he would give his sources). Not having Holmes' scruples, he presses boldly on up to August 1980.

Murphy's attitude to John Paul seems to be that he hopes for the best, is reluctant to believe the worst, and in the end settles for a prudent agnosticism: "It is impossible to foresee in which direction the Polish pontiff will lead tomorrow's church."

I am not quite sure what future event or pronouncement would permit Murphy to reach a more definite conclusion. He assembles enough telling evidence to justify pessimism: the setback to ecumenism, the hold-the-line policy on ministry, the emasculation of the synod as a counterweight to the curia.

But having thus filled us all with gloom, Murphy then does a neat little Indian rope trick to extricate himself from pessimism. It is a revival of the myth that the-bad-guys-in-the-curia have got hold of him. It applied, more or less, to Pope John XXIII, for whom it was invented (by Murphy's alter ego, Xavier Rynne, among others). It is a bit of a surprise to find it being wheeled out again and applied to John Paul II.

Yet here is what Rynne — oops! Murphy — says, speaking of *Redemptor Hominis*, John Paul's first encyclical: "Replete with extravagant terminology and idiosyncratic doctrinal terms, the 18,000-word document gushed forth in vigorous ways of language that gave the Vatican Congregation for the Doctrine of the Faith fits, as its scriveners endeavored to pull it into shape and cope with its theological content." This is the sort of thing that gives Vaticanology a bad name. Is there any evidence that the text was submitted to the CDF at all?

But if Murphy seems to be writing from memory — admittedly a well-stocked memory, Malachi Martin, in *The Decline and Fall of the Roman Church*, seems to be making it all up. Having in a previous book predicted the demise of the Roman Catholic church "well before the year 2000," he is now eager to prove how right he was.

He has little to contribute on John Paul II, whom he reaches after 250 pages devoted to the history of the papacy from the beginning. The narrative is vivid but the argument is confusing. Martin can't make up his mind when the decline set in.

Sometimes he blames Pope John XXIII, and he does this by gravely misquoting the old man. Elsewhere he tells us that "from the days of Luther" the history of the Catholic church has been "a 400-year decline and fall." But that is canceled out by his suggestion that the rot really set in with the conversion of Constantine in 311. This last point is underscored by his use of Dante's famous phrase, "the curse of Constantine."

So it is difficult to detect any pinnacle from which the church could decline and since it seriously got under way. The bottom line is the only line. Thus John Paul's capacity for adding to its troubles is distinctly limited. He has to face, according to Martin, "a new theology which is distrustful of Roman authority and imbued with the spirit of experimentation."

The secret aim of these innovators, now exclusively revealed by Martin, is to survive into the next pontificate. That doesn't seem reprehensible; it is an ambition that most of us might reasonably share. But in Martin it becomes further evidence — I use the term analogously — of a diabolical plot. For he attributes to Pius XII the belief, and appears to believe it himself, that Marx was a "Satanist." That disposes of Marx.

From the Satanism of Marx it is only a step toward saying that today "many bishops ordaining candidates for the priesthood have no intention of creating priests with the sacramental powers to offer the sacrifice of the Mass and to absolve penitents of sins, and many candidates do not have the intention of receiving such powers." Consequently, "it is now impossible to reckon how many validly ordained priests there are."

If you find the last two paragraphs incoherent, that is simply because I am rehearsing Martin's line of argument, in which unexplained jumps prevail. Unlike Murphy, he is dogmatic rather than agnostic about the future. The pope should repress all these dangerous progressives, renew seminary professors, appoint sound bishops, fire those who disagree with him, and so on.

At the same time Martin appears to doubt whether such a vigorous policy would succeed. Satan is too firmly entrenched in the church. "This task," he explains, "will keep John Paul busy for life. If he can do it at all." No facts must be allowed to disturb Martin's apocalyptic vision of catastrophic decline and fall. I cannot imagine why it gives him so much satisfaction.

I have kept the best of this batch until last. *The Pope's Divisions* is by Peter Nichols, for 25 years the Rome correspondent of the London *Times*. I have to declare an interest and say he is an old friend whose olive grove at Lake Bracciano I visited last August. There he keeps a pig with whose aid he hopes to survive a nuclear attack and rebuild civilization. I also figure as the man who, "in rather an intense way," inquired over lunch whether writing the book had changed his mind about the church, of which he is not a member.

So if I tell you he writes like an angel, you don't have to believe me. But he does. John Paul is not his principal subject; on the contrary. While others went (or should have gone) to Rome to find out about the pope, he wanted to get away from Rome to see what was happening in the field. He was able to do this because the London *Times* was on strike for nearly a year.

His main conclusion was that there are two growth points in the church today. The first is in Latin America, where the slumbering giant is awakening, and the church has become a powerful factor for social change. He sees the women's movement as the second major factor for change. The emergence of sisters from the cloister has led, he says, to new forms of "collaborative ministry," which are changing the nature of ministry itself, making it more clearly a matter of service than power and control.

But if that is true, then the initiative has clearly passed to the local churches, and all the Vatican can do is impotently fume. This creates a dilemma for John Paul to which Nichols is acutely sensitive.

These differences between the "center" and the "periphery" (to use the jargon of the 1960s) would not matter so much if, as was confidently predicted, the successors of Paul VI had adopted a low profile, concentrated on their task as bishops of Rome and gradually shifted the government of the church away from the Roman curia to the Synod of Bishops (described by Nichols as "a Sleeping Beauty awaiting a papal kiss to arouse it to full dominance"). If these policies had been pursued, then this "renewed papal ministry" could have played an important role as the focus of the unity of most if not all Christians.

But far from conforming to this program, John Paul, the hyperactive pope, has done exactly the opposite. He has emphasized Catholic identity and difference, turned ecumenism into a distant spiritual dream and, by his travels, made the papal office more "visible" than ever.

"In terms of power and authority," says Nichols, "Rome has been the gainer from the papal habit of traveling." He aptly quotes Thomas Stearns Eliot's *Murder in the Cathedral* on the impending arrival of Thomas à Becket:

He comes in pride and sorrow, affirming all his claims,
Assured, beyond doubt, of the devotion of the people,
Who receive him with scenes of frenzied enthusiasm.

Is that what we will see on our TV screens when John Paul goes to Canterbury next year? Will he affirm all his claims? Or scale them down?

Guesses at the answers to these questions will no doubt be found in the books on which British authors are working in preparation for "the visit." Journalist Paul Johnson is hard at it; out-of-office Conservative politician Norman St. John Stevas has the leisure to work away at his book; the noble Lord Longford, otherwise known as Frank Pakenham (or "Lord Porn"), is also up to something; and your Vatican affairs writer is looking for another way of renewing this by now much battered topic.

Modesty allows me to say my idea is to write a book on what John Paul thinks on various important questions. Two conclusions I can share with you already. The first is that most of the differences we ("Westerners") may have with him are not so much theological as "cultural"; and the second conclusion is that most writers have been so impressed and awestruck by the "phenomenon" of John Paul that they have hardly listened to what he was saying. Attention to the content of John Paul's utterances is important in the second, post-shooting phase of his pontificate.

Sources of Renewal, Karol Wojtyla. Harper and Row, 437 pages, $14.95

Love and Responsibility, Karol Wojtyla. Farrar Straus Giroux, 319 pages, $15

The Mind of John Paul II, George Huntston Williams. Seabury, 392 pages, $26.95

The Papacy in the Modern World, J. Derek Holmes. Crossroad, 275 pages, $14.95

The Papacy Today, Francis X. Murphy. Macmillan, 269 pages, $13.95

The Decline and Fall of the Roman Church, Malachi Martin. Putnam, 336 pages, $14.95

The Pope's Divisions, Peter Nichols. Holt, Rinehart and Winston, 382 pages, $16.95

22

Pope's visit to Fatima casts new church role for Mary

(May 21, 1982) This always was meant to be the most personal of Pope John Paul's pilgrimages. He was going to Portugal to thank Our Lady of Fatima for saving his life just one year ago.

At 5:19 p.m. on May 13, 1981, the bullet of Mehemet Ali Agca rang out around St. Peter's Square; at 5:19 p.m. one year later the pope was lost in silent prayer at the foot of the gold-crowned statue of Our Lady of Fatima.

We do not know what his thoughts were. But some of them can be guessed at from his public statements.

On arrival at Lisbon airport punctually at 1:13 p.m. on May 12, he kissed the rather damp ground of "this noble land of Our Lady." In his speech he said that his coming was "the realization of a long-cherished dream." He had always wanted to see Fatima at firsthand.

That evening he realized his dream. He stood in the square outside the Basilica of Fatima before a vast crowd carrying candles that twinkled more brightly as dusk fell. "I want to share with you a confidence," he said. There was an expectant hush.

"As soon as I recovered consciousness after the attack in St. Peter's Square," he went on, "my thoughts turned to this shrine and I wanted to express here my gratitude to our Heavenly Mother for having saved my life."

The reason he turned to Our Lady of Fatima rather than to, say, Our Lady of Czestochowa, was the date, May 13. There were altogether too many coincidences for comfort.

May 13, 1917: date of the first appearance of Our Lady to the three children at Fatima. It was also the date on which Eugenio Pacelli, later Pius XII, was ordained bishop.

May 13, 1967: Paul VI visited Fatima on his fifth-year anniversary.

May 13, 1981: the assassination attempt.

"In this coincidence," said John Paul, "I recognized a divine call." He then added perhaps the most important remark he made in Portugal for those who want to understand his psychology of faith: "But in the designs of divine providence there are no mere coincidences."

As though to drive home this point he visited not only Fatima, but Vila Vicosa, near the Spanish border where King John IV proclaimed our Lady of the Immaculate Conception queen of Portugal in 1646. And on the last day of his trip he visited the Marian Shrine at Oporto. In this way he tried to root Fatima in the Portuguese national tradition.

Anyone who thought he was going to reveal at last the famous "third secret" of Fatima — Paul VI is said to have turned pale when he opened the dread envelope — was disappointed. John Paul treated it almost playfully.

"Would you like to hear a 'secret,' " he asked, "that will enable you to preserve this good and rich inheritance?" Naturally they would. "It is simple," he said, "and has really never been a secret anyway: Pray, pray often, pray the rosary every day." This sally was greeted with great applause.

In another of his "confidences," John Paul revealed that in all his world journeys, "the greatest moment of contact with the people of God" had been at Marian shrines. He instanced his recent visit to Equatorial Guinea — a nice compliment, as it is a former Portuguese colony. One wondered about his visit to Britain, still scheduled for May 28: There is no planned visit to a Marian shrine — though Our Lady of Walsingham, either the Catholic statue or the Anglican statue is due to be carried into Wembley stadium.

So ended John Paul's first day in Portugal. There had been one bizarre incident that I set down strictly for the record. A 32-year-old Spanish priest, Fr. Juan Fernandez Krohn, broke ranks, is said to have brandished a knife (a bayonet in some accounts) and cried, "Down with the pope," or something similar. He was quickly overpowered, and John Paul benignly blessed his struggling form.

"Thank God he's not Portuguese," said the Portuguese journalists around me. From Spanish colleagues I learned that Krohn — the name is of Alsatian origin — was ordained three years ago by Archbishop Marcel Lefebvre. He is a fanatical right-winger who believes that Pope John Paul is dangerously liberal and enamored of Vatican II.

In particular he blames the pope for military rule in Poland. No one who knows him believes that it was a serious assassination attempt. Someone who interviewed him recently said: "He is very aggressive, but spiritually, not physically."

Krohn was quickly disavowed by Lefebvre. He has joined a rival sect called the Sede Vacante group, which regards Lefebvre as too left-wing and holds that there has been no true pope since the death of Pius XII in 1958.

On May 13 the skies cleared, the absurd incident was forgotten, and as if to get the priorities right, it was the statue of Our Lady of Fatima, not the pope, that circulated through the crowds to be greeted by fluttering handkerchiefs, strewn petals and immense applause.

The pope's homily was different in tone from the impassioned meditation of the night before. Now he presented an apologia for devotion of Our Lady of Fatima, addressed not so much to those present, who did not need it, as to the wider world, which evidently required a word of explanation.

His starting point was the text of John 19:27: "Woman, behold your son; son, behold your mother. And from that hour the disciple took her to his own home." John was a representative figure. It followed that all "disciples" of Christ, like John, are sons and daughters of Mary, their mother.

The "homes" of Mary are innumerable, ranging from humble wayside shrines to vast pilgrimage centers. The latter are places where "the mother's presence is felt in a particularly vivid way." Preeminent among such places is Fatima.

Then came what I can only describe as a conceptual leap.

The son is naturally impelled, said John Paul, to bring all his problems to his mother. He was quite specific: "The problems of the family, of societies, of nations and of the whole of humanity." The human analogy, however, does not work: though sons (or daughters) may bring some of their problems to their mothers, they are not in the habit of bringing them all.

But by now John Paul had soared away from all such mundane considerations. Mary's motherhood, he asserted, was a sharing in the power of the Holy Spirit. It followed that Our Lady, in her revelations at Fatima, had "discerned the signs of the times": her vision of a world of sinners heading for perdition unless they repented was just what the modern world needed.

Here John Paul inserted a cautious theological qualification. There can be no addition to the stock of revelations which ended with the death of the last apostle. That is routine teaching. The status of so-called "private revelations," such as that of Fatima, "is judged according to their conformity with that single public revelation."

Fatima triumphantly passes that test, he said. "Repent and believe the gospel" is the message of Mark 1:15 and of Fatima. "The call of Fatima," he went on, "was uttered at the start of the 20th century, and was thus addressed particularly to the 20th century."

It was also a call to prayer and, said the pope, "particularly to the rosary, which can rightly be defined as 'Mary's prayer,' the prayer in which she feels particularly united with us." It is also a universal prayer: "The rosary embraces the problems of the church, of the See of Peter, and the problems of the whole world."

The message of Fatima is in effect: pray the rosary or else. In what may be called the "ideology" of Fatima, the "sinners" are elsewhere. Though never clearly identified, they are those responsible for what John Paul called "societies menaced by apostasy and threatened by moral corruption." Concretely that means the communist countries of Eastern Europe and elsewhere, and Western societies insofar as they succumb to the plague of divorce, abortion and other evils.

John Paul, claiming to speak as "the heir of Vatican II," said that Fatima had accurately judged the church's relationship with the world. The message of Fatima is more urgent and important than ever. That is why, he explained, the theme of the 1983 synod will be repentance and conversion.

So what began as a personal pilgrimage of John Paul to Fatima to thank Our Lady for saving his life, was transformed into a commitment on the part of the pope to a version of recent history in which Vatican II is interpreted in the light of what happened at Fatima 65 years ago.

Vatican II, with its sober Mariology, attempted to subordinate "private revelations" to the supreme norm of Scripture — as it had to do if ecumenism was to be anything more than friendly noises. In Portugal, at Fatima, John Paul has deliberately reversed this process.

None of this seemed to worry anyone in Portugal in the slightest. In Lisbon, John Paul had the most enthusiastic welcome he has so far received in a European capital. All roads in Lisbon lead down to the port, and they were crowded to welcome him Tuesday and again on Friday when he celebrated a Mass for youth in the Edward VII park. Tears flowed.

What did they mean? Most immediately, they meant that the Portuguese were happy at being recognized and put on the map by a papal visit. This is a small nation — nearing 10 million population — which created and then, less than a decade ago, was forced to abandon a vast colonial empire.

When Paul VI came here in 1967, Portugal was still ruled by Antonio Oliveira Salazar, a dictator who ran a highly efficient police state with, on the whole, the blessings of the church. In 1974, a revolution restored Portugal to democracy.

Portugal is still shakily democratic, governed by a center-right coalition. It has the most Stalinist communist party in Western Europe. The Portuguese Communist Party heartily approves of the invasion of Afghanistan and military rule in Poland. It collects 10 percent of the votes at elections, but it has a capacity for making trouble far in excess of that.

On the day before the pope arrived it called for a general strike. The whole country came to a standstill. It was a display of muscle before the papal visit. It was a protest against the government's decision to peg pay raises at 17 percent. Figures were produced to show that consumer goods in the first three months of this year were up by 25.4 percent and food prices up by 30.1 percent compared with the same period last year.

The three factors which influence Portuguese society today are tourism, the major industry; emigration, which masks the reality of unemployment; and industrialization. All of them contribute toward the weakening of family ties and growing secularization, which John Paul predictably denounced. The fourth decisive factor is that present-day Portugal — having contributed to the creation of Brazil,

Angola and Mozambique — has now turned inward and applied for membership of the European Economic Community.

The economic and political realities of Portugal were recognized by John Paul when he addressed the episcopal conference early in the morning of May 13. But they were seen through a glass darkly, partly because he chose to speak to them in Fatima. Fatima, a kind of Catholic enclave within Portugal, is not the best vantage point for considering the fate of the Portuguese church.

The Portuguese church is handicapped by having been too closely associated with the regime of Salazar, by an elderly clergy, and by returned missionaries from Angola and Mozambique who feel bitter about the Marxist government which threw them out. They are easy victims for the doom-laden, anticommunist ideology of Fatima.

In his speech to the bishops John Paul correctly identified the chief paradox of Portugal: it is a country of deep religious faith and yet this coexists with agnosticism among intellectuals and a large section of the youth.

Portugal, he noted, was in a state of "profound cultural mutation," and when this happens, one needs to "reaffirm, if not to recover, the solid values of the past."

This would be achieved, he suggests, if bishops, following the example of the Good Shepherd, "led from the front." Bishops are to be leaders and not followers of their people. Their task is, he said, "to go ahead and reconnoiter the way, to measure the depths of the currents, to seek out the dangers and guarantee the road ahead." This, which sounds more like the prophetic than the episcopal task, was more than ever necessary in an unstable world and a mutable society.

Some of this was code language. It was a way of praising the bishops for their last pastoral letter in which they had denounced "politically motivated strikes." But John Paul said nothing quite so crude. He did not need to denounce the Communist Party. It was enough for him to say that the bishops should reject "certain of the thoughts and ideologies which impede progress."

So in Portugal John Paul firmly committed the church to the Mariology of Fatima. He asserted the values of popular religion against the complaints of intellectuals. He showed that the attempt on his life and his remarkable convalescence have confirmed him in the wisdom of his policies. With divine providence on his side, he will now be irresistible.

The visit to Portugal bodes ill for his visit to Britain, for it is evident that he feels much more at home in Fatima than ever he could in Canterbury. To visit the first was a long-standing dream; to visit the second is a chore.

One was left wondering just what a liberation theologian — they are numerous in Portuguese-speaking Brazil — would make of the pope's emphasis on Fatima. Pope Paul VI made it more intelligible than John Paul. After visiting the place, Paul said, "Fatima made sense in the light of what happened at Hiroshima." ❏

23

'Popular cause' ecumenism espoused by 'John Paul III'

(June 11, 1982) It was always known that Pope John Paul's visit to Britain would be different. For the first time he was going to a country where Catholics were in a minority — 9 percent — in relation to other Christians. For the first time a trip had been arranged on the theme of the seven sacraments rather than according to categories. And for the first time he was going to a country at war.

But no one expected to see a new model Pope John Paul — John Paul III, as one Vatican expert put it. John Paul disconcerted, in a most welcome way, his habitual camp followers. It was as though, having established his authority in the church, he can afford to ease up and show "the smiling face" of the papacy.

The key factor was that he followed the English bishops' advice. If they said: "It would be tactless to put it that way," he put it another way. He behaved like a thoughtful first-time guest, which he was, rather than the inspector general come to restore order and discipline. Even his references to contraception were vague and noncommitting.

He flattered the English as "a fair-minded and generous people." He said: "I have always admired your love of freedom, and your generous hospitality to other peoples in their adversity."

He said that in Westminster Cathedral, a few hundred yards from the Hotel Rubens, where Polish commander Gen. Wladyslaw Sikorski had his headquarters during World War II. He quoted the late Cardinal John Heenan's remark: "Polish pilots saved us during the battle of Britain." But this nostalgia was more than sentimental.

It permitted John Paul to concentrate, without giving offense, on the prophetic message he had come to deliver. It was that war is "totally unacceptable as a means of settling differences between nations." He said this, in one form or another, every day of his trip.

Nor was he talking merely about nuclear war. The "scale and horror of modern warfare, whether nuclear or not," ruled it out. It should be confined to the "tragic past of humanity." This was spoken in Coventry, where a single air raid in 1940 destroyed the inner city and the medieval cathedral.

The gaunt, ruined frame of the old cathedral still stands alongside the new cathedral consecrated 20 years ago. It has a chapel of reconciliation that the children of the Germans who bombed it helped to build. John Paul the catechist used this as a symbol: we have all to build up, stone by stone, "the cathedral of peace."

This was applauded. Yet the newspapers that Sunday morning were filled with news of the capture of Goose Green and the heroism of Lt. Col. Herbert Jones, who died silencing a machine-gun post. The cathedral of peace was being torn down in the South Atlantic.

How can one explain the paradox? On the one hand, English Catholics, along with 85 percent of the population, are prepared to support Prime Minister Margaret Thatcher's war, and yet to cheer the pope when he quite explicitly deplores it.

I am not sure it can be explained. Here is a guess. The British people are rather like St. Augustine saying "chastity — but not yet." They are saying, "Peace — but not yet." The prospect of victory confirms that mood. But in their heart of hearts, they know John Paul is right: war is an anachronism, and only by luck has escalation been avoided.

It is also fair to add that the war in the South Atlantic seemed a long way off in the summer sunshine. It has not obsessed or dominated minds in Britain the way it evidently has in Argentina. It has been possible to think of other things. England played Scotland at soccer while the pope was speaking in Wembley Stadium, London; the Derby was run on the day he left. Distant events did not affect the partylike atmosphere of the papal visit, especially as John Paul moved into the Catholic heartlands of the north, to Liverpool, Manchester, York and Scotland.

History was made at Canterbury, not just in the obvious sense that this was the first time a reigning pope had visited the cradle of

Christianity in England. (Celtic Christianity antedated it, and came from the north, from the monks of Iona.) History was made in the deeper sense that the rich and polyvalent event will be pondered and commented upon for many years. It must lead to a new relationship between the Roman Catholic church and the Anglican Communion.

"Along with the Second Vatican Council," said one highly placed Anglican, "this was the greatest ecumenical event of the century." The euphoria was understandable. The liturgy spoke directly, through its symbols. Here are some of them.

- Dr. Robert Runcie, archbishop of Canterbury, wore his miter and carried his crosier, symbol of his jurisdiction. John Paul had no symbols of office. He was there as a guest, a brother bishop. The bishop of Rome would not upstage his host.

- Together they venerated the gospel of Canterbury, alleged to have been brought here by Augustine in 598. This established the link between Canterbury and Rome, and their common submission to the word of God. Ministry in the church is not above the word of God, but at its service.

- John Paul proclaimed the gospel, the Gospel of John: "that all may be one." This disclosed the essential function of the bishop of Rome as sign and symbol of unity.

- Together, and with the Anglican primates gathered there, they renewed their baptismal vows. Baptism into Christ is the foundation of Christian unity. Its natural completion is the Eucharist; that is where we are tending.

- Together they prayed in silence at the tomb of Thomas Becket, at the place where he was murdered in the 12th century. But then they moved to the chapel of the modern martyrs. John Paul lit a candle for Maximilian Kolbe, whom he will canonize in October; Runcie lit a candle for Archbishop Oscar Romero, killed two days after Runcie's enthronement; and the widow of the Rev. Martin Luther King Jr. lit a candle for her husband. The blood of martyrs is the seed of the unity of the church.

The acclamations, the fanfares, the flags, the applause made this an almost medieval scene, worth of T. S. Eliot's *Murder in the Cathedral*, first performed here in 1935.

It needed an effort to recall that just a few weeks ago, the Congregation for the Doctrine of the Faith had given a faintly damning verdict on the final report of the Anglican-Roman Catholic International Theological Commission, ARCIC. John Paul did not mention the final report. He did something much more significant.

He expressed the meaning of his own Petrine office in the language of the final report. We may conclude that in preparing his Canterbury visit, he had followed the advice of the Secretariat for Christian Unity and set aside that of the CDF and Cardinal Luigi Ciappi.

Moreover, he used ARCIC language not merely when addressing Anglicans. Speaking in Westminster Cathedral, he echoed the vision of a church built up from below through the communion of churches. "I come to remind all believers," he said, "that in each diocese the bishop is the visible sign and source of the church's unity. I come among you as the visible sign and source of unity for the whole church." So unity is not an imposition from above. It is the fulfillment of the drive toward *koinonia*. That was precisely the starting point of ARCIC.

In Canterbury John Paul avoided the controversial "Thou art Peter" text and preferred to define his office in terms of Luke 22:32. He had come "to confirm the faith of his brethren." He cited patristic texts from the time when Rome and Canterbury were in communion. The function of the church of Rome, as Ignatius of Antioch said, is "to preside in love."

These remarks were also a practical commitment to "the next steps" toward unity. The CDF had concluded that the "next step" could only be yet more discussion. John Paul and Runcie concede the need for more discussion on particular questions, but insist on two conditions that change the whole ball game.

The new commission, Ben ARCIC or Son of ARCIC, will also have to recommend "what practical steps will be necessary when, on the basis of our unity in faith, we are able to proceed to the restoration of full communion." "Practical" means what it says; what is to be done about overlapping parishes and dioceses?

The second decisive commitment is the invocation to local churches "to pray for this work and adopt every possible means of furthering it through their collaboration in deepening their allegiance to Christ and in witnessing to him before the world."

"Every possible means." For example, joint theological studies have already happened in some places. Joint projects in social actions. Perhaps joint meetings of bishops. It would be good if Roman documents were automatically sent to Anglican bishops so they could find out how useful or handicapping they were. Conversely Anglican statements should be shared with Catholic bishops. The joint declaration does not give any of these examples. But it appeals to the imagination and may be said to imply them.

By his visit to Britain, John Paul has turned ecumenism into a popular cause. His previous ecumenical encounters have been with prelates and professionals. In the Anglican cathedral of Liverpool, close to where the Mersey sound of the Beatles was first heard, he received a standing ovation as he entered and departed. If he thought the English were cold and unfeeling, he is now disabused. And if he thought ecumenism was not a popular cause, he is now disabused of that, too.

I remembered his poem, "The Birth of Confessors." It is about a bishop administering confirmation in a remote mountain village. It is dominated by imagery of energy and electric currents. The key line is: "I am a giver/I touch forces that expand the mind." Here, John Paul has done exactly that. The high hopes at the start of his pontificate were recalled.

In Coventry he spoke of John Henry Newman, naturally enough because Newman had set up his Oratory in a derelict gin factory in nearby Birmingham in the 1850s. Newman shocked the Church of England by his conversion to Catholicism in 1845. He was not greatly appreciated by traditionalist Catholics, he opposed the infallibility definition of Vatican I as inopportune, but at 78 was made a cardinal by Leo XIII.

Once Newman was a divisive figure, a betrayer or a Trojan horse. John Paul saw him as a prophet of unity, "not only in this country but throughout the world."

Newman is now reconciling because he taught Anglicans that the logic of their faith led to communion with Rome. But he also taught Catholics that they would have to reform for that unity to be possible. "It is important to prepare converts for the church," he once wrote, "but it is equally important to prepare the church for converts." His historical and existential approach to theology is the method ARCIC followed.

One disappointment here, though. The English bishops have petitioned Rome for Newman's beatification. John Paul did not mention this: a bad omen.

This raises in suspicious minds the larger question. Granted that John Paul has presented in Britain the smiling face of the papacy, is not this a mask for the centralizing papacy we have so far seen?

True, there is a kind of schizophrenia in much pontifical discourse. In a Catholic context John Paul speaks firmly about his own infallibility in a way he studiously avoids in an ecumenical context. This was verified in Istanbul and now in Canterbury. But it does have a positive aspect. If the pope learns to speak with the difficulties of other Christians in mind, he may learn something useful about the ecumenical potential of his office. He may discover what is essential to it. He may find out that the Vatican definitions are a burden rather than an asset.

In which case this on-off-on visit will have been the turning point of the pontificate.

It has not been without its moments of humor. Cardinal Basil Hume, the Benedictine monk plucked from relative obscurity to be archbishop of Westminster, was asked by the 8-year-old son of the dean of Canterbury, "Why don't you become the next archbishop of Canterbury?" Hume thought for a moment and said: "Well, Thomas, when you grow up, you'd better become prime minister, and then you can fix it." ❑

24

Opus Dei 'rejoices' in its new autonomy

(September 10, 1982) Rejoicing was great but discreet recently among the 72,375 members of the religious organization Opus Dei. They are involved in 604 newspapers, 52 radio or TV stations, and 36 news agencies throughout the world. With one accord they agreed that Aug. 23 was the greatest day in the history of the movement since it was founded in Spain by Msgr. Jose Maria Escriva de Balaguer in 1928.

What happened? Pope John Paul had agreed that Opus Dei should be considered a "personal prelacy." But what does it mean?

Opus Dei had long had a sense of its originality and uniqueness. It believed it did not fit into the available Procrustean bed of canon law. It resented being lumped together with religious orders and secular institutes — a secular fish among religious fowl.

Opus Dei had a good point. Its members do not lead a "consecrated life." They do not take vows. Instead they have something

they call "appropriate contracts or agreements." Their priests —
about 1,500 — are "secular" priests.

But they do have common features that give them cohesion and
unity. As their current president Alvaro del Portillo, explained:
"Opus Dei is made up of men and women, celibate and married,
intellectuals and workers who have the same spirit and vocations,
and enjoy the same regime, education and discipline."

The fact that its membership is a mixed bag has led Opus Dei
canonists to claim it is more like a diocese than a religious order.
This has now been conceded to them. The Vatican council defined
the diocese as "a portion of God's people which is entrusted to a
bishop to be shepherded by him with the cooperation of the priests"
(*Decree of Bishops*, No. 11.).

Opus Dei members see themselves in this description. They are
"a portion of God's people." They are not "entrusted to a bishop,"
but their president-general is their "ordinary," so he acts as a quasi-
bishop. The third condition is most easily met: the "ordinary" is
helped in his shepherding by the priests, who have been trained in a
seminary organized by him.

This argument has now been accepted. Opus Dei is a personal
prelature, a quasi-diocese and therefore it is removed from the Congregation for Religious and Secular Institutes, and placed under control of the Congregation for Bishops (whose prefect is the pro-Opus
Dei Cardinal Sebastiano Baggio). So it looks like an attempt at bureaucratic tidying up.

But as such, it is not very successful. One anomaly has been
removed: another has been created. Canon lawyers will puzzle for
years about this hybrid monster.

For Opus Dei does not resemble a diocese in every respect.
Like the diocese, it is "a portion of God's people," but a diocese is a
random portion of God's people, united in the first instance by geography alone. Opus Dei is not united by geography but, as they say,
by a common spirit.

Second, the notion of a self-selecting, self-recruiting group —
which Opus Dei is — is contrary to what a diocese is. Who belongs
to it? Do the children of married Opus Dei members belong to the
quasi-diocese of Opus? Who is to baptize them?

Where there is a will, there is a canonical way. Opus Dei rejoices because at last it has what it wanted. The door on which it has
been pushing for so long has finally ceded.

Pope John XXIII rejected the idea of a personal prelacy in 1962. Pope Paul VI stalled for as long as he could and his last recorded enigmatic remark was in June 1978, seven weeks before his death, when he said: "The question is open."

Pope John Paul II had no such hesitation. He became pope Oct. 17, 1978. Within a month, Nov. 15, he had conveyed to the president-general his view that "the resolution of the juridical status of Opus Dei is a matter of immediate necessity." The rest followed, delayed only by the need to go through a form of consultation so the eventual results would appear "collegial."

What does the church gain, if anything, from this long-desired change? Del Portillo says there are two positive gains. First, the Holy See will have at its disposal "a mobile body of priests and well-trained laity." This is the old "shock troops" idea, which used to be used by the Jesuits.

However, the mobility of Opus Dei is somewhat restricted. One does not expect to find members toiling in the danger spots of Latin America, as they claim they can work "in civil society and in professional milieux which the church cannot normally reach." They mean, in various establishments.

The second advantage of the change of status — still according to del Portillo — is that it preserved Opus Dei's identity, threatened by its association with Religious and Secular Institutes.

But these two arguments are so feeble that even the least suspicious mind would suspect some unstated advantage accruing to Opus Dei from the change. What that is is fairly obvious. One cannot become a diocese, even of the quasi kind, without in some way withdrawing from the existing, geographical diocesan structure. If that does not follow, there is no point to the whole exercise.

Consequently, this move strengthens Opus Dei's autonomy, divides it from the local churches still more and makes Opus Dei risk being a "church within the church." That may not be the intention; it is the effect.

Last December Cardinal Basil Hume of Westminster, England, issued some guidelines on Opus Dei. All were concerned with the freedom of the individual. An estimated 70 percent of Spanish bishops are said to oppose Opus Dei.

None of this worries the new personal prelature. Members are constantly citing the blessings they have received from this or that cardinal. In their naiveté, they do not appear to realize they are revealing their conservative political hand. Here are three examples from their own sources.

Archbishop Alfonso Lopez Trujillo, secretary of the Latin American episcopal conference (CELAM) said: "Opus Dei in the Latin American church represents a progress in fidelity, which is the only form of progress there is in the church."

Cardinal Sebastiano Baggio, Lopez's Roman protector, wrote: "Monsignor Escriva invented a new and original chapter in Christian spirituality."

And, finally, Cardinal Terence Cooke of New York said: "I can say with certainty that when the history of Catholicism in the 20th century comes to be written, the name of Monsignor Escriva will appear as one of the most committed, zealous and farsighted among the leaders of our era."

And now Pope John Paul has added his name to the list of prestigious Opus Dei patrons. One always knew he would. He went to pray at Escriva's tomb before the conclave that elected him. He has hastened the progress of his beatification, setting aside the 50-year rule. Now he has given Opus Dei what it wanted all along.

But why now, and why has the news been announced without the usual justifying accompanying letter? One can only surmise that John Paul wanted to get this matter out of the way before his visit to Spain, scheduled for Oct. 14. If the Spanish bishops were hoping to seize the opportunity to make representations about the harmfulness of Opus Dei, they can no longer. They have been presented with a *fait accompli.* ❏

25

Unhappy days for Marcinkus' men

(October 29, 1982) The Vatican Bank is very hard to find. The official handbook *Annuario Pontificio* gives neither its address nor telephone number. The theory is that those who need to know already do know — and the others can stay away. But if you go inside the Porta Santa Anna on the right of St. Peter's Square, you will see up on the left, beyond the barracks of the Swiss Guard, the turreted Nicholas V Tower. It's in there.

Strictly speaking, it is not "the Vatican Bank." Its proper title is the Institute for the Works of Religion (IOR). Archbishop Paul Marcinkus has been its president since 1969. The IOR must be carefully distinguished from another financial body known as the Administration of the Patrimony of the Holy See (APSA).

Housed in the Apostolic Palace (where the pope lives), the APSA has two sections: the "ordinary" section deals with everyday expenses; the "extraordinary" section oversees the investment of the money given to the Holy See in 1929 as compensation for the loss of the papal states. Well invested in the past, it is now far more than the original $80 million.

Marcinkus has nothing to do with APSA, nor can APSA control him. In both bodies the line runs directly to the pope. When it is said "the Vatican" is in deficit, this refers to the "ordinary" section of APSA, and not to anything else.

Outsiders — mostly religious orders, including Mother Teresa of Calcutta — have invested in IOR. This is why it is not accurately called the "Vatican bank." It would be more accurate, if a trifle pedantic, to call it "the bank in the Vatican." I shall continue to call it IOR.

Up until this year, Marcinkus was better known as the impresario of papal trips than as a banker. But now he will not be able to go to Spain for the pope's November visit. He has moved out of the Villa Stritch, where Americans working in the curia tend to live, and into the Vatican. His managing director, Luigi Mennini, and chief accountant, Pellegrino di Strobel, have taken the same precaution.

Mennini is Marcinkus' front man. He was on many of the boards of companies in which IOR had an interest. He has 10 children. One of them is a priest, Don Antonio Mennini. He is said to have heard the final confession of Aldo Moro, former leader of the Christian Democrats, before his execution by the Red Brigade.

The tactic used by Mennini senior when challenged is to deny everything. The judge Bruno Apicelli said he had the feeling that Mennini "would have denied his own name," if he thought he could get away with it. So long as Marcinkus, Mennini and di Strobel remain inside the Vatican, Italian law cannot touch them. What has happened to make them "prisoners of the Vatican"?

In July, the investigating judge, Luigi D'Osso, sent them "judicial communiqués" advising them that they were under investigation.

This was not a summons to court, nor a charge, but a warning that they could be called in for questioning about the collapse of the Ambrosian Bank of Milan. Its president, Roberto Calvi, was found hanging from scaffolding under London's Blackfriars Bridge June 18, with stones in his pockets (the work of masons?).

There is also another inquiry, of a less menacing kind, set up with astonishing speed June 13, a few days before Calvi's mysterious death. Cardinal Agostino Casaroli, secretary of state, named a committee of three wise men — an American, Joseph Brennan; a Swiss, Philippe de Weck; and an Italian, Carolo Cerutti. They were to report "before the end of the fall," and have done so. But despite alleged leaks their report has not yet been published. Their brief was to discover the links between the IOR and the now bankrupt Ambrosian Bank.

* * *

To unravel this spider's web, it will be as well to begin at the beginning. The Banco Ambrosiano is named after St. Ambrose, bishop of Milan at the end of the fourth century and the man who baptized St. Augustine. It was founded in 1895 by the farsighted Msgr. Giuseppe Tovini. It was meant for the support of charitable and pious works. Baptismal certificates had to be produced by prospective shareholders.

Though Tovini's prospects did not say so explicitly, his aim was to set up a proper "Catholic bank" at a time when the financial world in Italy was dominated by anticlericals and Freemasons. The bank prospered in a sleepy sort or way. It was provincial in the nicest sense of the term. Its president in the 1930s was Franco Ratti, nephew of the man who was then pope.

Cut now to the boom years of the 1960s, the period of the "Italian miracle." The Sicilian financier, Michele Sindona, was on the crest of a wave. He met Roberto Calvi, at that time a junior executive at the Ambrosian Bank, in 1967. Calvi admired Sindona, who opened up to him a whole new world of banking.

Sindona taught him in particular how to use the tax havens of Switzerland, Lichtenstein and Panama. Together they plotted the takeover of the Ambrosian Bank and its transformation from a steady, reliable, provincial bank into an international merchant bank, borrowing and investing all over the world. They took risks, but the rewards were high. Sindona introduced Calvi to Marcinkus in 1971.

Meanwhile, the plot had begun to succeed, and Calvi became president of the Ambrosian Bank. This was not too difficult. The directors were old, monolingual and staid. Calvi offered them vision and excitement; and he could cite, if not count upon, his friendships in the Vatican. He and Marcinkus helped each other. Marcinkus became a member of the board of Cisalpine, Ambrosiano's Nassau bank.

In 1974 Sindona crashed. He was declared bankrupt, resisted the law for as long as he could (the Italian system of appeals makes for endless delay) and finally "vanished" in August 1978. His disappearance is said to have been engineered (though Sindona has always denied this) by Licio Gelli, founder and grand master of the Masonic lodge known as P2 (Propaganda 2), and Col. Antonio Viezzer of SID, the Italian secret service.

What, one might well ask, were these eminently Catholic bankers and advisers to the Vatican doing in a Masonic lodge? It would be easier to answer if one knew what goals P2 was supposed to serve in the mind of Gelli, its founder.

When the list of 953 names of its alleged "brothers" was revealed in May 1981, they provided a cross section of the Italian "establishment" — bankers (including Sindona and Calvi), politicians, media men, generals, admirals, secret service people. In short, the kind of team you would need for a *coup d'état.* †❑

26

John Paul in Central America: The papacy and reform

(March 18, 1983) Pope John Paul's visit to Central America began, deceptively, with flowers and a chaotic fiesta atmosphere. He barely had time to notice that he was in Costa Rica, and failed to congratulate it on not having an army: a unique instance of unilateral disarmament.

But there were thorns amid the roses, as he had predicted in his eve-of-visit television message. Central America, John Paul said, was undergoing Gethsemane and Calvary. The judicial murder at dawn of six alleged terrorists in Guatemala on his first day in Central America proved this intuition was perceptive: Christ is being daily recrucified in this region. It was Lent.

Local papal nuncios had explained that this was a purely pastoral visit with no political implications. Yet the events of March 4, as the sun set over the July 19 Plaza in Managua, Nicaragua, proved them disastrously wrong.

Pope, Sandinistas at Odds

Abandoning the evenhanded condemnations of both unrestrained capitalism and dogmatic ideologies, John Paul declared open war on Marxism in general and the Sandinista government in particular. His hosts were taken aback. Never before in the pontificate had he used such harsh, uncompromising and authoritarian language. And never before had he met with such public opposition.

Throughout his homily John Paul had to compete with the chanted slogans: "People's power," "We want peace," "They shall not pass" and "It is possible to be a Marxist and a Christian" (it sounds an unlikely slogan, but it works in Spanish).

John Paul just about held his own, because he has a strong voice and was in possession of the most powerful microphone. But it was touch and go. A lesser man would have stomped off in anger.

The Sandinistas were immediately blamed for orchestrating the slogans and "politicizing" the Eucharist. Their behavior was inexcusable. Yet they were provoked by John Paul's total rejection of their revolution and even more of Christian participation in it. Their disrespect was the measure of their disappointment. The crowd melted away as they listened to the thumped-out message of papal disapproval.

Perhaps the Sandinistas had pitched their expectations too high. Their spokesman at the airport, Daniel Ortega, called on the pope to condemn U.S. aggression against their country: only the previous day they had mourned the death of 16 college students killed by ex-Somoza guards near the frontier with Honduras.

Ortega had resourcefully dug out a letter from the bishop of León in 1921 to U.S. Cardinal James Carol Simpson. He protested the U.S. Marines who were occupying the country. To no avail.

Sixty-two years later, said Ortega, the story is being repeated. The Nicaraguans still feel vulnerable before President Reagan's repeated attempts to topple them. They hoped the pope would recognize the novelty of their revolution, "of which Christians were an integral part to an extent that is unprecedented in any other revolutionary movement in Latin America and perhaps in the world."

They also hoped the pope would at least assert Nicaragua's right as a small (two and one-half million population) Third World country to make its own way, untrammeled by big power pressures. They were sadly disappointed.

Disquiet set in from the opening flourish of the homily, a conventional compliment. John Paul greeted "the beloved land of Nicaragua, so tried, so heroic" — and here applause broke out, but it was misplaced, for he was congratulating them on their heroism "in face of the natural catastrophes that have afflicted you." This seemed to belittle their other achievements, notably the removal of the dictator Anastasio Somoza and the literacy campaign, neither of which was mentioned.

Salt was rubbed into the wounds when John Paul said he wished to address all, "old and young, rich and poor, workers and employers." Later he added his own gloss on Galatians (3:22), "in Christ there is neither Jew nor Greek, slave nor free man, male nor female, poor nor rich." With such a starting point, it was likely the "preferential option for the poorest" reaffirmed during the Latin American bishops' 1979 meeting in Puebla, Mexico, would be lost sight of.

But his was merely a softening up. John Paul repeated what he had said in his letter to the Nicaraguan bishops (June 29, 1982), though he knew perfectly well it had been rejected by many in the local church as an inaccurate description: "Whenever a Christian, whoever he is, prefers any other doctrine or ideology to the teaching of the apostles and of the church; when he proposes to reinterpret catechesis, religious doctrine and preaching according to his own categories; when parallel magisteria are set up . . . then the unity of the church is weakened." So it is. The question was: had this happened?

Priests in Government Castigated

The five priests in the Sandinista government were not spared — and the pope refused ostentatiously to shake hands with Fr. Ernesto Cardenal, the venerable poet now minister of culture.

The pope said: "No Christian, still less one who has received special consecration from the church (i.e., ordination), can make himself responsible for breaking this unity and acting on the fringes of the church, against the will of the bishops."

So the dominant concern, then, was the threatened unity of the church. John Paul offered the priests an ultimatum, his voice rising to a passionate crescendo: "The unity of the church can only be saved when each one is capable of giving up his own ideas, plans and commitments — even good ones — for the greater good of communion with the bishops, with the pope."

The denunciation of the notion of *iglesia popular*, alleged perversions of the Eucharist, and wildcat ecumenism followed automatically from these premises. They are all fallacious and "thanks to human myopia and false criteria become a source of new and worse division."

It is easy enough to summarize the papal message in Managua. It is more difficult to convey the ferocious intensity with which it was delivered. All John Paul's oratorical skills were brought into play. His right hand soared the air in trenchant gestures of negation. It was as though he had long been burdened with these thoughts, and had come to Central America to say this above all else.

He went far beyond the Latin American bishops' (CELAM) report, which he had used as a general guide. The CELAM report, however, distinguished between "light" and "shade" in its account of Nicaragua. John Paul discarded its positive points and accentuated the negative.

Pope Repudiates Liberation Theology

The gravity of his stand cannot be overestimated. He set out to reverse the trend from anathema to dialogue that began with John XXIII. It was continued in Medellín and Puebla and the liberation theologians. It was now repudiated in the only place that can plausibly claim to have had a revolution with reconciliation, the Christian revolution allowed for by Pope Paul VI in *Populorum Progressio*. If Nicaragua is not a candidate for a revolution according to liberation theology, then hope is extinguished throughout Latin America. Authoritarian governments can rejoice. They can play the anti-Marxist card as official papal doctrine.

The Nicaraguans were too thunderstruck to have any other immediate reaction than disappointment. If John Paul is to be taken seriously, then the only role for the church is to oppose the Sandinistas. Because they are clearly determined, as one of their posters said, "to defend the revolution laboriously achieved after 20 years of struggle," the likely result will be greater control over the church and even real persecution.

Persecution is no doubt bracing for the church — as the example of Guatemala shows — but it should not be recklessly sought. Certainly John Paul intends to be taken seriously: he announced in his homily that the forthcoming *ad limina* visit of the Nicaraguan bishops to Rome will be an opportunity to check how well they have responded to his exhortations.

The priests and laity who have opted for the revolution are placed in a cruel dilemma. They can no longer claim the pope has been misled by bad advice or that he was talking about someplace else, or that he was speaking in general terms. He was addressing them, inviting them to eat their words and betray their deepest convictions.

Their only recourse — admittedly a rather desperate one — is to challenge John Paul's ecclesiology. They can point to what he said to the Central American episcopal conference (SEDAC) in Costa Rica March 2: "To preserve and enrich the unity of faith in the church and, by the same token, ecclesial identity, the spirit of Christ sustains the dynamic life of the magisterium, a vital service for the church."

Theologians close to the Sandinistas will want to maintain that the spirit of Christ animates the church generally; the role of the magisterium can be upheld without assigning to it any monopoly of the Holy Spirit. There is room for them, too. They believed the Spirit was at work in Nicaragua.

But because this is precisely what Pope John Paul denied, their theological loophole will be treated as a subtler form of disobedience. An unstoppable force meets an immovable object. The result could be a real and possibly irrevocable division in the church. The pope said he came to Central America "to change inner attitudes." As they are unlikely to be changed, in this instance, by the mere exercise of papal authority, one can form provisional hypotheses about the future.

The more pessimistic is to predict a new breakaway reformation. Apart from disagreement about "where the Spirit is," there are other similar factors. The experience of basic communities has shown that Christ can be encountered directly in the scriptures, with or without benefit of the official ministry of the church. Luther, after all, began with a form of *iglesia popular*, and then political influences consolidated the breach.

But the solidity of the Catholic tradition in Central America makes this unlikely. The defense of the poor and the Indians can be traced back to the Dominican Bartolomé de Las Casas in the 16th century.

In any case, the "Protestant" alternative in Central America consists mostly of U.S.-funded sects that stress personal salvation and disdain political commitment. They provide personnel and motivation for military dictators such as President Efraín Rios Montt of Guatemala. That is an unappetizing prospect.

Previous Papal Condemnations Ineffective

History offers other solutions for cases where the papacy has tried to impose unpopular solutions in matters not clearly of faith. In the 1830s Pope Gregory XVI told the Poles they were not to revolt because they had a duty of obedience to the czar of Russia. In the 1890s Pope Leo XIII condemned "Americanism," an error that fortunately was never satisfactorily defined. There is not much evidence that either condemnation had any effect.

After initial bewilderment and some heart-searching, Poles and Americans went their own way, convinced the Catholic church was broad enough to accommodate them. The difference, however, is that neither Gregory nor Leo delivered his message in Warsaw or Washington. John Paul has not confined himself to sending warning letters from distant Rome. He has spelled out his message in the July 19 Plaza in Managua. Television and the jet age permit the pope, for all practical purposes, to replace a local bishop.

Later that night, over supper in the nunciature of San José, Costa Rica, John Paul looked worried and preoccupied. The local archbishop, Roman Arrieta, tried to console him by saying the demonstration had been rigged and 95 percent of those present had been on his side. "Rest assured, Holy Father," he said, "that you have sown good seed in fruitful soil. Christ, whose vicar you are, has asked you to sow in tears that you may reap in joy."

John Paul said what worried him most was "the deliberate profanation of the Eucharist." He was observed spending extra time in the nunciature chapel, making reparation.

This line was faithfully followed in the Central American press outside Nicaragua. The Sandinistas had behaved disgracefully, barbarously, outrageously. They were said to be as bad as Joseph Stalin. The vice president of Costa Rica came close to blasphemy when he said the events of Managua were "a second Good Friday." Everyone agreed the Sandinistas were to blame for "politicizing" the visit.

"Politicizing" Ignored in El Salvador

Yet two days later, after a quiet interlude in Panama, a similar "politicizing" took place in El Salvador, and there were no complaints. President Alvaro Magana's exploitation of the papal visit was less crude, but that made it all the more effective.

Magana used his welcoming address to the pope at the airport to announce the next stages of his peace program. This the U.S. State Department has been urging him to do for some time as a way of regaining the lost initiative. Sober-suited, in dark glasses, he intoned like a sleepwalker: "Our program of peace includes respect for human rights and an amnesty law to facilitate the peace commission, the setting up of the necessary conditions for elections and establishing mechanisms that assure full and democratic participation." In a paragraph of almost impenetrable Vaticanese added to his prepared speech, John Paul said in effect that he hoped they would succeed.

But his main contribution to the government case lay in the way he shared its assumption that the situation in El Salvador was almost "normal." The fiction was that the guerrillas practically did not exist, and that if only they would behave reasonably, peace would break out.

Any guerrillas who listened to the pope's homily in the noon-day sun at the Metro Centro would have no difficulty cracking his code language. The reference to Archbishop Oscar Romero set the tone for the rest.

Romero's successor, Archbishop Arturo Rivera y Damas, had called him "prophet and pastor." But John Paul disagreed. "Romero," he said "together with other brother bishops, called for violence to cease and for reconciliation to be established. In remembering him, I plead that his memory should be respected and that no ideological interest should try to exploit his sacrifice as pastor."

This was delivered on the passionate high note John Paul uses for important statements. It left some of his hearers perplexed as a summary of Romero's life and death. For he had not been backed up by his "brother bishops," had urged the troops to disobey unjust orders and had thought the time for legitimate insurrection had come. That was why he was killed.

But perhaps the main reason John Paul wanted to rewrite the Romero story was that Romero had undermined in advance the anticommunist campaign the government uses to justify itself.

In a text addressed to the pope, quoted on the back of postcards suppressed by the government just before John Paul's arrival, Romero had said: "Holy Father, it is very difficult to speak of anticommunism in my country because the anticommunism proclaimed by the right is not based on love or Christian sentiments but on an egoism which defends its own interests."

There was no way around that statement. The issue was not whether it could be ideologically exploited; it was whether it was true or false. John Paul believed it to be false.

Government Peace Program Blessed

His solution to the civil war in El Salvador was "true conversion to Jesus Christ" leading to a reconciliation that would "break down the political social, economic and ideological barriers." The application of the church's "social doctrine" would make this possible. The democratic way was the way forward. The government peace program was blessed.

One significant last-minute change in the pope's homily made this clear. In the text prepared in Rome he had said: "No one should be excluded from the dialogue for peace." But the government document, "Basis for Peace in El Salvador," remarked that "the dialogue proposed by the opposition does not contribute to peace and will be transformed into a negative factor." So "dialogue" is a guerrilla term. In the end John Paul read: "No one should be excluded from the effort for peace."

Any lingering doubts about John Paul's position were cleared up when he addressed priests in the College of San Salvador later on Sunday, March 6. He invited them to give their lives for the authentic gospel. A priest cannot give his life "for a mutilated or exploited gospel or for a party political option."

The liberation the church calls for, he said, "is a change of heart bringing about a peaceful but decisive revolution, the fruit of Christian love." John Paul rehearsed his usual theme on the priesthood. Priests should say Mass "above all on an altar." They should be dressed in the way "that makes them easily identifiable." They are not called to be "social workers, political leaders or civil servants of any temporal power."

Applied in a peaceful situation, such exhortations are harmless enough. Applied where a civil war is raging, such as that of El Salvador, they place the priests in a position of imaginary neutrality, somewhere above the battle, and thus support the status quo.

John Paul's reinterpretation of Puebla's "preferential option for the poorest" confirmed he intended this. It does not allow one to ignore, he said, "that there is a radical poverty wherever God does not dwell in the hearts of men and where they are enslaved by power, pleasure, money or violence. Your mission reaches out to those forms of poverty as well."

"To that end," he added, "the priests should preach not only justice, but also proclaim God's mercy." So the repudiation of liberation theology, begun by John Paul at Puebla, was completed in San Salvador March 6, 1983.

Perhaps the only person who can contemplate these events with unalloyed satisfaction is President Reagan. For he has now secured papal backing on two cardinal points of his Central American policy: destabilization of the Sandinistas in Nicaragua, and the attempt to provide the El Salvador government with a fig leaf of democratic respectability.

Recent U.S. moves have concentrated on stepping up the cross-border raids against Nicaragua from Honduras, and increasing the number of U.S. military advisers in El Salvador from 45 to as many as 55. But these are paltry measures compared with the psychological weapon of a pope who, in Managua, refused to pray for the victims of the national guard and, in San Salvador, tried to deprive the guerrillas of their only real advantage: the justice of their cause.

Theme Changes in Guatemala

Then, in Guatemala, John Paul departed from this script and sprang a surprise. His homily in the Campo de Marte was on faith. It was an impassioned and eloquent plea for social justice, a defense of the rights of the poor, an unambiguous commitment of the church to development in society.

In the pope's eyes there was no contradiction with his previous statements, for the justice he was proclaiming was based — he repeated this — not on some "ideology" but on the gospel and the social teaching of the church. The pope's speech was different here because the setting was different.

In Guatemala the church is gravely persecuted. The number of priests has declined by death or exile from 700 to 450. Clergy phones are tapped. Anyone can be arrested on the basis of denunciation or mere suspicion of "aiding the subversives." Execution follows. The Geneva Convention does not apply because there is "no declared war."

Moreover, Gen. Rios Montt, born-again Christian, has not disguised his hostility to the church and his preference for the 30 percent of the population who are "Protestant." So in denouncing "violence, torture, arbitrary arrests and killings" as crimes and a grave offense against God, John Paul was also making a polemical anti-Protestant point.

He seems to share the view of the local cardinal, Spanish-born Mario Casariego, who said the missionaries have brought "faith and the Spanish language" to Guatemala (even though 80 percent of the population are Indians, speaking about 20 other languages).

"Christian faith," said John Paul, meaning Catholic faith, "is the glory of your people and the soul of the Central American countries." But that makes the "sects" (as they are always called here) a foreign importation, an anomaly in these historically Catholic countries.

So John Paul reminded his hearers that "not everyone who says Lord, Lord, will enter the kingdom of heaven," that faith without good work is vain, and that "man is justified by work, not by faith alone." The "sects" notoriously concentrate on individual salvation and are politically docile.

John Paul was speaking under a banner that proclaimed the "homage of the Guatemalan army to the messenger of peace." That was not the least of the many ironies on this Central American trip. He hoped to leave behind him, he said in Guatemala, "a climate of justice." One can wonder about that, while being quite sure he made his presence felt. From now on in Central America, they will talk about "before" and "after" the papal visit. ❑

27

Rome meeting 'blow to national conferences'

(April 29, 1983) We now have a full and official account of the secret meeting held in the Vatican Jan. 18-19. It is the work of Fr. Jan Schotte, secretary of the Pontifical Justice and Peace Commission. A Jan. 25 memorandum from Archbishop John J. Roach and Cardinal Joseph Bernardin adds some more details.

The U.S. bishops insist they were not being called on the carpet for their views on nuclear weapons. The specific conclusions in the second draft of their pastoral letter, they say, "were not criticized, questioned or addressed." This is hard to believe, because the meeting's entire purpose was "to hear the concerns of the European bishops and to receive guidance from the Holy See." What concerns? Guidance about what?

Moreover, the U.S. bishops are congratulated in the Schotte report on their "courage and humility" in agreeing to go to Rome for this "open exchange." They can have displayed these virtues only if they were under some attack. Courage was needed to face criticism, humility to accept it.

If, afterward, they preferred to describe the consultation as "a positive and helpful exchange of views," one feels bound to attribute this to ecclesiastical diplomacy, born of a reluctance to admit that real divisions exist.

The Schotte report, however, makes clear that disagreements existed and what they were about. The most serious and radical objection came from Cardinal Joseph Ratzinger, whose opening shot was that the National Conference of Catholic Bishops (NCCB) was not competent to write such a pastoral letter.

He said, "A bishops' conference does not have a *mandatum docendi* (a mandate to teach). This belongs only to individual bishops or to the college of bishops with the pope."

This is a disconcerting remark. Common sense suggests that a group of bishops, provided they work a bit, are likely to produce more effective teaching than bishops in lonely isolation. Memories of Vatican II confirm that an episcopal conference carries more weight than the individual bishops who make it up. The rediscovery of collegiality was one of the great achievements of Vatican II.

Yet Ratzinger's remark is theologically defensible: it represents one possible interpretation, a narrow one, of Vatican II. It is made more plausible by playing with marked cards. If he had spoken, as would be more natural, of the *munus docendi* (the teaching office) of bishops, he would have to concede that it flows from episcopal ordination.

By changing this to *mandatum docendi* (a mandate to teach), he insinuates that someone has to give it to them. There is all the difference in the world between a "duty" (another meaning of *munus*) and a "concession."

Behind this lies the debate about the nature of an episcopal conference. The council defined it this way: "An episcopal conference is a kind of council in which the bishops of a given nation or territory jointly exercise their pastoral office by way of promoting that greater good which the church offers all mankind, especially through forms and programs of the apostolate which are fittingly adapted to the circumstances of the age" ("Decree on Bishops," 38, 1). Further, the document on implementing the council, *Ecclesiae Sanctae*, recommends: "The bishops of nations or territories which do not have episcopal conferences will see to their setting up as soon as possible."

Clearly, episcopal conferences were regarded as a good thing. Yet, from the start, not all commentators regarded them as a wonderful expression of collegiality. Dominican Fr. Jerome Hamer wrote in 1963 of "partial realization of collegiality which has to be referred to the whole" (i.e., the whole college, united with the pope).

Writing in *Concilium* in 1965, Ratzinger himself conceded that episcopal conferences were "one of the possible variants of episcopal collegiality," which is more than he is now saying. He is, of course, cardinal prefect of the Congregation for the Doctrine of the Faith, and Hamer, now Archbishop Hamer, is its secretary.

Yet despite this sniping, episcopal conferences had a good press until the 1969 synod, called to deal with the confusing aftermath of *Humanae Vitae*. Episcopal commentaries on the encyclical had been far from uniform; some introduced considerations about "conscience" which modified or blunted its impact.

One 1969 speaker who wanted to restrict the autonomy of episcopal conferences was Cardinal Karol Wojtyla of Kraków. He warned against the peril of "nationalism," which "always and everywhere is and will be most dangerous to the unity, faith and charity of the church."

In a 1971 book, Jesuit Fr. Henri de Lubac (created a cardinal Feb. 2 this year) quoted Wojtyla with approval and launched a vigorous attempt to cut episcopal conferences down to size. He conceded that they could be "practically useful," but that was not high praise in his vocabulary.

They are denied true theological status. Their common decisions are said to be merely "collective" and not really "collegial." They can undermine the individual bishop's role by subjecting him to the bureaucratic structures that go with setting up an episcopal conference.

In 1983 Ratzinger does not spell out these criticisms in any detail. But with his starting point ("no mandate to teach"), he does not need to. Teaching in the church is done either by individual bishops or by all the bishops in union with the pope. There is no properly collegial role for intermediate bodies such as episcopal conferences.

Ratzinger says only individual bishops have a mandate to teach, short of another general council. But because there are more than 3,200 of them, it is impossible for the pope personally to oversee that their teaching is in harmony with his. Perhaps papal diplomats acting in his name could do it. But that would be to return to the preconciliar situation.

Moreover, the Ratzinger theory contradicts church practice since Vatican II. "Intermediate bodies" have been regarded as the key to renewal and have been taken seriously as "teachers of the faith."

The decisions of the Latin American episcopal conference (CELAM), for example, have been regarded as "collegial." In this instance, the "union with the head of the college" has been explicit: Paul VI went to the opening of CELAM's Medellín, Colombia, meeting 1968 and John Paul II to the sessions in Puebla, Mexico, in 1979. But the CELAM was left to get on with its work.

Again, in practice, John Paul prefers to deal with episcopal conferences rather than with individual bishops. There are too many U.S. bishops for all to make their *ad limina* (periodic) visit to Rome at the same time. But smaller, more manageable conferences go together and are addressed as a group.

Further, on every papal visit so far, the most important speech has invariably been that addressed to the episcopal conference.

Never televised, it is an intimate occasion that sets the pastoral keynote for the visit. And it is, as John Paul never tires of saying on these occasions, "an expression of affective and effective collegiality."

The January 1980 Dutch synod was a clear example of the way bishops are treated as a serious theological entity. If individual bishops in their dioceses were all that mattered, they could have been "dealt with" on an individual basis. But all were summoned to Rome and reminded — incidentally — of their teaching office.

It is difficult to guess why Ratzinger, who knows this recent history as well as anyone, should ignore it so signally in this instance.

A second source of astonishment is the way some argue that bishops should only propose teaching that is "binding in conscience." Where controversial matters arise, "they should offer several options or express themselves hypothetically." It is also said "it is wrong to propose the teaching of bishops merely as a basis for debate." Neglect of these principles leads, we are told, to "confusion among the faithful."

The implications of these remarks are far-reaching and preposterous. They assume that bishops are only ever called upon to pronounce in open or shut cases where they can "bind in conscience." That means they can only repeat what is already known: a somewhat redundant exercise.

In controversial matters, they would be reduced either to silence or to a noncommittal summary of the options — what has been called the bland leading the bland. It does not seem to be realized that there are other, equally valid and important forms of teaching that fall short of the ultimate deterrent of "binding in conscience." People have to be encouraged to think morally to be prodded into sensitivity, in short, to be woken up.

Moreover, the recognition of this distinction of levels of teaching helps the bishops' authority and credibility. They score no marks for silence of platitudinous summary. It does not help if they are thought of as omni competent judges infallibly solving moral conundrums from a lofty eminence.

Much better to see them as moral guides as involved in the struggle toward moral judgment as anyone else, who share their reflections after hard work and extensive consultation.

The third astonishing feature of the Schotte report is that although "fidelity to the tradition of the church and the teaching of John Paul II" is presented as the criterion of sound doctrine, what John Paul II's teaching is on the matter is nowhere made clear.

What makes this — evidently premeditated — absence of the pope from the discussion even more astonishing is that his own position was discussed and regarded as of vital importance. So the absurd situation was reached in which Cardinal Agostino Casaroli filled the gap by offering "a personal commentary" on the June 11, 1982, U.N. message.

"He did so," the Schotte report explains, "not as an authorized interpreter of the Holy Father's statement, but on the basis of his knowledge of the text and context of that message." So he was not wiser than anyone else. He was placed in the unenviable position of having to "deduce" what papal teaching might be and hedged it with cautious qualifications: "this was doubtless in the thought of the Holy Father," etc.

This seems a rather odd way of doing things. It is as though John Paul set the bishops a difficult riddle, then left them to speculate about what it might mean. No doubt it will be said this was done to leave the bishops free to make up their own minds.

But no such inhibitions were apparent in the Dutch synod. In any case, although the U.S. bishops were not worsted in arguments — they stated their case well, and the countercase was merely set in parallel against it — they then returned home to modify their pastoral according to what they had heard in Rome.

So the secret meeting in Rome raised without resolving questions on the morality of nuclear war. But its deeper significance is ecclesiological. What price collegiality now? And how *can* doctrine develop? ❏

28

'Spiritual defiance' infuses pope's Poland visit

(July 1, 1983) Just before the papal visit to Poland, Cardinal Józef Glemp gave an interview to an Italian weekly, *Il Sabato*. He said that "any protests of demonstration during the pope's visit will be the result of deliberate provocation and will not have the people's approval." He could hardly have been more spectacularly wrong. Anyway, he forgot to tell Pope John Paul about this supposed "agreement."

Even the weather reflected the difference of mood in the two papal visits. In 1979 the June sun beat down mercilessly, and the message was one of release and hope. In 1983 the sky was gray and gloomy, and the message was one of endurance, spiritual defiance and suffering.

John Paul announced this theme from the moment of his arrival. The kiss on the airport tarmac was, he said, "like the kiss placed on the hands of a mother, a mother who has suffered much and who suffers yet again." This was not sentimental tear-jerking. It was a sober statement about the historic vocation of Poland, where the passion of Christ goes on being relived.

So the pope's visit to Poland was like a medieval mystery play in which the characters act out their predestined roles. It dramatized the question: who really rules Poland? At the heart of it was a confrontation between Gen. Wojciech Jaruzelski and Pope John Paul. The contest was very uneven. No wonder Jaruzelski twitched nervously as he read his prepared text. "I confirm our will to lift martial law," he intoned, "and to find humanitarian solutions."

The last time John Paul was in the Belvedere Palace, Warsaw, the man he looked across at under the chandeliers was Edward Gierek, now retired and disgraced. Since then there has been another first secretary of the Polish United Workers' Party, Stefan Kania. He has been forgotten.

Where have all the leaders gone? Jaruzelski's rather forlorn appearance suggested that he knows he is in a high-risk profession. The pope treated him with elaborate courtesy, referring not to the leaders of Poland but to "the highest representative of the state authority in Poland," a term he usually reserves for upstart military dictators in Latin America.

So the unequal contest went on. Jaruzelski could appeal only to "38 years of socialism." Not only has it not achieved the promised paradise, but martial law was the ultimate admission that the communist regime has no popular base and no democratic legitimacy. Its sole justification is geopolitical: the Soviet Union is next door and will not admit any other regime in Poland. That was Jaruzelski's case.

Against it John Paul weighed in with all the prestige of the papacy, the Polish mystique of suffering, his international fame as the defender of human rights and above all the sense that he had a thousand years of Polish history on his side. Faith, freedom and national identity were woven into a powerful and irresistible case.

Jasna Gora and Piekary have seen it all before. In the 19th century, when Poland was partitioned, it was said that at these Marian shrines, "Our Lady spoke Polish." In Poznan, the memories stretched further back to the two first Polish kings, Mieszko and Boleslaw the Bold, who are buried in the Cathedral of Ss. Peter and Paul. John Paul had this history on his side.

So the visit exposed the contrast between the fictional country over which Jaruzelski officially rules and the real country where Poles are free. In the fictional country Solidarity is outlawed, finished, dead and buried. Lech Walesa is a nonperson, a mere "private citizen," an ordinary electrician going about his work (accompanied admittedly by the most televised security police in the world) in the Lenin shipyard in Gdansk.

The real country was on display from the first evening after mass in St. Ann's Cathedral, Warsaw. Crowds filled Nowy Swiat Street giving "V" for victory signs and shouting slogans about Solidarity, Lech Walesa and Zbigniew Bujak — the Warsaw underground leader. "The pope is with us," they chanted, meaning not just that he was present in Warsaw, but that he was on their side.

The Zomo or riot police looked impotently on. Wisely they kept their water cannon and batons out of action. The crowd cheerfully wished them "good night" and advised them to "go to the church." There was something of the good humor which marked the beginnings of Solidarity and which, briefly, disarmed the security forces. As Aldous Huxley said: "You can do anything with bayonets except sit upon them."

The government news agency hastened to explain that the Warsaw demonstration was "the work of a small handful of agitators." We were back in the fictional world. Not for nothing is the government news agency called PAP.

The next day — Friday, June 17 — the government backed down on its refusal to let Walesa see the pope. An audience was in principle granted "for humanitarian reasons." It did not mean that his status had changed, or that he was once more a partner in dialogue.

There it was again, this curious term, also used by Jaruzelski: "humanitarian." The Polish rulers cannot do anything because it is simply a good thing or required by common decency. They have to dress it up in "humanitarian" clothes in order to assert the moral superiority of Marxism. That is another piece of fiction.

John Paul dealt with it swiftly at Niepokalanow, the Franciscan "City of the Immaculate One," where St. Maximilian Kolbe was guardian until sent to Auschwitz in February 1941. There are physical victories, said the pope, won by force of arms. They can create a desert and call it peace (or "calm," to use Jaruzelski's favorite word).

But Poland needs and in a sense already has "a moral victory," built on self-control which leads to "living in the truth, integrity of conscience, love of one's neighbor, the capacity to forgive."

By Saturday, June 18, in Czestochowa, the moral victory had been won and the whole visit began to slip out of control. The youth Mass outside the ancient battlements was a pro-Solidarity rally. The theme was freedom. "We may envy the French, the Germans or the Americans," said John Paul, "because they are so easily free, while our freedom costs so much."

"True freedom," he went on, "is not possible without values." The phrases came twice over the loudspeaker — a curious and accidental form of emphasis: "We do not want — do not want — a Poland that costs us nothing — costs us nothing." At any mention of freedom, workers or human rights, Solidarity banners were unfurled.

Then for the first time, John Paul used the word *solidarity* with a small *s*. "I give thanks for the proofs of human solidarity given by Poles," he declared, "especially by young people in the difficult period not many months ago." As examples of human solidarity, he gave "care of those interned in prison or fired from work." Prepared in the quiet of the Vatican, this use of the term "solidarity" may have seemed like a good joke: this was how the Russians used to be fooled in the 19th century. But in the context it took on critical significance.

Two things happened Saturday, which showed how rattled the government was becoming. As the pope arrived in Czestochowa, the Catholic Intellectuals' Club (KIK) was dissolved; previously, it had been merely suspended. Such clubs have provided most of the advisers to Solidarity.

Next, government spokesman Jerzy Urban cried foul. The church was breaking its agreement not to politicize religious events. The church marshals were supposed to report Solidarity demonstrators to the authorities. They were failing in their work. Urban then resorted to threats: if this kind of display continued, the lifting of martial law would be still further delayed. But by now the crowds had decided that they might as well be hanged for a lamb as a sheep.

So, too, had Pope John Paul. On the evening of June 18, it was announced that he would "improvise." No text was distributed in advance. The unscheduled speech took the form of an apostrophe or prayer addressed to the Black Madonna of Czestochowa.

It began: "Mary, in this moment of sincerity, when I open my heart to you, I cannot remain silent on a number of painful questions . . . that is why I beg you to intercede for those who suffer — and for those who inflict suffering" (applause), "for your Son rejected no one."

Still in his prayer, John Paul suggested that the Gdansk agreements of 1980 should be taken up again and made the basis of a "social dialogue." This was greeted with tremendous applause.

After that, there was no looking back. In his speech to the Polish bishops Sunday, June 19, John Paul said dialogue should be reopened with those who "represent the true aspirations of the workers and the need of honest solidarity among them." More fundamentally still, "Poland has the right to hear the truth."

The first specific reference to Solidarity came in Poznan Monday, June 20, at a Mass for farmers. But again it was indirect, taking the form of a quotation from the late Cardinal Stefan Wyszynski. In the fall of 1981 he said the right to found a labor union "is a right conceded by someone — it is innate and therefore inalienable." Because the state cannot concede this right, neither can it take it away. The conclusions followed relentlessly.

Trybuna Ludu, the Communist Party daily, reacted fiercely with a long article blaming the failure of the Gdansk agreements on Solidarity "extremists." The "political opposition" was responsible for the breakdown, not the government.

In Katowice, on an airfield lashed by thunderstorms, John Paul spoke more bluntly than ever. Relatives of the miners shot after martial law were close to the altar. They were remembered in the homily and the prayers of the faithful. John Paul also recalled that in 1981 a delegation from Solidarity had gone to visit him in Rome, "accompanied by a representative of the Polish government." He hoped that kind of cooperation would be restored. It was in Katowice that he spoke of Our Lady, Mother of Social Justice, a new title to add to the litany of Loretto.

Finally, on Tuesday, June 21, the sun came out in Wroclaw and prepared an emotional reception and farewell in Kraków. Citizen Walesa got his audience in the end.

General Jaruzelski will have some explaining to do after the visit. It did not go according to plan. It signally failed to demonstrate that "normality" has returned to Poland. It did not win the "legitimation" or blessing that had been hoped for. So he is exposed as a hollow man. He is worse off than before. The consequences are unpredictable. In Poland, the unpredictable is usually tragic. ❏

29

John Paul five years later: Reassertion and restoration

(October 14, 1983) Pope John Paul's pontificate has now lasted longer than that of Pope John XXIII. Its direction has been clear from the outset: reassertion and restoration are its watchwords. After five years, it seems useful to ask how much John Paul has learned about being pope from the two predecessors whose names he adopted.

There is no training program for future popes. Their idea of the papacy is influenced by tradition, the cultural atmosphere, and by the way popes in their lifetime behave. They learn the metier of pope by watching others at work.

Sometimes, they learn what not to do. There is a well-attested story that John, asked by a new and anxious archbishop of Le Mans how he could possibly succeed the wise, good and learned Cardinal George Grente, member of the French Academy, comforted him by saying: "Don't worry: just be like me — the opposite of my predecessor."

It is true that John did not attempt to compete with Pius XII on his own ground — those 20 volumes of magisterial and encyclopedic teaching. He did not aspire to exercise infallibility. Instead he inaugurated a new pontifical style, less hieratic and remote, more fraternal, pastoral and "collegial" (a forgotten word he revived).

John and Paul provided the immediate "models" for John Paul. These were the popes he knew personally, though he was not as close to John as he was to Paul. He remembers John at the beginning and above all the end of the Vatican council — when "his intended *au revoir* turned into a farewell." Paul, on the other hand, he can call "my great predecessor and true father."

But despite this difference, their two names are usually linked together. In *Redemptor Hominis*, a programmatic first encyclical, John Paul said he would take up their inheritance and complete their work: "John XXIII and Paul VI are a stage to which I wish to refer directly and a threshold from which I intend to continue" (2). So much is obvious: though the metaphor is clumsy and mixed, popes do not openly contradict their predecessors.

Both predecessors are praised for possessing what John Paul calls "the charism of transformation." It has something to do with the crucial question of "change" in the church. In trying to understand this concept, one has to recall that Pope John Paul is by professional training a philosopher. On the first anniversary of Paul VI's death, he spoke of this "charism of transformation" thanks to which "the figure of the church, familiar to all, showed itself to be identical and yet different. This diversity did not mean a distancing from its own essence, but rather a deeper penetration of its very essence."

The language is that of the late Edmund Husserl and phenomenology, but the attitude is that once described by Michael Novak (in younger and better days) as "nonhistorical orthodoxy." John had believed that the key discipline was history, not philosophy. He told the council that "history is the teacher of life." Rather than seek out some intemporal essence of the church, he preferred to see it as a living community which had to look out for the favorable breeze of the Holy Spirit and "discern the signs of the times."

Lacking such a sense of history, John Paul tends to pack together into one "essence" institutions and traditions that took centuries to develop. In John's city of Bergamo, for example, he exhorted priests and religious worried by "all these changes" to remember that "We are what we have always been — and by that I mean we must remain as Christ the Lord wanted." But it is difficult to leap with seven-league boots from the first to the 20th century.

So in John Paul's interpretation of Vatican II, continuity is stressed rather than change. Again in Bergamo April 26, 1981, he said: "The church emerged from this council — which Pope John summoned, guided (as he himself confessed) by the clear inspiration of the Holy Spirit — with renewed faith in the power of Christ's word. It emerged with a new certainty about its mission. It emerged toward the future."

Undoubtedly the "future" came next. Perhaps the most important remark there is that the council was "a clear inspiration." One could argue about what it means, but it cuts the ground from under those such as Cardinal Giuseppe Siri, who regarded the council as a mistake and "the greatest disaster in recent ecclesiastical history" (the cardinal has since changed his mind and testified that Pope John opened doors no one else could).

Obviously any description of Pope John must pay some attention to his openness to change. But Pope John Paul is remarkably unspecific about the details. John is presented in a series of paradoxes: like the man in the gospels, he brought "things new and old" out of his treasure-house; "a man in love with tradition gave the impulse to a new age in the church"; "at 80 he demonstrated the ever-renewed youthfulness of Christ's spouse."

Everyone is agreed, however, on John's "goodness. "Speaking at his birthplace, Sotto Il Monte, John Paul referred to "the good and smiling figure of Pope John, so dear to the hearts of all Italians" and explained that his popularity showed that "the world has need of goodness, and so it loved Pope John and still venerates and invokes him." So the "cult" was acknowledged, though nothing was said about beatification. However, the cliché of "Good Pope John" is not without dangers: in the wrong hands it can be used to imply he was pious but rather simpleminded and impractical.

John Paul's portrait of his predecessor is not controversial, but it is incomplete and selective. In four sermons in Bergamo, there was only one quotation from the *Journal of a Soul:* it comes from John's October 1910 retreat and is the most "anti-modernist" statement in the whole book. It needed to be balanced by other passages in which the young Angelo Roncalli speaks of "the wonderful progress that has been made in scientific history in the past few years." And a historian, if not a homilist, would want to add that Roncalli was himself absurdly suspected of "modernism."

John Paul's account of Paul is committed and polemical. It is based on one interpretation of what has been happening in the modern church. He believes Paul was the victim of monstrous injustice and calumny. So he advised the executive committee of the Paul VI Institute in Brescia, a body committed to the historical study of Pope Paul, to go to work with scientific rigor, certainly, but above all with love because "in the course of his life he was not always understood. He had his cross, bore 'insults' and was 'spat upon.' . . . Love is therefore an act of reparation to his memory" (Jan. 26, 1980).

To a group of pilgrims from Brescia, Pope Paul's home city, he explained where he thought the insults and the spittle came from: "Faced with the secularization that was invading society and the ferments which caused unrest within the church, Paul VI, misunderstood and sometimes calumniated, remained a beacon of light for everyone" (April 24, 1979).

With this analysis of the recent past, it is unlikely that "dissent," even of the loyal variety, will have much place in the church's life. Pope Paul's optimistic idea that theologians communicated both upward and downward has been lost sight of. The "critic," whatever his motives (among which love of the church is not allowed to count), is a troublemaker to be dealt with.

Although in *Redemptor Hominis* Paul is praised as a splendid "helmsman of Peter's barque, who knew how to preserve a providential tranquillity and balance, even in the most critical moments," the dominant image is one of agony rather than tranquillity. In some texts Paul appears as a tragic and almost mythical figure of immense stature.

John Paul told the Brescia pilgrims: "The gigantic figure (*la figura gigantesca*) of this great pope taught us — at a difficult period in the life of the church and through a daily martyrdom of worry and work — what it really means to love and serve Christ and souls." The portrait is of a martyred, agonized and suffering pope.

What is missing is any recognition that part of Paul's anguish came from his admirable ability to see several sides to a question. It was not solely the product of secularizing infiltrators in the church.

As the bulky dossiers on birth control mounted on his desk, Pope Paul confessed, "How easy it is to study, to study, how hard it is to decide." Up in Kraków, Archbishop Karol Wojtyla had no such inhibitions, and his 1960 book *Love and Responsibility* was eagerly taken up by Pope Paul as an anticipation of *Humanae Vitae*.

There can be no doubt that Paul and John Paul agreed on major issues. But John Paul behaves as though he believed his predecessor was unable to carry through his ideas either because he was hesitant, vacillating or weak.

To confirm this, one has only to consider how swiftly the inherited dossiers were dispatched. An extraordinary synod was called to deal with the church in the Netherlands. The Jesuits had imposed on them a "personal delegate of the Holy Father." Fr. Hans Küng lost his license to teach as a Catholic theologian. All these "problems" had been hanging about for years. They had been dealt with by lamentations.

Only someone whose mind was already made up on these and other questions could have acted with such decisiveness and clarity. If this is true, it would be another illustration of the law that pontificates go by contrasts.

One is forced to conclude that in the style of his pontificate, Pope John Paul has taken over little from his predecessors. He has devised his own "model" of the papacy in which international travel to trouble spots plays a great role. Even here, however, he has claimed a rather implausible continuity: "John XXIII had foreseen this development, Paul VI gave it full realization on a vast scale, and John Paul I would certainly have developed it further" (interview in *L'Osservatore Romano*). But Paul VI's last journey was in 1970, and his modest little trips had neither the heroic scale nor the marathon tempo of John Paul's great religious spectaculars.

Probably neither pope realized there was a half-quotation here from Alfred de Vigny, the French romantic poet: "A great life is the realization of a dream of youth." The idea of the pope as the church's champion, up there on the smoke-shrouded battlements, in single-handed combat with the forces of evil, does not derive from Italian culture at all. It is found in Roman Slowacki, the Polish romantic poet who — Pius IX having fled Rome — in December 1849 looked prophetically forward to a Slav pope in the 20th century:

This pope will not — Italian-like — take fright
At sabre thrust
But brave as God himself, stand and give fight —
His world — but dust. . .
Love he dispenses as great powers today
Distribute arms:
With sacramental power — his sole array —
The world he charms. ❏

30

Pope's visit to Agca sets model of mercy

(January 13, 1984) Pope John Paul went to the maximum security prison at Rebibbia in Rome Dec. 27. There he met Valerio Malucci of the Red Brigade, the man who supplied the gun that killed Aldo Moro, the Christian Democratic leader in 1978. He met the 200 women prisoners and was surprised to find that they were accompanied by 18 children under the age of 3. He met terrorists, hardened or repentant, famous criminals, minor offenders and people waiting for their trials to begin.

He shook hands with them all. "I have come among you," he explained, "as a sign that you have not been abandoned, that you are not alone in the world, and that somebody thinks about you and loves you."

But the most dramatic meeting in this three-and-a-half-hour visit was with Mehemet Ali Agca. It lasted longer than 20 minutes. Agca knelt and placed his forehead on the back of John Paul's hand — a Muslim sign of respect. They talked in Italian, helped by a little English.

Their conversation was private and confessional-like. All Pope John would say about it later was that it was "providential." Providence led Agca to make the assassination attempt and to bungle it. That was May 13, 1981. A year later, to the day, John Paul explained that he had been saved by Our Lady of Fatima, whose feast it was. So he went to Fatima to give thanks for his deliverance.

And now he was meeting his would-be assassin in his prison cell. That, too, was in the hands of Providence. It was like a medieval illumination: the servant of God embraces the man who tried to kill him. In the storybooks, Agca would end up by being converted. Though he is said to have "repented," that has not yet formally happened.

But already the emblematic scene teaches that mercy is stronger than justice, and that mercy is at the heart of the Christian gospel. John Paul wrote about this in his second encyclical, *Dives in Misericordia*, before he had a chance to apply it in practice.

In that Advent 1980 encyclical, John Paul says mercy causes "uneasiness" in modern people. In a technically well-organized world, there is no room for mercy, which disturbs the order of things and acts as the joker in the pack. This is why the Turks complained about the pope's visit to Agca. Even if released by the Italians, he would still be wanted for murder in Turkey and must expiate his crime.

Dives in Misericordia also dealt with another common objection to "mercy": that it "belittles the receiver, and offends against the dignity of man." But there is no need for the one who receives mercy to feel humiliated or for the one who bestows it to feel superior.

The parable of the prodigal son helps one to grasp this point. John Paul sees it as "the tragedy of lost dignity and the awareness of squandered sonship." So the prodigal son, on his return, has no need to feel demeaned. Rather he is "found again and restored to value."

This was the point of the pope's talk with Agca in his prison cell. *Dives in Misericordia* says "conversion to God always consists in discovering his mercy." Agca does not have to become a Christian to make that discovery.

One thing — we may be sure — the pope did not waste time on whether the KGB or Bulgarian secret service placed the gun in Agca's hand. It is possible, in any case, that Agca does not really know — the Turkish right-wing Grey Wolves were penetrated by East European agents. But this was not on the papal agenda because a dialogue of reconciliation such as this differs fundamentally from a police interrogation. Both the aim and the methods are different.

In any case one would need more than 20 minutes to unweave the web of Agca's lies. He seems to have tried out various plots to see what the effect would be. His latest story is that he originally came to Rome to kill Lech Walesa, making the pope only a second choice victim. That would have disturbed the symmetry of the scene in the prison cell, if true.

A final quote from *Dives in Misericordia* to show the political importance of mercy: "Society can become ever more human if it introduces into personal relationships not merely justice but also that merciful love which constitutes the messianic message of the gospel."

Mercy takes the first step. It seizes the initiative. It risks rebuff. It offers a way out to those trapped in the spiral of violence. It is the practical condition of disarmament, for as the message of World Peace Day reminded us: "It is man who kills and not his sword or, in our day, his missile." ❏

31

Vatican treats Boff, Gutiérrez differently

(October 5, 1984) Not all liberation theologians are being treated the same way. Brazilian Franciscan Fr. Leonardo Boff was summoned for an interview at the Congregation of the Doctrine of Faith (CDF) Sept. 7.

Peruvian diocesan priest Gustavo Gutiérrez, in Rome last June to publicize *We Drink From Our Own Wells*, his recent book on the spirituality that came out of liberation theology, would never have had an interview at the CDF, no matter how hard he knocked on the door.

Why this difference? The Gutiérrez case is being left in the hands of the Peruvian bishops so they can exercise controlled collegiality.

There was no point in entrusting Boff to the Brazilian bishops, because they would have gotten the wrong answer: the majority of them are known to be on his side. The presence of Cardinals Aloísio Lorscheider and Paulo Evaristo Arns at each elbow Sept. 7 proved the point: no wedge can be driven between Boff and his bishops.

The Peruvians were a different matter. Peru's only cardinal, Franciscan Juan Landazuri Ricketts, 71, is sympathetic to liberation theology and used Gutiérrez as his personal expert at the 1968 Latin American bishops' meeting in Medellín.

But Jesuit Fernando Vargas Ruiz de Somocurcio, 66, bishop of Arequipa, is a doughty opponent of liberation theology in all its forms. The question was how many of the 51 other bishops (including auxiliaries) could he bring round.

The process of pulling over the Peruvian bishops began in March 1983, when Cardinal Joseph Ratzinger, CDF prefect, sent them 10 critical "observations" on Gutiérrez's theology. This was merely, he explained, "to help them complete their examination of his theology and compose a document on it." It went without saying that the document would be negative.

Gutiérrez was told what was going on. In June 1983, he submitted a 60-page defense of his work to the bishops. They met in plenary sessions in August and again in January 1984 but found themselves unable to agree to the sort of text Ratzinger desired. To resolve the impasse, they set up a commission of six.

Five turned out to be pro-Gutiérrez; only one was against. Two more bishops were added to "strike a balance." This commission sat down to work with a CDF team Sept. 24. It was hoped the document that could not be put together in Peru might be completed in Rome.

Great pressure is being put on the Peruvian bishops. Officially, they are merely making an ordinary *ad limina* — but because 12 of them made their last *ad limina* visit as recently as May this year, what is happening is far from routine. It resembles, in some ways, the "extraordinary synod" that tried to bring the Dutch church to heel in January 1980.

All the Peruvian bishops were in Rome Sept. 26 to Oct. 4. The last time they voted on the Gutiérrez question, 18 were in favor of "corrections," 18 against and five abstained. That was in April. It would be no surprise to discover that the lapse of time or the Roman air has changed some minds.

Just before the Peruvian bishops arrived in Rome, the nuncio to Lina, Archbishop Mario Tagliaferri, had a private audience with Pope John Paul. Tagliaferri would have been able to offer a personal assessment of the chances of pushing through a successful condemnation.

Gutiérrez remains cheerful, though a little apprehensive. He admits he has suffered but says it would be blasphemous to compare his sufferings with those of his people. "I'm tempted to say what they say," he said. "These are questions that only concern the palefaces." Gutiérrez is an Indian.

All these events should be seen against a background of violence and guerrilla war back home. Although the coming to power of President Fernando Belaunde Terry in 1980 marked a return to civilian government, the harsh counterinsurgency measures he has ordered have contributed to the guerrilla movements they seek to destroy and have weakened his own authority.

It is difficult to foresee a tranquil papal visit to Peru in January, supposing it happens. ❑

32

Curia 'defenders' undercut pope's message: Ratzinger, others use pope's weight, not words, to slam church opponents

(April 12, 1985) While I was down under in Australia last month, spreading the word about Pope John XXIII, something strange was happening in the Vatican. Prominent people had been making statements well to the right of anything Pope John Paul II had said. One wonders why.

The chief offender is Cardinal Joseph Ratzinger, prefect of the Congregation for the Doctrine of the Faith (CDF). Unlike his predecessors who maintained a poker-faced silence in all that was not the official line of duty, Ratzinger seems to enjoy giving interviews.

When he speaks in his own name, his opinions carry no more weight than anyone else's. He cannot expect the afterglow of the magisterium to rub off on his off-the-cuff remarks. Once he descends from the CDF chair, he has to justify his opinions as any theologian does. Mere assertion is not enough. He has to produce evidence.

Take his view that an episcopal conference has "no theological status or reality." He stated this most clearly when addressing the Jan. 18, 1983, consultation of the U.S. bishops' pastoral letter.

Ratzinger then said, "A bishops' conference as such does not have a mandate to teach. This belongs only to the individual bishops or to the college of bishops with the pope."

One can see the *practical* reason Ratzinger wishes to propound this thesis. An episcopal conference (typically the Brazilian or the U.S. Catholic Conference) can stand up to him, but individual bishops find it much more difficult. They cave in at the first threat of a withdrawn imprimatur.

Alternatively, the theory is useful to Ratzinger when he thinks a conference has gone collectively soft. In that case, the individual "sound" bishop (let's say Archbishop John J. O'Connor) can redeem the whole pack. It is a risky operation and depends for its success on no one's knowing what is really happening.

It should be said firmly, however, that Pope John Paul does not share in Ratzinger's private theological opinion. For 20 years, 1958 to 1978, Karol Wojtyla was a member of the toughest and most cohesive episcopal conference of them all.

In Poland, no individual bishop dared or sought to get out of line. Because any hint of division within the church would be ruthlessly exploited by the Communist Party, arguments among the bishops — and there were some epic ones — were kept strictly under wraps. To the world, the Polish bishops presented an impressively united front.

If some outsider such as the Vatican diplomat they have not had since the war were to inform them that, as a group, they have no mandate to teach, I fear they would have invited him to jump with his theory into the Vistula River.

Again, Wojtyla's emergence on the international scene came through the Roman synods of the 1970s. In each case, his peers elected him to speak on their behalf. Wojtyla always stressed this point: his strength came from the fact that he was not speaking merely as an individual but in the name of the Polish church.

The institution of the synod depends directly upon the episcopal conferences. They elect the representatives who go to Rome and brief them before they depart. The synod is a meeting of episcopal conferences gathered around the pope, not an assembly of randomly chosen individual bishops. That makes it a quasi-collegial event.

Nor has Wojtyla's practice as pope strayed from his practice as archbishop. On every international trip, the meeting with the episcopal conference is always the high point (also the only one that is not usually televised). John Paul invariably speaks on these occasions of the "affective and effective collegiality" that binds them. It would be the height of absurdity to say that on these occasions the pope gathers the bishops together, then addresses them merely as individuals.

On the contrary, the pope always speaks to bishops as if they have a special mandate, as a group, to teach and apply the faith in this country or region. Wherever he can, he quotes the joint pastoral letters produced by the episcopal conference.

So one can say that, in practice, John Paul accepts the theological reality and presence of the episcopal conferences. The weakness of Ratzinger's position is that it is based on a narrowly juridical view of things (that telltale phrase "as such" gives the game away). The pope, on the other hand, bases himself on the experience of being in communion with his fellow bishops.

The second main divergence between Ratzinger and John Paul concerns the interpretation of Vatican II. Ratzinger has talked explicitly of the need for a "restoration" of pre-conciliar values.

He has enumerated a number of "cries" of faith that allegedly followed in the wake of the council: a tendency to reduce belief in God to Christology alone; to see the church as a merely human organization; to treat theology as a private activity starting from "limited human experiences"; and to read scripture apart from the witness of the church.

Some of these complaints are no doubt justified (though unpacking them would take a long time). But just because they happened, if at all, after the council does not imply that the council must be blamed for them. Our old friend "secularization" is a more promising candidate for this role. Ratzinger has fallen into the oldest fallacy of all: *Post hoc, ergo propter hoc* (after this, therefore, because of this).

John Paul has not fallen into this trap. Whenever he speaks of Vatican II, he speaks positively. Although he sometimes denounces (as did Paul VI) erroneous interpretations of the council, the event itself remains majestically untouched.

That is why it can be commemorated and celebrated next November. There would not be much point in commemorating a wrong turning or celebrating an ambiguity.

My last examples of statements well to the right of the pope come from two Dominican professors at the Angelicum — once the pope's own university.

Fr. Daniel Ols, as you read in *Time* magazine (March 11, 1985) wrote an "editorial" in *L'Osservatore Romano*, the Vatican daily, in which he attacked the book on Christian unity written by Karl Rahner and Heinrich Fries.

Reunion cannot occur, said Ols, without other churches' "assent to all and every one of the dogmas" professed by Rome (including those of Vatican I). If that were to be taken literally as a statement of current Vatican policy, one could close down the Secretariat for Christian Unity straightaway. It would no longer have any function.

It would also imply that the pope's words in Istanbul, Turkey, were hypocritical. For there, John Paul committed himself to realizing unity with the Orthodox, spoke of "our two sister churches" and quoted Acts 15:28 about "not imposing anything which is not necessary."

"It seems to me," said John Paul, "that the question we should be asking is not whether we can reestablish full communion, but rather whether we have the right to remain apart." In this spirit, the properly theological dialogue with the Orthodox began.

The pope should be worried when his own newspaper undermines clearly stated papal positions. It might comfort him to know that Ols, though a Frenchman, was refused religious profession by the French Dominicans and had to flee to the conservative bastion of the Bologna province in Italy, whence he drifted down to Rome.

Another Angelicum professor — are they all propping each other up? — has a better track record. British Fr. Aidan Nichols is a more liberal spirit than Ols, but in a column in the London *Tablet*, he gave vent to the now fashionable Euro-pessimism: "The fact of the matter is that in more than one part of the world, the Catholic church is manifestly falling apart."

It is not a fact at all, but a judgment in the eye of the beholder. It would help us to know where the falling apart was supposed to be occurring. Unless we know that, we do not know what the fact means. But it is here used as a sword of Damocles hanging over all our heads. If the church is "manifestly falling apart," the most energetic measures are required to retrieve the situation.

Nichols was trying to "defend the pope," so presumably he thinks the pope agrees with his statement. Maybe John Paul does agree that "the church is manifestly falling apart," but he has not said so. Publicly, he is bullish.

Thus, one is left with two questions.

Why should these learned men vilify the recent past and behave as if the Holy Spirit were absent from the church in the pontificate of Paul VI? And what persuades them that the pope is on their side when all his explicit remarks suggest the contrary?

It is high time to tell the Holy Father what is being done in his name. ❏

33

Dutch, pope butt heads over church

(May 24, 1985) To evaluate whether Pope John Paul's visit to the Netherlands was a success, we need to know why he went there. The four-day visit was the climax of a long process of regaining control of a church believed to be slipping into error.

First came the special synod held in Rome in January 1980, which set the ground rules for the future development of the Dutch church. Then, conservative bishops were appointed to carry out these new policies. Finally, the pope came in person to invest them with his authority. This was, so to speak, the last card in the Vatican pack.

Moreover, the pope thought he would succeed. He made this clear on arrival when he thanked Cardinal-designate Adriaan Simonis for emphasizing "the close attachment of Dutch Catholics to Rome." The pope said, "This attachment is deeper than might appear from any account of the contemporary history of the Dutch church."

In other words, the pope was going to bring all his charm, authority and charism to bear on Holland, and thus he would reach out to the "silent majority" of Dutch Catholics who have suffered in silence for so long. Then the "dissidents" in command of the media would be isolated, good sense and normality would be restored and the new era could begin.

The actual visit proved that this plan was based on a faulty analysis of the current state of Dutch Catholicism. There was no evidence that the hungry masses were eagerly waiting to hear the pope's message on crispness and authority.

Even in the southern province of Limburg, Bishop Joannes Gijses' territory, the crowd was estimated at 40,000 to 50,000 — a mere one-third of the prediction. This was despite the fact that Limburg is close to Belgium and West Germany, from where 1,000 more might have been expected.

Gijses himself admitted that Limburg is practically another country and was no guide to Holland, generally. It was the only place at which a mass meeting was attempted.

In fairness, it should be said that the pope had bad luck with the weather — May is normally tulip time in Holland. But on the morning of the Mass at Maastricht airport, thunder rolled, lightning flashed and huge hailstones crashed through roofs and windows. Insurance men would have called this "an act of God."

In Den Bosch, another southern town, the turnout was negligible. This, said Dutch sources, showed the people's disapproval of the recent appointment of Bishop Joannes Ter Schure. Naturally, there was no means of proving this, but most agreed that, until the arrival of Ter Schure, there had been very little "polarization" in the diocese of Den Bosch.

So why did John Paul give Den Bosch such a manifestly unpopular bishop? That was the question in everyone's mind. Astonishingly, in the Basilica of St. John, cathedral of the diocese, the pope began to answer it.

This was unprecedented. John Paul was defending an episcopal appointment with his nominee sitting sheepishly 10 feet away. John Paul said, "I should like to say in all sincerity that the pope attempts to understand the life of the local church in the appointment of every bishop. He gathers information and gets advice in accord with ecclesiastical law and custom. You will understand that opinions are sometimes divided. In the final analysis, the pope has to take the decision himself."

This offered a rather farfetched picture of the pope poring over endless lists of names and personally selecting bishops in every corner of the world. It was also not true that "opinions were divided" about Ter Schure. On the contrary, they were united against him.

But having gotten this far, one expected that the pope would justify the appointment by explaining the criteria he had used. That possibility was envisaged, only to be rejected: "Must the pope explain his choice? Discretion does not permit him to do so." (These words were cut in delivery, but they remained in the script.)

The Dutch would have liked to hear his explanation, no matter how tough. He might have said for example, "Since the council, you have been on a wrong track in Holland. You have interpreted it wildly and abusively. You have made errors in ecumenism, liturgy and ministry. I have therefore given Den Bosch a bishop to set things right and lead from the front." I think the Dutch would have preferred an honest statement of that kind to the evasiveness of "discretion does not permit him to do so."

At the risk of being wearisome, I must insist on this quality of Dutch frankness and outspokenness. It is part of the national tradition. Thus, Prime Minister Ruud Lubbers, a rich Catholic Christian

Democrat, coolly informed the pope at their official meeting that "sometimes Rome seems a very long way from here, and, to be frank, the very word *Rome* makes some people uneasy, if not downright suspicious."

To which the pope replied, somewhat hesitantly, "I feel already at home in your country." It is the sort of remark that visitors are expected to make. But, in fact, in the previous 48 hours he had already heard much that would be unwelcome to him.

For the important new fact about the visit was that "criticism" is not something outside on the streets. It is built into the very fabric of the Dutch church, presided over by its rather hapless bishops.

Before the pope arrived, Simonis made the Freudian slip of referring to "the papal problem" instead of "the papal visit." He laughed, too, but not for long. He explained the exclusion of Catharina Halkes, the feminist theologian from Nijmegen, from the meeting with the pope as a matter of "fairness."

It would be unfair to make provocative remarks and expect the pope to answer them off the cuff in a language he has not fully mastered. The pope "speaks for centuries," he observed. One cannot ad lib the magisterium.

True, but behind Halkes were apparently hundreds of liberal volunteers ready to stem the imperiled dikes. There is a cohesiveness (and sometimes a boring predictability) about Dutch Catholic opinion, which means it is the bishops who are now isolated, not the so-called "dissidents."

A Dutch theologian said to me, "It's a pity the pope spent so much time learning the Dutch language instead of trying to understand the Dutch people." One saw his point.

Much of the pope's effort was misdirected. He spoke far too often and far too long. The Dutch wanted him to listen. Simonis declared beforehand, "The pope is coming to celebrate the faith, not to discuss it."

But if they were not to discuss the faith while he was here, when could they? So they muscled in with varying degrees of brutality or ineptitude. The discussion was mostly conducted in code.

Speakers would praise "dialogue" or "pluralism" or "openness," and the pope would reply that, alas, there was not time for dialogue, that pluralism had its dangers and that "openness" was a highly ambiguous notion.

Holland was free from Nazi rule 40 years before, he noted. "But what have you done with your freedom?" was his very Polish question.

This could have gone on for several hours, and indeed it did, in the Jaardeurs, a vast trade fair and exhibition center in the city of Utrecht, where Primate Simonis lives. It is a 21st century building, linked to a railroad station by the largest shopping district this side of Singapore.

But it provided a controllable and air-conditioned environment in which the pope could meet, successively, social and health care workers, missionaries, development experts and parish workers.

The only time the pope put his nose out of doors May 12, he was jeered at and insulted by the anarchist fringe who thought it great fun to dress up as pregnant nuns. They were spoiling for a fight with the police, and they duly got it.

That press agents and TV reports should have presented this as "liberal Catholics protesting the papal visit" is, I think, an absurdity. The protest was against authority in general. Next morning, the protesters took off their nuns' garb, put on sober suits and went back to work in the banks.

The real battle was taking place not on the streets, but in the Jaardeurs. Enter Nevrouw (Dutch for Mrs.) Hedwig Wasser, who boldly "departed from her prepared text." She informed the pope (who may not have understood her), "Speaking personally, I should like to add this: Are we preaching the liberating Gospel in a credible way if we lay down the law rather than extend a helping hand? If we exclude rather than make room for unmarried people living together, divorced people, homosexuals, married priests and women?

"Are we critical and performing the pastoral work of Christ if bishops show themselves above us instead of among us and in our midst as we proceed? Developments in the church in recent times have forced many of us, because of our faith and in obedience to Christ, to be critical and disobedient toward the Church."

This statement was meant to be in the Catherine of Siena and Sister Theresa Kane tradition of admonishing the pope, but Wasser's intervention was too vague and too emotional to do anything more than confirm the pope's view that Holland is in bad shape.

But she had given the pope a piece of her Dutch mind and revealed the rawness of her wound, and that was enough.

Then came an interesting twist. The last surviving "liberal" bishop, Hubertus Ernst of Breda, was introducing "parish workers"

— all those from priests to choir members who "help out in parishes." They have grown in numbers, he declared, in the past 10 years, and they all appeared for the pope.

But Ernst then echoed, in more restrained language, what Wasser had just said. He urged the pope to have a special love for "those believers who find it difficult to stay in the church and yet remain faithful." He sought understanding for those who "suffer from the church."

I doubt this is a thought that greatly appealed to John Paul. After all, he has just added Leonardo Boff to the roll call of those who "suffer from the church," largely for saying that there are some who "suffer from the church." But Ernst, knowingly, had brought us to the heart of the institutional problem of the Dutch church. It is not about bishops who are parachuted down from above. It is about who does the day-to-day pastoral work in the parishes.

Priests — ordained ministers — are a vanishing breed in Holland. True, Gijsen ordained seven last year in his diocese of Roermond. But the remaining six dioceses had to be content with six priests among them (and Haarlem had none at all).

This vacuum has been filled by "pastoral workers," laypeople who have theological training equivalent to that of priests. At the moment, they number 324, one-third of whom are women.

The pope's worry, already expressed at the synod of the Dutch church, was that the "pastoral workers would become a parallel clergy which would appear to be an alternative to the priesthood and the diaconate."

This is a serious threat in Holland, where the five theological colleges have no lack of candidates. But the men want to be pastoral workers because they reject celibacy, and the women have, at the moment, no other option.

Edward Shillebeeckx has provided the theological rationale for this movement, which is the reason his work on ministry is suspect. As priests grow older or disappear altogether, the work of the parishes can be carried on only if women and married men are ordained.

So in the end, the question posed by Holland is which matters more: the preservation of the tradition that insists on celibacy and the exclusion of women, or the pastoral service of the people of God? The pope's answer is that the preservation of the tradition is more important.

This was the crunch question posed by the Holland visit. The Dutch are not yet ready to cry "uncle." The pope is not going to budge. So the irresistible force met the irremovable obstacle, and Polish determination encountered Dutch stubbornness.

Simonis admitted the difficulties when he said that implementing the synod "is taking longer than we expected." The reason? "Reality teaches us that, measured in human terms, the Holy Spirit does not always work at the same time and in the same way among the shepherds and large sections of the flock."

The conflict would be resolved in the pope's sense if, somehow, priestly vocations emerged. But exaltations and speeches are not likely to produce that result in the near future.

There is wild talk of importing German or Polish priests from across the borders of Holland, or even for calling upon Opus Dei to provide the manpower. The Dutch have had in their history enough experience of Spanish and German occupation to doom any such idea from the outset.

So where do we go from here? The pope has committed himself, used the ultimate deterrent, and the situation remains unchanged. Some Vatican observers say that the pope tried too hard and that he has discredited the papacy by expecting too much of it and exposing it to rebuff.

The alternative is to say the Dutch are merely incorrigible. Take your pick of explanations. What seems certain is that the psychodrama of the Dutch church, far from being a little local affair, concerns all Catholics.

It involves two contrasting views of the church, of the role of the laity in the church and of the interpretation of Vatican II. If that is so, then the pontificate has reached its turning point. ❑

34

Brazilian bishops meet in Vatican to 'clear the air'

(March 14, 1986) Representatives of the Brazilian Bishops are meeting in the Vatican March 12-15. The meeting has been presented in an optimistic light. The Brazilians requested it.

In February, the round of *ad limina* visits of the 14 pastoral regions of Brazil came to an end. All had presented their cases to the Roman offices. The pope's addresses, written in advance and very critical of liberation theology, seemed to reveal a misunderstanding of what they were doing.

It seemed to be sound collegial sense to ask for a general meeting to clear the air and remove misunderstandings. That was the original purpose.

But the nature of the meeting has been changed by the papal invitation to all Brazilian cardinals to come along. These include 83-year-old retired Cardinal Alfredo Vicente Scherer, other conservatives such as Eugenio Sales of Rio de Janeiro and centrist Avelar Brandao Vilela of Sao Salvador da Bahia.

If the inclusion of all Brazilian cardinals changed the composition of the meeting, a further invitation to all prefects of Roman departments (known as dicasteries) to intervene as required gave rise to the fear that the meeting's conclusions had been written in advance.

So, although all analogies with the special synod of the Netherlands church in January 1980 are being strenuously denied, the operation seems designed to achieve a similar purpose: to regain control of the Brazilian church, deemed unruly and too independent.

It seems, then, that the initiative of the Brazilian bishops has backfired. A Rio newspaper, *O Globo*, which is part of the conservatives' network and sometimes carries stories biased toward conservatives, March 1 published a summary of the agenda for this meeting.

This alleged agenda is light-years away from the open-ended discussion originally envisioned. It puts the Brazilian bishops firmly in the dock and lists the following allegations against them:

- They have allowed sociological factors to prevail over religious considerations.

- Their proposal for a joint Bible with Brazilian Protestants is considered extremely hazardous.

- The involvement of bishops and priests in land reform proposals and the coming constituent assembly is to be queried.

- A review of the Leonardo Boff case may be envisaged, but only on condition that it prolongs the ban on him. His Franciscan superiors agreed to silence him for "a convenient period." That was taken to be about a year. The year is now up.

At the same time, questions are being raised about the long-promised second document on liberation theology. Brazilian bishops objected that Cardinal Joseph Ratzinger, head of the Congregation for the Doctrine of the Faith, published the first (*NCR*, Sept. 7, 1984) without consulting them. Later, in Ratzinger's presence, the pope told Cardinal Paulo Evaristo Arns of Sao Paulo that the Brazilian bishops would be consulted before a second, "positive" document was published.

Last fall, the Brazilian bishops received a draft that bishops' conference members assessed as fairly good. Leonardo Boff also thought it positive. The bishops expected it to be issued in December. Because it has yet to appear, they speculate that criticism from German bishops and Latin Americans at last fall's synod and elsewhere, made drafters afraid to publish a positive document. The Brazilian bishops are not likely to let the impasse pass. ❑

35

Encyclical on Holy Spirit judged pessimistic

(June 20, 1986) *Dominum et Vivificantem,* released by the Vatican earlier this month, is Pope John Paul's fifth encyclical. It is written as a letter in the first-person singular. It is a personal letter, reflecting the ideas found in the pope's 1976 retreat to the Roman curia, later published as *Sign of Contradiction.* Some passages are directly borrowed from this earlier work.

For example, the idea that those who reject God do not simply fall into error but devise an anti-truth and an anti-word recurs. There seems to be no middle ground between God and Satan.

Unbelievers are not just bewildered agnostics who do not know. They are inevitably caught up in a dramatic anti-God struggle: "Opposition to God, who is an invisible Spirit, to a certain degree originates in the very fact of the radical difference of the world from God."

Moreover, Satan is infiltrating and omnipresent in modern society, appearing as the agent of death: "Social factors, instead of fostering the development and expansion of the human spirit, ultimately deprive the human spirit of the genuine truth of its being and life — over which the Holy Spirit keeps vigil — in order to subject it to 'the prince of the world.' "

Watch television for an evening — or walk down Broadway — to be persuaded of this sterility from so many sides. Yet, there is a deep pessimism in our brother the bishop of Rome. He denies this and says he is merely "calling sin by its name."

Consider, for example, his use of the term "discernment." *Gaudium et Spes* invites the church to "discern" the presence of the Holy Spirit in human activity, which does not require an explicit reference to God to be sanctifiable. The Holy Spirit speaks through the men and women of our time, through movements, trends, events.

Discernment implies seeing in difficult circumstances. It does not mean blessing every recent fad. It involves saying no as well as yes. But on the whole, it involves approaching the contemporary world in the confident hope that the Spirit will be found at work there.

John Paul does not deny this, but he invites us to "learn how to 'discern' the fruits of the Spirit . . . from everything that may, instead, come originally from 'the prince of this world.' "

Time and time again, one expects a positive development, only to be let down. One has to wait until page 120 (out of 141) before the exciting text, Romans 8:2, is cited: "Where there is the Spirit of the Lord, there is freedom."

John Paul's commentary is narrowly restrictive: "This revelation of freedom and hence of man's true dignity acquires a particular eloquence for Christians and for the church in a state of persecution." So it does. But is that its exclusive meaning? Is there not a traditional contrast between institution and Spirit that could come in here?

Linked with this omission is the absence of any discussion of the charismatic gifts showered upon the whole people of God. They are referred to once — but only in a quotation from *Lumen Gentium*, which is not further exploited.

This means the dynamic aspect of the action of the Holy Spirit — empowering for mission or ministry — is overlooked. The principal task of the Spirit in the encyclical, it appears, is to convict us all of sin.

No doubt this is a salutary warning. But we have to wait a long time before hearing a word about being adopted sons and daughters in the Spirit — an important Pauline theme — and the positive "fruits" and "gifts" of the Holy Spirit are treated skimpily.

At least one-third of the encyclical is devoted to demonstrating that materialistic atheism is an anti-theism and, therefore, "the sin against the Holy Spirit." But it does not seem to be addressed to ordinary Catholics, for it is written in a difficult, complicated style, full of underscorings, the exact import of which is often hard to figure out.

An example: "Already the 'giving' of the Son, *the gift of the Son*, expresses the most profound essence of God who, as Love, is the inexhaustible source of the giving of the gifts. The gift *made by the Son* completes the revelation and giving of the eternal love: *The Holy Spirit*, who in the inscrutable depths of the divinity is a Person-gift, through the work of the Son, that is to say by means of the paschal mystery, is given to the apostles and to the church in a new way, and through them is given to humanity and to the whole world."

Although reading this passage is rather like wading through wet concrete, if you battle through it contains the gist of the encyclical.

Maybe the key point for understanding John Paul's thought is to grasp that he is not concerned with exegesis, but with a *philosophical* reflection on the scriptural texts — a literary form rare, indeed unknown, in the West.

One hears the voice of the Lublin philosophy professor in the following passage: "In the texts of St. Paul, there is a superimposing — and a mutual compenetration — of the *ontological dimension* (the flesh and the spirit) and the *pneumatological* (the action of the Holy Spirit in the order of grace)."

So, John Paul goes on, "the Holy Spirit will insure that in the church, there will always continue *the same truth* which the apostles heard from their Master." But here, said a Brazilian theologian, the Holy Spirit seems to be playing the same role as that of the Congregation for the Doctrine of the Faith.

There is another way of seeing the Holy Spirit as the principle of surprise, discontinuity and novelty in the church.

Cautious though he is, John Paul knows this, too. That is the reason the finest passage of the encyclical is concerned with prayer.

"The breath of the divine life, the Holy Spirit, in its simplest and most common manner, expresses itself and makes itself felt in prayer. It is a beautiful and salutary thought to recognize that, if prayer is offered throughout the world in the past, in the present and in the future, equally widespread is the presence and the action of the Holy Spirit."

Christians cannot pray at all — except in the Holy Spirit. In this understanding, we must all grow. ❑

36

Pope wins gamble as religious pray in Assisi for peace

(November 7, 1986) About 200 of the world's religious leaders prayed here in the birthplace of St. Francis Oct. 27. As Pope John Paul II — this time cast in the role of genial host — repeatedly explained, they were not there to "pray together" but "to be together and pray."

It was important to say this clearly in view of the Catholic tradition that, until 30 years ago, would not even allow the Our Father to be said with other Christians (on the grounds, explained a British bishop in 1948, that they did not mean the same thing when they said "thy kingdom come"). Two forlorn Archbishop Marcel Lefebvre traditionalist priests handed out leaflets at Assisi charging that the pope was an apostate and that ecumenism had gone mad.

In Assisi, the bishop of Rome and various cardinals looked gravely and reverently on as Muslims chanted the Quran, two American Indians (popular with the crowds) smoked their pipe of peace and animists from Africa addressed God as "the roaring thunder that splits mighty trees, the all-seeing Lord up on high who sees even the footprints of an antelope on a rock mass."

"Let peace reign in the Vatican," prayed the animists, a prayer the U.S. church could take up, provided one adds the thought in the Christian prayer that "our religious commitment to peace implies a simultaneous commitment to justice."

This was the only prayer read by a woman — and she did not compose it. It was written by French Cardinal Roger Etchegaray, who orchestrated the event. The entire world of religion is male-dominated, as if the religious debates were about whether one should wear beards (Orthodox) or mustaches (Shintoists) or be clean-shaven.

This is not a frivolous point. If the Orthodox are among those most implacably opposed to women's ordination, this is largely because they hold the priest to be the *eikon* or image of Christ. Therefore, the priest must be capable of growing a beard.

It is hard to decide whether what happened at Assisi was a media event, an eight-hour wonder, a flickering, forgettable *eikon* (in another sense). It had some odd features. During the first meeting, the world's religionists (as the Shintoists call them) stood around in a silent circle while Pope John Paul told them they had not come to discuss, but to pray.

The circle was designed to solve problems of protocol and precedent, but it also became a symbol of eternity, having neither beginning nor end. On the other hand, because at this point they were all behaving like dummies, and concentrating on a religious stillness, it was like being in a waxworks museum. One was tempted to touch them to make sure they were real.

And they were all in costume. It struck me how little real relation there is between dress and religion. What we choose to call "religious garb" is a matter of convention. There is nothing intrinsically Orthodox about stovepipe hats (black for Russians, white for Uniates) or distinctively Sikh about a turban or definitively Shintoist about Makado gear or essentially Catholic about the pope's white soutane (borrowed from the Dominicans in the 16th century). These are cultural accidents.

Maybe the exception is the Buddhist monk, whose saffron robes and shaved head indicate poverty and abnegation rather as Francis' rough cloth garb and sandals did. Which brings us back to the local man.

Halfway through the events, I met briefly with Archbishop Achille Silvestrini, the Vatican's foreign minister, who waxed eloquent about St. Francis. This was the right place to pray for peace, he said, because Francis opposed the fourth Crusade and met the sultan of Egypt. That is the reason Franciscans, and no one else, were allowed to work in the Turkish empire.

It was a little hard to follow Silvestrini's argument. But I did grant the following points of great importance for peacemakers. In Francis' time, the pope offered mighty indulgences as an inducement to go on the Crusade to fight against unbelievers in the Holy Land. Francis persuaded the pope to confer the same indulgences on his little church, the Portiuncula, thus making the need to go to war in the Holy Land redundant.

Francis, in other words, devised a peace parable for his time that struck the imagination of his contemporaries. I tentatively suggest that the Assisi meeting could prove to be Pope John Paul's peace parable for our time. It will, therefore, prove to be of great historic importance.

It was a brilliant idea to invite the world religions to *pray*. Prayer is a noncontroversial activity. It is beyond criticism. If they had paused for a moment to discuss what they meant by prayer, the old antagonisms would have been at once revived. To pray is to say something about a power higher than Ronald Reagan and Mikhail Gorbachev.

It was a brilliant idea to invite the world religions to pray for *peace*. For that, too, is incontrovertible. It is the deepest aspiration of humankind. It transcends race, religion and color. It is an irrefutable cause. Some left-wing protesters carried a banner proclaiming, "You Don't Pray for Peace, You Have to Fight for It." That seemed paradoxical and odd.

It was a brilliant idea to get the Christians of the world to pray for peace in this *company*. Never have Christians realized so vividly how much they have in common. While the other religions scattered for prayer in various locations in the hilltop city, the Christians were bused to the Cathedral of San Rufino, where they experienced, even if briefly, the irrelevance of their division.

As they trudged back down the hill after their non-lunch (the pope insisted on fasting), the sense of Christian togetherness grew. On his right, John Paul had Robert Runcie, the archbishop of Canterbury, and on his left, Metropolitan Methodios, representing the ecumenical patriarch of Istanbul.

It was a brilliant idea to assemble the world religions at Assisi. John Paul could not have invited them to Rome, because it has been the city of anathema.

Assisi was still home ground for him, but a home ground where he, too, has to submit to the norms of the gospel and confess that "Catholics have not always been peacemakers" — a remark that would not be worth commenting upon were it not so rare.

Thus, the highly conservative John Paul has completely shattered the traditions of Vatican diplomacy. Much too risky to invite the world guerrillas to lay down their arms for a day, said conventional wisdom, because one might be rebuffed. Although the response was patchy, there was no rebuff. John Paul played for high stakes. He has — modestly but implicitly — made himself a spokesman (the right word) for all the world religions. His words shaped the meaning of this event.

Here they are: "While we have walked in silence, we have reflected on the path our human family treads: either in hostility, if we fail to accept one another in love or as a common journey to our lofty destiny, if we realize that other peoples are our brothers and sisters. . . . Either we learn to walk together in peace and harmony, or we drift apart and ruin ourselves and others." ❏

37

Warsaw warms to Rome while Moscow winks, but pope wrote his own script in Poland

(June 19, 1987) Pope John Paul II is a different man in Poland. He is at home. There are no apparent ecclesiastical problems. He knows the language and just how far he can go. He can make a point with an allusion, a quotation, even a raised eyebrow.

So a visit to Poland is like a stately pageant in which memories are unfurled and Polish identity is reaffirmed. On his last visit in 1982, he asked a little girl, "Where is Poland?" She didn't know how to reply. He gently put his hand on her heart and said, "There is Poland."

At the same time, each trip to Poland has its own special emphasis. The first, in 1979, was a celebration of his surprise election to the papacy. Along with most Poles, he believed this to be a providential compensation for the terrible sufferings of Polish history.

In 1982, he came to comfort a nation dismayed by the imposition of martial law and the shattering of the hope that was Solidarity.

The 1987 agenda is different, and it seems to have been agreed on between John Paul and Gen. Wojciech Jaruzelski at their meeting in the Vatican Jan. 13 this year. The message is that church-state relations have reached an unprecedented new stage of friendliness.

This does not mean ideological differences have been abolished, but they have been subordinated to a higher value.

This was graphically illustrated in their first meeting in the newly restored Royal Palace in Warsaw, which the pope was seeing for the first time. The palace was seriously damaged in September 1939 and deliberately razed in 1945 before the Germans retreated from Warsaw.

In restoring the palace so meticulously, the communist government was not making a point about monarchy, but rather was saying something about Poland. Jaruzelski's opening words as he greeted John Paul could equally well have come from the pope: "As long as our lives last, as long as our memory lasts, these walls will always bring to mind the drama of the historical experience of our nation."

Ringing words. But the pope and the general do not remember exactly the same things. Both have selective memories. Jaruzelski's memories are in a way more interesting because less familiar.

Holy Father, you are going to Lodz, said Jaruzelski, "a city of the great class struggle of the proletariat." It once epitomized the pitiable condition of Polish workers suffering under the "domestic and foreign bourgeoisie," and he named the Scheibler and Bussac companies that exploited the workers in the past.

John Paul was hardly expected to devote much time to "the great class struggle of the proletariat" during his Lodz speech. He only mentions it to denounce it. On the other hand, John Paul can also understand the reason Jaruzelski has to make these remarks.

But he will not have the general write his script, and on occasions has behaved subversively. He was in Tarnov June 10, in the foothills of the Carpathian mountains, ostensibly to beatify Karolina Kozka, a 16-year-old girl killed in 1914 "while resisting rape by a Russian soldier" (as the official handouts say).

That was fairly provocative, though mitigated perhaps by the thought that the Russian soldier was part of the imperialist, czarist army. But there was a lot of rape in 1945, too, which is no doubt hinted at in this beatification. But the main thrust of the Tarnov sermon concerned peasants. John Paul claimed peasants were the backbone of the nation. To make this point, he quoted Wincenty Witos, leaders of the Polish Peasants' party (PSL) in the years after the recovery of independence.

"We must not only seek to base our future on these peasants," the pope quoted Witos as saying, "but must also, at all costs, win their fidelity and attachment to the state."

That is probably the first time Witos has been quoted in socialist Poland. His works have been published only by exiles in Paris. He was a sympathetic figure who, though prime minister, left Warsaw in the middle of the 1920 war crisis to get his harvest home.

But it was difficult to see his relevance to contemporary Poland, so this was probably a rather sneaky allusion to rural Solidarity and an expression of regret that their agricultural fund was blocked.

So both John Paul and Jaruzelski used coded memories. On one memory, they can agree wholeheartedly. Friday, June 12, the pope was to go to Westerplatte, where World War II began. "As head of the armed forces," Jaruzelski proudly declaimed, "I have ordered a gun salute. Colors will be displayed, and the horns of the republic's navy will resound." No doubt the pope would talk about peace.

More recent memories are controversial. Jaruzelski's version of the crushing of Solidarity is that "the fires, often fueled by an alien hand, have now died down." He means Solidarity was financed from abroad. There now exists in Poland, he says, "a socialist pluralism" and a "spirit of reform," such that the goals of Solidarity are being reached but without the anarchy to which it led. I have not yet found any Pole who believes this, but again, they understand why the general has to talk this way.

He has to say it because, like every Polish leader since the war, Jaruzelski looks over his shoulder toward Moscow. Hitherto, every rapprochement with the church has been viewed with suspicion in Moscow.

What is new in the current situation is that Mikhail Gorbachev seems not to be so worried about better relations between the pope and the general in Poland. The evidence for this is found in the first-ever interview given by Cardinal Józef Glemp, Polish primate, in *Literaturnaya Gazeta* (Feb. 4, 1987).

Glemp uttered little more than banalities about peace. The significant thing was that the interviewer, astonished at finding himself in a country that was both communist and Catholic, remarks, "We find this incomprehensible. Over the years of Soviet power, we have grown in the conviction that adherence to religion is evidence of cultural and intellectual backwardness. Yet, even communists embrace it — a paradox?"

Yes, he admits, it is a paradox: "There is no other word for it. But a reality, too. And one that must be reckoned with. This is required by the new political thinking."

So recognizing the "reality" of religion in Poland is part of "the new political thinking" in the U.S.S.R.

John Paul read that interview, too. It may even have been set up during his meeting with Jaruzelski three weeks before. It is important to get the right signals from Moscow. They seem to be saying that what was once said about religion as "the opium of the people" no longer applies. There has been retreat from this interpretation of Marxism.

If that is true, then this 1987 visit to Poland comes at a crucial turning point in 20th century history. I believe it is true, and offer as evidence the following statement from the Polish official press agency: "The Polish People's Republic is a secular but not an atheistic state."

It remains to work out the consequences of this dramatic change. One is that John Paul could conceivably go to Moscow next year for the 1,000-year celebration of Christianity in Russia. ❏

38

To fathom pope, look to Kraków

(*September 11, 1987*) *As Pope John Paul II arrives on U.S. soil, he is at work to reshape the Roman Catholic church to meet the needs and challenges of the 21st century. This trip is part of that effort. The pope is having an important influence on the church, yet even after nine years as bishop of Rome, he remains a mystery. What makes him think the way he does? What fuels his faith? How does he view his pontificate? How is he doing as Peter's successor?*

It was, I am fairly sure, in 1971 that I first met Karol Wojtyla, then the future Pope John Paul II. I was a regular visitor to Poland in those days and had many friends in the Znak (Sign) group of Catholic intellectuals in Kraków. "You should go and meet the cardinal," they urged.

I was not in the habit of talking with cardinals, preferring to seek the truth about a local church on humbler levels. Why should I go see Cardinal Wojtyla?

The Znak people assured me he was a most remarkable man, that he was beginning to organize meetings of philosophers, film-makers, writers and scientists to lay the basis of a modern Christian culture in the midst of communist Poland.

He was also said to posses "the gift of tears" (a grace that used to be asked for in the old liturgies): The contemplation of the Passion of Christ sometimes brought tears to his eyes — in private and even in the pulpit. If he had a weakness, it was that his sermons tended to go on and on.

So along I went to the episcopal residence at ul. Franciszkan-ska 3 and took my place in the line, along with the *monsignori* and old ladies in shawls. For two hours most mornings, he received who-ever wanted to see him. It was a bit like a doctor's clinic.

I was last in line and got in with only five minutes to lunch. He asked me what I was doing in Poland. I said I was trying to understand the situation of the church in Poland so as to write about it in the West. If this were hagiography, he ought then to have said, "Come to lunch."

He did not. He said, instead "Come back at 5 o'clock. I'll give you an hour." I prepared my questions throughout the afternoon. But when I presented myself promptly at 5 p.m. Wojtyla asked all the questions. Whom had I met in Poland? What did they say? What was my experience of the Pax movement, a pro-government faction whose leader, Bodeslaw Piasecki, had once been excommunicated? And so on.

It was rather disconcerting. I felt scrutinized, inspected, interro-gated, laid bare. I gathered not the faintest hint what he felt or thought about anything. I had nothing to put in my notebook.

Then — with a glance at his watch and five minutes to go — he began to speak. "If you wish to write about Poland for the West," he began, "there are two misunderstandings you must avoid."

I was all agog. "We are often described as the 'church of si-lence,' " he explained, "but a church that has 11,000 pulpits from which the gospel is proclaimed every Sunday morning cannot accu-rately be described as silent. The party envies us this method of communication." That was news to me.

What was the other misunderstanding? "People call us a perse-cuted church," he went on, "but that is no longer true. We were persecuted in the Stalinist period up to 1956. Since then, we have been restricted, impeded and harassed (*harcelée*), we don't have enough paper for our publications, they are anyway censored — but that is not the same as persecution."

"Tell the people in the West that," he concluded, rising and thus indicating it was time for me to go. I fell to my knees, received his paternal blessing and departed. I couldn't know I was meeting the next-but-one pope and did not for a moment imagine it.

Later that night, discussing the meeting with the Znak people, I was told how privileged I was to have received such "revelations" from him, for what was really going on in our conversation was that he was distancing himself, ever so gently, from positions held by Stefan Wyszynski, primate of Poland.

Wyszynski once said at a Rome press conference, "You call us the 'church of silence,' but here I find a church of the deaf." He meant the Vatican did not understand Poland. And Wyszynski always kept alive the sense of persecution because, in that way, he could keep his troops in order.

Up there on the battlements there must be no murmuring, no hint of disloyalty, no notion of loyal opposition. The Polish bishops' unity was the rock on which the waves of communism would lash in vain. The Polish bishops met in secret and announced their unanimous conclusions. The laity then obeyed them. The priests saw to it that they did.

If only we could have access to the minutes of the Polish episcopal conference! It would show, says one witness, vigorous and sometimes even violent debate about how far one could go in "helping" the regime.

All agreed that the communist regime was an alien imposition that, for reasons of geopolitics (Soviet Russia is next door), could only be undermined from within.

They agreed, too, that Mary, the mother of Jesus, was queen of Poland. This title, celebrated at the shrine of the Black Madonna of Czestochowa, was not a pious honorific, but an assertion about where true sovereignty lay. Did this mean the gray men in Warsaw now holding power without popular consent were, in effect, usurpers?

No one ever dared say that — but it was implied. That was the reason Solidarnösc, exactly 10 years later, was so threatening: Through the free labor union, the people of Poland expressed themselves and their aspirations for the first time since World War II.

But within the common approach, there were differences about tactics. Wyszynski preferred defiance and ceding as little as possible;

Wojtyla saw the benefits that could accrue from prudent accommodation. But these differences remain buried in the archives.

The irony is that in 1987, Wyszynki's successor as primate, Cardinal Józef Glemp, appears accommodating, while Pope John Paul from his Roman fastness gives nothing away.

. On his third visit to Poland, in June 1987, John Paul disdained to "help" First Secretary-General Wojciech Jaruzelski. The unfortunate was reduced to saying at the airport, "You take away with you an image of your homeland in your heart, Holy Father, but you leave us with all the problems."

There were other implications of the 1971 interview — if one can call it that — which become clear with hindsight. I do not claim to have discovered them at the time. But if one could be momentarily endowed with divine omniscience, the 1971 meeting in Kraków would provide the key to understanding John Paul II's entire pontificate, both in its style and in its policies.

First, one must note how extraordinarily "rooted" in Kraków is Karol Wojtyla. He lived there from age 19 to 58. The episcopal residence where he received me was his home during World War II, when he was an "illegal seminarian." Unlike Warsaw, Kraków was mostly spared the devastation of war.

As Wojtyla walked around the city, he could recall where his friends were seized in random roundups and where the ghetto was. Nearby Auschwitz is also imprinted indelibly on his memory.

In Holy Week 1940, he wrote a play based on the Book of Job. It reflects poignantly all the disasters that had befallen Poland and Kraków in the previous six months: the deportations, the arbitrary killings, the breakup of families, the decimation of Polish elites, the clergy and the intellectuals.

Poles were reduced to slave labor — until they were no longer needed, when they would follow the Jews into oblivion. Hans Frank sat in Wawel Castle where Polish kings are buried, as governor of this rump state, and there prepared the destruction of the people. ❏

39

Pope in United States more teacher than learner

(September 25, 1987)

> *Well, what are the prospects for your exhibition?*
>
> *I suppose they will cut me to pieces. Max promises me that most decisively.*
>
> *You shouldn't take much notice. How many times have I cut Adam to pieces, who is my close friend. Without censure, life would be so boring.*
>
> — From "Our God's Brother,"
> a play completed by Karol Wojtyla in 1949

All papal trips have the same pattern: The pope moves around the country, he is visiting, talking to different categories of people. Yet all papal trips are different: The pope deals with what he perceives to be the major problems facing the local Catholics.

In the case of the United States, the usual category-by-category approach — educators, health workers and so on — was complicated and enriched by ethnic diversity. This was recognized in the pope's meetings with blacks in New Orleans, Hispanics in San Antonio, Texas, and Native Americans in Phoenix, Ariz.

And that was only a sampler, a beginning. But it already makes a striking contrast with John Paul's last trip, to his homeland.

While Polish Catholicism equates Catholicism and national feeling, the U.S. church has to bring together almost as many peoples as are found in the United Nations; its Catholicism, therefore, cannot be exclusive and defensive. To be truly Catholic, the U.S. church has to be inclusive, welcoming, all-embracing.

The pope knows this on the international level. Yet he had a curious phrase in New Orleans which seemed to deny the existence of an American church. "It is important to realize that there is no black church, no white church, no American church; but there is and must be, in the one church of Jesus Christ, a home for blacks, for whites, Americans, every culture and race."

One sees the point: There must be no separated American church any more than a separated black church. But it would be perverse to deny that there is a distinctively American approach to being church. Talk of the American church is at least as valid as talk of the French church or the Polish church — and John Paul does not recoil from these expressions.

Before the visit, Archbishop John L. May, president of the National Conference of Catholic Bishops, said it would serve to reestablish Catholic identity: "Many of the 53 million Catholics in this country are dusting cobwebs off their Catholic identity and renewing their religious commitment to their church, to their pope as vicar of Christ, to one another and to the nation and the world."

By "Catholic identity," May was thinking in doctrinal terms. There is fuzziness in people's minds about what the church teaches. Restoring identity means therefore "identifying Catholic doctrine and what it means to be a truly committed Catholic." But few have been in much doubt about what was official Catholic doctrine; the problem was not knowing what it was but accepting it, and the papal visit leaves that problem untouched.

But "Catholic identity" has another meaning, which takes us out of the realm of alleged "dissidence." It answers the question: How do U.S. Catholics characteristically set about tackling their problems?

Through carefully prepared "structured dialogues" and video presentations, the various categories — notably those in higher and secondary education, in charities and health — introduced themselves to John Paul.

Whether he was listening or not — and he needed to — some were blunter than others. Fr. Thomas J. Harvey, executive director of Catholic Charities USA, addressed the pope directly in San Antonio: "From you, Holy Father, we ask continued and unrelenting commitment to a social doctrine which expands the horizons of human development. Where people are being exploited, we ask that you be unyielding in your cry for justice. Where people are suffering from such debilitating problems as divorce, diseases such as AIDS and the ambiguity of changing lifestyles, we ask patience of the church's teachings so that we do not close the door to opportunities for better solutions to these pressures of our changing world than our present wisdom easily affords."

John E. Curley, Jr., president of the Catholic Health Association, told the pope in Phoenix that "our nation's health care environment increasingly poses ethical dilemmas that defy simple answers" and warned that "our ministry may well be placed in jeopardy if it cannot come to terms with such issues."

These are just two examples. One could cite many more. The approach is one that tries to read "the signs of the times" and to serve the needs of the present. While being firm on basic principles, it does not claim to "have all the answers" and admits there is a place for "exploration" (to use the word popularized by Fr. Frank J. McNulty on the trip's opening day). It recognizes that there are open questions such as the place of women's ministry in the church.

These are not revolutionary statements — far from it. They do not come from wild, boat-rocking dissidents. Yet the pope seems to regard them at best as "letting off steam" and at worst as further evidence of how far the U.S. church has slumped into moral relativism.

The central problem of the trip was always: What "image" did the pope have of the United States before he came? And given that he has no useful firsthand experience, what were his sources in the United States?

Without identifying them closely, it is evident that he was given alarmist reports from conservative circles. In the plane on the way over, he tactfully said the U.S. church was "very good," conceded that dissent was a serious problem, but claimed that "the great silent majority is faithful."

A similar attempt to minimize the reality of dissent came from Archbishop Justin Rigali, head of the Vatican's school for diplomats: "The idea that there is tension between Rome and the church in the U.S. was promoted by a tiny group of American Catholics . . . manipulated and nurtured with a lot of help from the media."

This was the mood in which the speeches and homilies were prepared. The pope would try to reach out, in populist fashion, to this supposed "silent majority."

On every topic, John Paul stressed the dangers that could arise. Abstract principles were stated — and when it looked as though he had said something concrete on the sanctuary movement, for example, his spokesman hastened to explain that he had not.

The result was a "dialogue of the deaf," as the Rome-prepared speeches failed to engage with the experience-based reports. The pope and his interlocutors seemed to be talking past each other. When they said "pluralism," he said "truth."

John Paul is an either/or thinker. His account of pluralism turns it into the equivalent of "indifferentism." He told the college presidents: "Pluralism does not exist for its own sake; it is directed to the fullness of truth. In the academic context, the respect for persons that pluralism rightly envisions does not justify the view that ultimate questions about human life and destiny have no final answers or that all beliefs are of equal value."

But there are other ways of defining pluralism. Not all questions are ultimate questions. Some are definitely penultimate, concerned with matters of opinion on which there can be legitimate differences.

Whether there should be, for example, tighter episcopal control of Catholic colleges as the pope proposed can hardly be treated as a doctrinal matter: It is rather a question of prudent practical judgment.

On this, Fr. Theodore Hesburgh, former president of the University of Notre Dame, argued that "if church or state or any other power outside the university can dictate who can teach and who can learn, the university is not free and, in fact, is not a true university where the truth is sought and taught. It is rather a place of political or religious indoctrination."

John Paul introduced himself several times as "an old university professor." Yet his experience at the Catholic University of Lublin did not prepare him to understand the U.S. college scene.

Lublin is the only independent institution of higher education between the River Elbe and the Pacific. Everyone connected with it has to be a committed Catholic. If entry were not tightly controlled, the Polish government would undoubtedly seek to infiltrate and undermine it. But that is not an immediate threat to the 235 colleges of the United States.

When John Paul encounters someone who disagrees with him — even on evident matters of opinion such as communion in the hand — he does not seek the truth contained in the opposing position; he seems to regard that as consensus weakness. It is almost as though he is stimulated by opposition, thrives on it and regards it as the validation of his mission.

Sometimes he is positively truculent, especially in his treatment of history. So, for example, after agreeing to call off the beatification of Fray Junipero Serra in response to Native American protests, he went out of his way to present the "beloved" Franciscan as someone who "had frequent clashes with the civil authorities over the treatment of Indians."

This was a cool piece of apologetic sleight of hand. It was backed up by a wholly ineffectual text from his predecessor, Paul III, in 1537, which defended Indian rights. John Paul follows the maxim, "Never apologize, never explain." The papacy always has it right. In the present as in the past.

The same technique was applied in talking with the Jewish leaders. John Paul made the following claim: "I am convinced that history will reveal ever more clearly and convincingly how deeply Pius XII felt the tragedy of the Jewish people and how hard and effectively he worked to assist them during World War II."

It is hard, after the publication of the Vatican wartime diplomatic documents, to think of some future discovery in the Vatican archives that would notably change our picture of Pius XII. While one can agree that Pius' silences have often been misinterpreted, judgments on the "effectiveness" of his aid to Jews can be statistically tested. John Paul can hardly believe that he has privileged access to historical truth as well.

The Jews who heard this also knew that on the plane, he had said it would have been "impossible not to meet with Kurt Waldheim." John Paul is a philosopher by profession and knows there was no metaphysical or moral necessity about this meeting. So if "impossible" was not a slip in English (it is his fifth or sixth language), it was another way of saying he had done the right thing and was sticking by his decision.

Thus, John Paul operates from within a complete intellectual system. It has no gaps, no holes, no vacant spaces. Everything new is slotted into a preordained place. The system provides a reply in advance to every question. From within the system, one asserts more than one argues. The meeting with the U.S. bishops in Los Angeles illustrated the system in operation.

What about the prediction that the number of priests is declining dramatically? John Paul said one must "resist the pessimism of such prophets of doom." But supposing the numbers continue to fall? Never mind, "the basis of our hope is the power of Christ's paschal mystery. . . . He is strong enough to attract young men even today."

One gets the impression that John Paul is like a captain ready to go down with his ship, denying the statistical evidence as the vessel sinks beneath the waves.

Nor is it any use looking to women to fill the gaps in the priestly ranks. For the teaching that "women are not called to the priesthood" is "quite clear" can mean either "relatively clear" or "absolutely clear." The second meaning was no doubt intended.

There was a semblance of argument to justify this exclusion. All church consideration of women must be based, said the pope, on "two firm principles: the equal dignity of women and their true feminine humanity." "Feminine humanity" is a curious giveaway phrase. Either there is humanity or there is not. In which case it is difficult to see how the "equal dignity of women" can be combined with their exclusion from the priestly ministry. So a special category of humanity, "feminine humanity," has to be devised to maintain the exclusion.

So everything the U.S. bishops said in their reports was accepted, then stood on its head.

Geoffrey Chaucer said of his "poor student," "Gladly would he learn and gladly teach." John Paul in the United States has been more interested in teaching than in learning.

Yet he is not without a Polish sense of humor. In his meeting with Catholic secondary educators in New Orleans, he improvised a few remarks. "I have come here as a student," he said, "so as a student, I thank you for all you have taught me this morning." He hoped he would get good marks.

"By their sustained applause," concluded the news story, "the educators told the pontiff he had made the grade." ❑

40

Visiting pope listened, rejected 'lay ministry'

(October 2, 1987) During his visit to the United States, Pope John Paul listened almost as much as he spoke. This was the great originality of this trip compared with the 35 international journeys that had preceded it. The pope was undoubtedly the star, but other voices were heard as well.

The visit was, therefore, like a dress rehearsal for the synod starting in Rome next month. It mimed the synodal process in two ways.

First, the purpose of the synod is officially to "provide information and give advice" to the pope. The 23 speakers who addressed

John Paul all tried to do just that. They "opened their hearts" or invited to "walk along the way with him." The bishops reporting to the synod will do the same.

Second, the four U.S. delegates to the synod have been elected by their episcopal peers. They will speak not in their own name but in the name of the National Conference of Catholic Bishops (NCCB). They will follow the same procedure as in Los Angeles, where four bishops presented the point of view of the NCCB.

But obviously the visit and the synod are also linked by their content: the role and mission of the laity in the church and the world. This theme was addressed by, among others, Archbishop Daniel E. Pilarczyk, of Cincinnati, in Los Angeles, and in San Francisco by Patrick S. Hughes, pastoral minister director for the diocese. In each case the pope replied.

Pilarczyk said the U.S. bishops were worried about the future: Would there be enough priests to do the specifically priestly work the church needs? And where would the money come from to pay the growing number of laypeople who work as church professionals?

However, Pilarczyk went on, despite these worries there were definite signs of hope. The Holy Spirit is still at work in the church: "What we are experiencing is a broadening of the concept of church vocation and ministry, a concept which formerly included only priests and religious but which now includes laypersons in an ever-increasing number of capacities and religious in capacities different from those in which they served previously."

Pilarczyk welcomed this trend not merely because it helps to plug the gaps in the ranks of priests, but also because it is a good thing in itself. More and more laypeople are becoming aware of their vocation to ministry.

Hughes put some flesh on these bare bones. In his own San Francisco diocese, two of the archbishop's immediate staff are laypeople. Half the archdiocesan agencies are headed by laypeople. Two-thirds of departments and divisions have laypeople in top administrative positions. Parishes, schools and other institutions reflect the same reality.

San Francisco, Hughes claimed, is a microcosm of the whole country. More laypeople than ever are working within ecclesial structures. "Their ministry," said Hughes, "contributes tremendous time, energy and talent to the church. The entire church benefits greatly."

But there are problems for lay ministers, some of which stem from their sheer novelty. They are often the first laypeople to do the job, so there are no precedents for their ministry. Sometimes, they have to struggle to find acceptance and understanding. They may feel torn between family and ministry. They know that they will be on a lower salary than in some comparable secular job and regard this as an aspect of their special commitment.

However, the complete avoidance of talk of "lay ministries" in the reply to Hughes can hardly be defended on the same basis. For Hughes' entire presentation was devoted to lay ministries. So to devote two out of 25 paragraphs to them already made a point: This is not John Paul's favorite topic.

Still, he does begin with the positive statement that renewal since the council has led to increasing participation of laypeople in church life. Then he echoes, and modifies, Hughes' description: "An increasing number of laymen and women are devoting their professional skills on a full-time basis to the church's efforts in education, social services and other areas, or to the exercise of administrative responsibilities. Still others build up the body of Christ by direct collaboration with the church's pastoral ministry, especially in bringing Christ's love to those in the parish or community who have special needs."

No doubt all these people are doing good work, and the pope blesses them. They have been schooled to think of themselves as doing lay ministry. But the pope will not let this term pass his lips. "I rejoice," he concludes the paragraph, "with you at this great flowering of gifts in the service of the church's mission." Once again we have mission where ministry might be expected.

Why? Perhaps a clue is provided in the next paragraph, which warns about a danger hanging over the heads of these laypeople. They should stick firmly to the "sound ecclesiology" of Vatican II (it remains undefined). If they do not, "we run the risk of 'clericalizing' the laity or 'laicizing' the clergy, and thus robbing both the clerical and the lay states of their specific meaning and complementarity."

John Paul gives no examples of what "clericalizing" the laity or "laicizing" the clergy really means. It does not seem that he is describing some actual situation in the United States that has been brought to his notice where church roles have been reversed.

The epigram — so to call it — originated in Latin America. It was first used by Colombian Cardinal Alfonso Lopez Trujillo as part of his attack on liberation theology.

Every statement so far made about lay ministers applies equally to women. Hughes said that there has been some progress and that "women have moved into significant ministerial positions."

But there is still a long way to go. The promotion of women in the church, Hughes argued, was not just for the sake of women. On the contrary, "the church needs the feminine dimension if it is to bring the full power of God's creative energy to bear on the needs of our world."

Neither Pilarczyk nor Hughes imagined he was saying anything controversial, still less revolutionary. They were not talking theories, but were offering a description of what has been going on. What they said was based on experience.

That is a first reason that the pope's replies were disappointing. In answer to Pilarczyk, he carefully avoided using the term "lay ministries" while conceding that "the more active participation of the laity in the *mission* of the church is an eloquent sign of the fruitfulness of the Second Vatican Council."

What is the meaning of this shift from "ministry" to "mission"? It can be defended on the grounds that, although all Christians share in the "mission" of the church in virtue of their baptism and confirmation, not all are called to share in its ministry. So to talk about mission is to address all the laity, the whole church; to talk about ministry is to address what is likely to remain a small minority.

So whatever the phrase means, it is not descriptive of something going on in the United States. And it is not very clear what one is supposed to do to avoid this alleged "danger." As at other points during the U.S. trip, there was a strong sense of talking at cross purposes.

This is ultimately traceable to two different interpretations of *Lumen Gentium*, the council's "Dogmatic Constitution on the Church." Those who wish to encourage lay ministries stress Chapter 2 of *Lumen Gentium* on the church as the new pilgrim people of God.

There is a fundamental equality in grace. While a distinction should be made between the ordained priest and the other members of the people of God, this in no way entails division or separation, since they share in a common mission. Most commentators on the council documents thought that "people of God" represented the basic thrust and intention of the council.

Karol Wojtyla never did. For him, the key passage in *Lumen Gentium* is the statement that the priesthood of the faithful and the hierarchic priesthood are interrelated, yet "they differ from one another in essence and not only in degree."

In his commentary on the council, *Sources of Renewal*, Wojtyla says that this doctrine (of essential difference) "contains in a certain manner all that the council wished to say about the church, mankind and the world" (see Ronald Modras in *The Church in Anguish*, p. 48).

This is a remarkable statement. It means that the first thing to be said about the church is that it is hierarchical. Its hierarchic structure guarantees its apostolicity. It also ensures the subordination of the laity to the clergy, the clergy to the bishops and the bishops to the pope.

What, then, of the "true equality" of which Vatican II speaks? It exists, but only "in the invisible order of grace," where it is strictly unverifiable. A lay leader may be more effective in the order of grace than a member of the hierarchy, but we will never know.

There is no evidence that Karol Wojtyla has changed his mind since 1969, when he wrote this commentary. It remains, therefore, the necessary background to explain the reason, during his U.S. trip, he was so reluctant to endorse the concept of lay ministries. Does the pope deep down believe that the only "real" form of ministry is the priestly ministry?

It is difficult to see how the discussion at the synod can usefully proceed unless this matter is cleared up. For the two models of the church at work give different results; yet they cannot be contrasted as orthodoxy and unorthodoxy. Anyone who takes a different line cannot be labeled "dissident." ❏

41

Pope's plays throw light on his pontificate

(April 29, 1988) Michael Dummett, Wykeham Professor of logic at Oxford University, when asked what he thought about *The Acting*

Person, Karol Wojtyla's major philosophical work, said, "You know, it is very difficult for a Catholic philosopher to criticize the work of a reigning pope, especially when he commits a howler on the first page."

"What howler?" I nervously inquired. "He says here," the professor continued, sipping his sherry with relish, "that 'only man can act purposely and deliberately.' Well, of course, that's complete nonsense."

I never know quite where I am with Oxford philosophers. "Are you perhaps thinking of animals?" I tentatively suggested. "No, of course not — though it makes perfect sense to ask of a dog, *why* does he do this or that," he said.

I shrugged. Dummett shrugged. Then he went on. "It's not a matter of animals. It's much more serious than that. God, of course, can also act purposely and deliberately. The Holy Father has forgotten about God."

I recalled this cautionary tale (of which the moral is, "You can't be too careful") as I began to read the six surviving plays of Karol Wojtyla (*The Collected Plays and Writings on Theater*, translated, with instructions, by Bodeslaw Taborski, University of California Press, $35). I have taught French literature and reviewed plays for the *Times Literary Supplement*. But how could a mere literary critic dare pronounce on the work of an author whom he only knew in translation, and who later went on to higher things?

My inhibitions soon vanished as I noted Wojtyla's extraordinary chutzpah. If he, at age 20, could display such confidence in his own judgment, then so could I. The papacy doesn't come into it. Or shouldn't.

Wojtyla's self-confidence was striking. Just before Easter, 1940, this 20-year-old Polish would-be playwright wrote the famous director and founder of the "rhapsodic theater," Mieczyslaw Kotlarczyk. "I have written a new drama, Greek in form, Christian in spirit, eternal in substance, like 'Everyman.' "

No mock modesty there. His work is a synthesis of the entire history of the theater. He has the smell of success about him, but what makes the future Pope John Paul II's self-confidence quite extraordinary is the timing of this letter.

Consider the situation in Holy Week 1940, when he wrote his play "Job." Poland had been partitioned yet again, cynically fallen upon from the East by the Soviets just as the Nazis were victorious in the West.

The Jagiellonian University, where he had been enrolled in Polish philology and literature, was shut down, its professors packed off to concentration camps.

The sadistic Hans Frank was installed as governor of the rump of Poland in Wawel Castle in Kraków, the burial place of Polish kings and heroes. That added desecration to insult. The cathedral is part of the castle complex.

Poles, like Jews, were an expendable slave race, to be worked to death. Literally. Yet young Karol's thoughts turn to the theater. It had, of course, been abolished along with every other manifestation of Polish culture.

But that, precisely, is the point of his literary activity. "Job" and "Jeremiah" (like the lost "David"), far from being an aesthetic escape from the tragedy of Poland, were a spiritual resistance movement, an attempt to find some spiritual significance in the national catastrophe.

In his letter to Kotlarczyk, he claims that "Job" "develops the idea that suffering is not always a punishment but can sometimes be, and often is, a presage."

His "Job" ends with a vision of the risen Christ, the ultimate comforter. That is not so farfetched, given that, thanks to George Frideric Handel, the best-known verse of Job is "I know that my redeemer liveth, and that he shall stand at the latter day upon the earth" (19:24-5).

Pope John Paul's 1982 encyclical, *Salvifici Doloris*, which many Poles consider to be his most personal contribution to Christian thought, echoes the theme of his 1940 play:

> If the Lord consents to test Job with suffering, he does it to demonstrate the latter's righteousness. The suffering has the nature of a test.

> The book of Job is not the last word on this subject in revelation. In a certain way it is also the foretelling of the passion of Christ. . . .

> Love is also the fullest answer to the question of the meaning of suffering. This answer has been given by God to man in the cross of Jesus Christ (*Salvifici Doloris*).

The message of the pontificate in 1984 was the same as the message of the play in 1940.

"Jeremiah," also written in 1940, has the same theme as "Job," but now it is given a grandiose liturgical and national orchestration. We now move from an individual fate to the destiny of the nation.

Yet, both "fate" and "destiny" seem inept terms because Wojtyla believes that providence is directing the whole operation. As he wrote to the Kotlarczyk family Aug. 7, 1940, when he completed his drama, "Everything is the working of grace; one should know how, and above all want, to cooperate."

"Jeremiah" uses a lot of elements from the baroque tradition. Statues turn into speaking angels. Choirs of monks, singing the lamentations of Jeremiah over Jerusalem (as in the forgotten service of *Tenebrae*), act as a chorus.

Poland is Jerusalem and the Polish Jeremiah is the Jesuit court chaplain, Piotr Skarga. A famous painting by Jan Matejko depicts Skarga preaching in 1596. His theme is the fall and rebirth of the nation. Dissensions among noblemen have brought it to this pass.

Skarga's sermon is proof that the messianic vision of Poland was not the invention of 19th century romanticism. The play ends with Skarga, both hands raised in the prophetic mode, exhorting pregnant women to come to the tomb of the *hetman* (general) Stanislaw of Zlolkiew:

> Touch the coffin! — There is life,
> take the fetus to your womb.
> Swear the oath ere you depart!
> Come spring, oath takes root in tomb.
> Rise! — Much must be done, avenged.
> In this act you all unite!

Angels blow brass trumpets as the play ends.

Wojtyla thought of calling his play "The Covenant." He says he had the idea "in a flash, like a revelation, of a national drama." This would have meant that God had struck a deal with Poland or, in more noble language, assigned it a task, a vocation.

The vocation was to be the *antemurale Christianitatis*, the bulwark of Christendom, against the Turkish and Tartar hordes, not to mention the schismatic Muscovites who were regarded as "barbarian."

Poland entered the 17th century as a great power. Her troops occupied vast areas of European Russia and even entered the Kremlin itself in Moscow. Yet, by the end of the century, Poland was an economic and political wreck.

Wojtyla's play is full of literary memories. In the 1840s, Juliusz Slowacki used the image of the potter's wheel from Jeremiah 18: "O Jerusalem, Slavic Jerusalem, the hour is coming when you will be destroyed and broken like a potter's vessel" (although this poem was not published until 1924, Wojtyla would have known it).

The other great 19th century poet, Adam Mickiewicz, declared that the motto on the tomb of Zolkiewski, *"ex ossibus ultor"* (from the tomb an avenger), would one day be fulfilled.

But who were the "avengers" of 1940? "Jeremiah" does not answer this question. Nor has it been answered since then. So Poland remains "unavenged" to this day.

Wojtyla's next play, "Our God's Brother," written 1945-1950, is much more sophisticated. It is his masterpiece. It might, with cuts, succeed best on radio, where nothing visual distracts the imagination, and atmosphere can be easily evoked.

The play is set in Kraków in the 1880s and concerns a painter called Adam. Much of the action — so to call it — takes place in his atelier. His most recent painting, "Ecce Homo," shows a tortured Christ far removed from Pre-Raphaelite gentilities. It also reflects his own inner struggles.

His friends — painters back from Munich and Halina, an actress back from a world tour, a visiting Jesuit and his mother — anxiously discuss what has happened to Adam. He has discovered the poor. This unsettles him. He begins to work in the poorhouse, but his do-gooding is rejected as patronizing.

Enter a mysterious stranger, clad in black. The translator thinks this might just be Vladimir I. Lenin, who studied in Kraków 1912-1914. So he might. The way Wojtyla juggles with time, anything is possible. In any event, the man in black is a Marxist who assures Adam he is wasting his time: There can be radical change only when one harnesses the anger of the poor.

Wojtyla treats the dialectic fairly enough. One of the down-and-outs tells Adam his Christ is an "alienation," a broken reed for the revolution: "There was once one — remember — who swore that everything was just around the corner. He talked and talked. Then what? He went away, and we're still here. And we're the same as before. End of story."

In the end, Adam rejects the agitator's solution of inciting the poor from the outside and joins them like any Slav "populist" of the period ("I will follow them").

The Lenin-figure (if that's who he is) is discomfited. He is an intellectual leader who does not identify with the people he purports to serve.

Although mostly talk, it makes for good drama. The argument is serious and fairly conducted. They talk no more than characters in George Bernard Shaw. One can imagine how fresh and free such dialogue must have seemed in 1950, when grim "socialist realism" occupied whatever theaters were open.

Yet, it couldn't possibly be put on under Stalinism, and was even turned down by the Kraków Catholic paper, *Tygodnik Powzechny*. Its editors hastened to remedy this when the author became pope.

Life imitated literature when, in 1983, John Paul beatified Adam Chmielowski (in religion, Br. Albert), who was the hero of his play.

So there is obviously an autobiographical element: Adam gives up painting for religious life, Wojtyla gives up poetry and the theater to be a priest. If we accept that, then "Our God's Brother" becomes the key to the thinking of Pope John Paul.

What is Adam's greatest temptation? "The thought that one can love with the intelligence, and with the intelligence only, and that this will suffice." This remark Adam addresses, appropriately enough, to his father confessor.

But the continuity is striking. Thus, the pope's strictures on the "liberation theologians" of Latin America, whom he believes to be misled by the class war, display his consistency from 1950 to 1984.

The play could also be said to illustrate his difficulty in recognizing the originality of non-Polish situations. It would be very hard to maintain that the social problems of Austrian Galacia in the 1800s have anything to do with late 20th century Latin America. But they explain his violent anti-Sandinista reaction in Managua, Nicaragua, in 1983.

"The Jeweler's Shop" (1960) has been quite widely performed. It reflects the period when Wojtyla was known to his students in Kraków and Lublin as "*Wujek*" or "uncle." They told him about their unhappy love affairs, and he incorporated this material into this meditation on marriage.

Taborski's exegesis complicates the play needlessly. First, he tells us that "The Jeweler's Shop" is presented "from a metaphysically human viewpoint: The jeweler and his shop are there or not there, depending on our need or willingness to perceive them."

But then he explains that the jeweler stands for "divine providence, for the power of moral judgment. The wedding rings which he does not so much sell as dispense and which he refuses to buy back, symbolize the obligations of marriage." Ah-ha!

What we have are three interlocking situations that say something about human love. Teresa has to come to accept widowhood after the death of her husband, Andrew (Act I). Stefan and Anna are estranged (Act II). Teresa's son, Christopher, is about to marry Monica (Act III). Life and love go on for eternity — like the golden ring that has no end and no beginning.

Once again, we have a central character called Adam who is the authorial voice. Adam is a father confessor. He knows everyone, but he himself remains unknown and elusive.

Adam's concluding speech explains why human love (eros) is so disappointing.

> The cause lies in the past; the error resides simply there. The thing is that love carries people away like an *absolute*, although it lacks absolute dimensions. But acting under an illusion, they do not try to connect that love with the Love that has such a dimension. They do not even feel the need. . . .
>
> Sometimes human existence seems too short for love. At other times, however, it is the other way round, human love seems too short in relation to existence — or rather too trivial. At any rate, every person has at his disposal an existence and a love. The problem is how to build a sensible structure from it.

I do not pretend to understand this fully. It seems to refer to a contemporary debate about human love (eros) and divine love (agape). Only agape can lay an absolute claim on our love. Human loves are merely its shadows, forerunners, anticipations, dress rehearsals for the real thing.

Variants on this theme can be found in much Catholic writing of the period: Graham Greene's *The End of the Affair*, Evelyn Waugh's *Brideshead Revisited* and Paul Claudel's *Le Partage de Midi*.

But these comparisons do not really help, for these three authors were concerned with how God could "use" guilty sexual love to open people up to divine love. They showed how "God wrote straight on crooked lines." There is nothing "guilty" about Wojtyla's lovers. They are all properly and sacramentally married.

One could say that, for them, eros and agape are working in harmony. They are on the same side. No wedge can be driven between them. No woman is obliged to love her husband less in order to love God more.

So the interesting question in "The Jeweler's Shop" concerns not the pairs of lovers so much as Adam, the confessor and quasi-omniscient narrator. In the final scene, Adam names all the characters slowly, one by one. He then falls silent.

Teresa goes on: "Adam mentioned us one by one, left his own name out. He was, as it were, a common denominator of us all — at the same time a spokesman and judge. Somehow, we quietly entrusted ourselves to his thoughts, his analysis and heart. All this — all this was, and moved, or was moving slowly into another structure."

This is an idealized version the relationship Bishop Wojtyla (he became bishop in 1958) had with his students and friends in the late 1950s and early 1960s. He was an expert in matters of the heart, *because* he was not personally involved. Women felt "safe" with him.

But by the same token, he remained rather cryptic, mysterious, distant and aloof. This is the view of Halina Bortnowska, who knew him well at this time.

It can be confirmed from another source. In the same year, 1960, that he was writing "The Jeweler's Shop," Bishop Wojtyla published a book called *Love and Responsibility*. Its 1960 preface begins by answering the objection that "priests and persons living a celibate life can have nothing to say on questions of love and marriage."

His reply is that, in his pastoral work, the priest becomes so familiar with certain problems that "a different type of experience is created which is certainly less immediate and 'secondhand,' but at the same time very much wider."

One can agree that the experience of the married couple is limited to one marriage: their own. The confessor may well have a much broader knowledge of varied marital situations. But unless language is abused, he cannot stretch this "experience" to include, say, the experience of sexuality.

For that, you either have or you haven't. There is no "vicarious experience" of sexuality, no substitute for the real thing. Andrew Greeley's novels make the point vividly.

None of this would matter were it not for the fact that in the 1980 preface to *Love and Responsibility*, the author says that "experience" shows that the use of artificial contraceptives in marriage demeans the wife and means she is treated "like an object."

This proposition is said to be based on "experience," which is apostrophized in the most lyrical fashion: "This work is open to the echo of every echo of experience, from whatever quarter it comes, and it is at the same time a standing appeal to let experience, their own experience, make itself heard, to its full extent, in all its depth and breadth. . . . Experience does not have to be afraid of experience. Truth can only gain from such a confrontation."

Once again, there is continuity from 1960 to 1980. Now as then, Pope John Paul claims to speak in the name of the experience of the married. The plays are important as an unconscious revelation of the sort of person Wojtyla is.

He is a man who lives through many tensions. The last play, "Radiation of Fatherhood," is a long stream-of-consciousness reflection on overcoming loneliness. It includes what must surely be the first account of childbirth from the pen of a future pope.

There is much raw material for the psychiatrist here. One mother explains: "I love Adam and constantly restore to him the fatherhood he renounces. I discreetly turn his loneliness into my motherhood. . . . The radiation of fatherhood passes through me, acts through my motherhood."

Again, I cannot tell you what this "means." And "meanings" exist independently of the intentions of the utterer. But it is interesting for the first time in the modern period to have a pope who reveals his vulnerability so sincerely.

It is hard to think of any other pope in history who said, "I think in theatrical images." True, he first made the remark in 1940. But he has a remarkable consistency, and so it throws light on his pontificate.

The playwright and the actor impersonate others so much that they sometimes have a problem of identity. In 1957 he wrote a poem called "Actor" that admirably sums up the problem:

So many grew round me, through me,
from myself, as it were,
I became a channel, unleashing a force

called man.
Did not the others, crowding in, distort
the man I am?
Being each of them, always imperfect,
myself to myself too near,
he who survives in me, can he ever look at himself without fear? ❑

42

Pope, in Bolivia, excoriates capitalism

(May 20, 1988) After one week in South America, Pope John Paul launched his most devastating attack on capitalism May 11 in the continent's poorest country, Bolivia.

Speaking on a dusty field at Oruro to a crowd of 100,000, he said, "Certainly, one cannot deny the good results achieved by the joint efforts of private and public initiatives in those countries where a regime of liberty rules."

But this was his only concession to capitalism.

He went on, "These achievements, however, should not blind one to the defects of an economic system whose principal motive is profit, where man is subordinated to capital, turning him into a cog in an immense machine, reducing his work to a piece of merchandise at the mercy of the ups and downs of the laws of supply and demand."

In saying this, John Paul was backing the Bolivian bishops who wanted him to "question the structures that prevent people from overcoming their situation," as Bishop Julio Terrazas, president of the Bolivian episcopal conference, put it.

Besides speaking, John Paul also listened.

He heard a mine union leader evoke the unemployment in the tin mines: "Today, you have not been able to hear the calling of the sirens because our tunnels are empty, and in our mining camps you can hear only the cries of the children because they cannot put bread in their mouths."

The bishops have mediated the disputes between the unemployed tin miners and the government. But the coca plant has replaced tin as the staple industry. So John Paul's exhortation to youth to avoid "the temptation of easy enrichment by way of drug trafficking" was to be expected.

Days earlier, in the plane from Rome, however, John Paul referred to the international attempt to curb drug trafficking and said the profiteers had gone unpunished "so we must speak of everyone, and not just of the poorest." He added that, "in this complex problem, some are in need of help rather than sanction or a punishment."

In the Bolivian capital of La Paz, John Paul urged the bishops to help Catholics "defend themselves against active proselytizing of the sects." Bolivian television airs evangelists who offer faith-healing for money.

The pope noted that the "sects of a fundamentalist sort" are growing in influence in Bolivia. The bishops should "provide the faithful with an adequate capacity for discernment so that, with an attitude of sincere ecumenism with our brothers in other Christian confessions and with respect for all, they nevertheless remain and act like faithful children of the church in which they were baptized."

Earlier on his trip, John Paul had faced a different set of problems in Uruguay, a country of 3 million on the other side of the River Plata from Argentina. It is the most "secular" state of Latin America, even turning Christmas into "the Feast of Families." It returned to democratic rule in 1984 after 12 years of military rule marked by deaths, disappearances and much torture.

John Paul's main theme in Uruguay was to stress the Christian origins of the country and to call for a "new evangelization" that would overcome the secularist ideology inherited from the 19th century.

He denounced the separation of church and state and declared the need for "the public profession of Christianity."

His own visit with its two great outdoor Masses effectively ignored the separation of church and state. It was regarded as a coup to have President Julio Maria Sanguinetti, who belongs to no church, in the front row of a prayer meeting in Montevideo. Other ministers were present at each event.

A Vatican official remarked, "We have moved ahead 50 years in the course of two days." That may be so, but some Catholics had wanted the pope to support the campaign to bring the torturers from the military regime to justice. His silence on this issue may have bought the government acquiescence.

After Bolivia, the pope's next stop was to be Peru for two days, where he would conclude a Eucharistic Marian Congress. The "sects" were already objecting to so much Mariology.

The trip was to conclude in Paraguay, where a difficult encounter with Latin America's longest-serving dictator, Gen. Alfredo Stroessner, was expected. Stroessner insisted that the pope visit Encarnación, his birthplace. The bishops reluctantly agreed.

Speaking of his coming meeting with Stroessner in the plane on the way out of Rome, John Paul had said, "What he does is his responsibility; what I do is my responsibility. My responsibility is to preach the gospel of Jesus Christ and the social doctrine of the church."

That may have summed up, in advance, his first week in Latin America. ❑

43

John Paul's first decade: His many roles shift papacy

(October 14, 1988) Ten years have passed since Cardinal Karol Wojtyla of Kraków was elected pope, Oct. 16, 1978, taking the name John Paul II.

He is very different from the two popes whose names he took. He is unlike the shrewd, relaxed and cultivated peasant, John XXIII, who saw himself as an enabler of the Holy Spirit. That was the reason that he called Vatican II. John Paul would never have called a council.

Nor does he resemble the anxious, tortured Paul VI, who completed John's council. Where Paul was hesitant, he is decisive. Where Paul left "openings," he closes them.

So much so that one school of interpretation of John Paul's pontificate presents it as "correcting" the liberal "weaknesses" of Paul's pontificate.

To define more clearly the originality of John Paul's pontificate, I want to set down in no particular order 10 "roles" he has played in 10 years. I use "roles" in the sociological sense. This is what he has done. This is how he has functioned.

1. The upholder of tradition. By definition, all popes have this conservative role, because the Catholic faith is founded on tradition, according to St. Paul's formula, "I am handing on to you what I have received" (applied to the Eucharist and the resurrection).

But there is tradition and traditions, and in John Paul's case, the emphasis has been on the reiteration of established positions.

There has been little attempt — none, really — to interrogate the tradition to draw out from it "things new and old" and to see whether it might not have something different to say about aspects of sexual morality, women in the church, lay ministries. There has been no fresh reading of "the signs of the times," no listening to "what the Spirit is saying to the churches."

All the institutions Paul VI founded — typically the synod and the International Theological Commission — have lost their advice-giving function. Now they are pressed into service in the cause of upholding tradition.

2. The globetrotting traveling salesman of the church's unity. John Paul's journey to France last weekend was his 40th international trip. The visible head of the church has made himself visible to more people than any previous pope could have dreamed of.

Eight million people went to Rome for the 1985 Holy Year. That is less than 1 percent of the Catholic population. The pope's journeys, which he prefers to call "pilgrimages to the heart of the church," have put him within range of many millions of Third World people who could never imagine going to Rome.

Most Catholics have a "lump-in-the-throat" experience the first time they see the pope. That is not the same as listening to his message.

3. The international media star. This is the most criticized aspect of the pontificate. But Pius XII in his own way exploited the media: The thin, ascetic figure, his gaze turned heavenward, his arms extended in benediction, became the icon of the papacy in the post-World War II period.

Paul VI, a shy and private person, did not learn how to use television. John Paul is a master of the medium. He knows how to evoke applause with a sweeping gesture. His image is one of dynamism, certainties and compassion.

4. The leader in spirituality. He prays, visibly prays, and is keenly aware of human suffering and its redemptive value. He sees the 20th century not as the peak of human progress, but as an era of unparalleled suffering.

His encyclical *Salvifici Doloris* (Feb. 11, 1984) is his most "personal" document. It is a rebuke to "Western" superficiality for failing to grasp the reality of evil in a century that has known "an incomparable accumulation of sufferings, even to the possible self-destruction of the planet."

To someone who sees faith in such life-and-death terms, the "Western" concern with church structures and women's ordination is unintelligible. "The pope," said Halina Bortnowska, his editor in Kraków, "would like to put the whole church on a spiritual retreat."

5. The populist. John Paul is "populist" in the sense that he wishes to appeal to the "ordinary faithful" above the heads of theologians. He believes a "silent majority" in the church was disturbed by theological speculations and needs reassurance.

In his first encyclical, *Redemptor Hominis* (1979), he deplored the way "critical attitudes" had become widespread, assailing, from within, "the church, her institutions and structures, and ecclesiastics and their activities."

So why not "silence" those who rock the boat? The masses will not protest and might even cheer.

The revival of Mariology is another example of populist thinking. Paul VI was anxious that Mariology should not needlessly antagonize Protestants.

John Paul has no such inhibitions and claimed in his encyclical on the Marian year, *Redemptoris Mater* (1987), that devotion to Mary "cast an ecumenical light." That might be true for the Orthodox, but hardly for churches that emerged at the Reformation.

6. John Paul is a "populist" in another sense. On his international travels, especially to the Third World, he makes himself "the voice of those who have no voice."

Although unfailingly — sometimes disconcertingly — polite to dictators such as Gens. Alfredo Stroessner and Augusto Pinochet, he denounces their abuses of human rights and exhorts them to constitutional reforms.

It is arguable that the papal visits to the Philippines and Haiti helped create the mood that made it possible to topple the dictators. But papal "populism" in such cases is nearly always qualified by "diplomatic" considerations that reduce its impact.

Thus, there can be no doubt that his speeches in Mozambique articulated the people's deep yearning for an end to violence, but without indicating the path to peace with any precision. Were the South Africans being told to stop supporting the RENAMO guerrillas?

It was difficult to say. But it may be significant that none of the guerrillas John Paul has exhorted "on his knees" to desist from violence — in Northern Ireland, Peru and El Salvador — have shown any inclination to lay down their arms.

7. The teacher of Catholic social doctrine. John Paul appears as the pope who attempted to breathe new life into what used to be called Catholic social doctrine (CSD). Paul VI said in 1971, "In view of the varied situations in the world, it is difficult to give one teaching to cover them all or to offer a solution which has universal value" (*Octogesima Adveniens*).

John Paul believes this admission of incompetence is fainthearted. While Paul VI thought the task he found impossible was best done on the level of the local church, John Paul thinks he can offer "solutions of universal value."

This leads to misunderstandings. Paul VI would have welcomed the U.S. bishops' economic pastoral as an attempt to apply CSD to the local situation. John Paul pointedly ignored it when he spoke on justice in Detroit.

But if one pitches the CSD level too high and aims for universality, the result is a degree of lofty generality that leaves particular situations untouched. It is like looking at the earth from a plane: The particular features of the landscape are flattened out.

Laborem Exercens (1981), for example, declares that unemployment "is in all cases an evil and, when it reaches a certain level, can become a real social disaster." But though unemployment and underemployment are endemic, the condemnation of this "evil" remains generic.

8. The church's chief executive officer (CEO). The most striking feature of the first 10 years has been the attempt to centralize church government. Vatican II recognized the reality of the local church. It was expressed, in part, through the episcopal conference. But now episcopal conferences are reduced to being no more than a "practical arrangement," with no theological reality and no mandate to teach.

The relationship that now matters is that of the individual bishop with the curia. Whereas an episcopal conference — especially a large one such as those of Brazil and the United States — might have some chance of defending itself against the curia, the individual bishop is no match for it.

They are checked up on every five years in their *ad limina* visits to Rome, which are, said the preface to the recent revision of the Roman curia, "as it were, at the center of the pope's supreme ministry."

If all these controls fail to produce the required conformity, then other measures can be used, as Archbishop Raymond C. Hunthausen of Seattle and Bishop Pedro Casaldáliga of Sao Felix, Brazil, discovered to their cost.

9. The ecumenical leader. This is where John Paul appears so "progressive" that he has brought down on his head much right-wing thunder.

He is blamed for the Assisi meeting Oct. 27, 1986, when Buddhists and most of the world's religions were represented. Although John Paul carefully explained they were not "praying together" but "praying at the same time," he was still accused of "indifferentism" (the idea that "one religion is as good as another"). It would be difficult to find a more fatuous charge.

The same right-wing circles also reproach him for his visit to the Rome synagogue April 13, 1986. There John Paul said, "With Judaism, we have a relationship that we do not have with any other religion. You are our beloved brothers, and in a certain way, it could be said that you are our elder brothers."

This cut at the roots of anti-Semitism. It was important that a Polish pope should say that "no condemnation can be imputed to the Jews as if they were the people responsible for Christ's passion."

But after Vatican II, that was the least that could be expected. As for unity with other Christians, John Paul turns it into a mirage that might be realized once the others accept papal primacy.

That effectively postpones it for several generations.

10. The "man from a far country." This was his self-description the day he was elected 10 years ago. Two days later, he said the church valued cultural, historical and linguistic diversity and saw such diversities as an enrichment.

He added, "The particular nature of our country of origin is from now one of little importance; as a Christian, and still more as pope, we are and will be witnesses of a universal love." He seemed to be saying we should disregard his Polishness.

But this has proved extremely difficult to do. Looking out from Kraków and Warsaw, one has a different perspective on the world.

Looking eastward, one sees that "a key fact of our time is that . . . millions of our contemporaries yearn to recover the basic freedoms of which they were deprived by totalitarian and atheistic regimes" (*Instruction of Certain Aspects of Liberation Theology*, September 1984).

We may think of this from time to time; John Paul thinks about it all the time. This explains his continuing mistrust of liberation theology and the three priests still in government in Nicaragua. In his eyes, they have failed to learn the lessons of Poland and have become what Lenin called "useful idiots."

Innovations such as the Pontifical Council for Culture — set up May 28, 1982 — appear as a Polish idea that does not export well. In Poland, the church has become the sponsor of culture in the broadest sense, and exhibitions, poetry readings and historical lectures take place under its patronage.

But the same need for free breathing space does not exist elsewhere, artists refuse to be dragooned and a Catholic culture cannot be brought into existence by pontifical fiat.

I discussed this article with a Polish intellectual who bridled at the idea of "assessing" the first 10 years of the pontificate. "If someone wrote on this question in Poland," he said, "he would be concerned with how to apply the papal magisterium, not with how to evaluate it." ❏

Part III

The Later Years

44

Amid euphoria, Pope worries lest new Europe be merely secular

(April 13, 1990) Oxford, England — from the start of his pontificate, Pope John Paul, the first Slav pope, has shared a dream. He proclaimed the "spiritual unity of Europe," called for open frontiers and demanded religious freedom for Catholics of Eastern Europe and the Soviet Union.

In 1989, the year of peaceful revolutions, that dream came several giant steps closer to realization. Eastern Europe has become once more Central Europe. Democracy has poked through. Yet the Vatican's euphoria about the events has been muted and tempered by alarm at their possible negative consequences.

Of course Pope John Paul II rejoiced. "Warsaw, Moscow, Budapest, Berlin, Prague, Sofia, Bucharest," he told the diplomats accredited to the Holy See Jan. 14, "have become stages in a long pilgrimage toward liberty." The list was instructive.

Warsaw rightfully came first, because there the first breakthrough occurred; Moscow deserved an honorable mention, as a tribute to Mikhail Gorbachev; the omission of the capitals of Soviet republics such as Lithuania or Armenia was tactful in the presence of the Soviet diplomat Yuri Karlov, last week formally named as the Kremlin's man in the Vatican.

What made it all happen? John Paul said "the irrepressible thirst for liberty had speeded up developments, made walls tumble down and opened gates." He noted, without dwelling on it, the role churches played.

He struck a note of anticommunist triumphalism: "In countries in which for years a single party has dictated the truth to be believed and the meaning to be given to human history, these brothers have shown that it is impossible to stifle fundamental freedoms which give meaning to human life; freedom of thought, of conscience, of religion, of expression, of political and cultural pluralism."

The church had been vindicated by events, proved right. But any satisfaction this might bring has to be balanced by thoughts of the dangers created by the new situation.

"It is always possible," the pope went on to the diplomats, "that age-old rivalries will reemerge, that conflicts between ethnic minorities will be rekindled and that nationalism will intensify."

It has not taken long for this prediction to be verified. For more than 40 years, communism papered over ethnic differences and maintained a sort of stability, even if it was no more than a state of frozen immobility.

Repressed conflicts reemerge as ethnic and national differences combine with religion in Transylvania and the Ukraine. Identity tends to be defined against others as in the Baltic republics. The problems of liberty can be greater than the problems of oppression.

All this has made redundant one kind of papal discourse. A rhetoric conceived in opposition will not do in the changed situation. On his return home to Poland in June 1979, he said Providence had chosen him as pope to "proclaim the spiritual unity of Europe."

This was not a pious thought, but a steely claim that the frontiers of Europe were anomalous, artificial and should be opened as soon as possible. It was a clear political statement about the postwar Yalta division of Europe into two ideologically contending blocs.

But the pope's dream of a Europe without frontiers involved a restoration. He sketched out his medieval vision at the shrine of St. James of Compostella in Spain in 1982 and last summer invited thousands of young people to join him on pilgrimage there.

He said, "In the centuries when a homogeneous and spiritually united continent was being shaped, the whole of Europe came here to the 'memorial' of St. James. It was one of the places that favored the mutual understandings of the so many different European peoples, the Latins, the Germans, the Celts, the Anglo-Saxons and the Slavs." Europe was united because, like the diverse peoples who made it up, it was baptized.

So the pope has a sacralized view of Europe. It is the dream of Christendom, with a perfect unity between faith and culture. On his map he sees pilgrimage centers and Marian shrines. Everything and everyone that is not linked with this fundamental vision is omitted.

Evidently, this sacralized vision of Europe does not fit the realities of the secularized Europe in the late 20th century. The pope knows this and consciously challenges contemporary trends with his project of a "second evangelization" of Europe. The church must be a "sign of contradiction."

He particularly resented the way the European Community made off with the adjective "European," forgetting that the Slavs had just as much right to it. Not only that, but their experience of persecution meant they had a lot to teach the West about spirituality, orthodoxy and Christian fidelity.

In the East, "secularization" was the official state program and so Christians resisted it. In the West, God was edged to the margin by prosperity and the pursuit of technological progress, and the Christian response was feeble.

John Paul startled the European parliament in Strasbourg in September 1988 by saying "an ethics based only on social consensus and individual liberty" that allowed no place for God in public life would lead straight to another Auschwitz, another gulag archipelago.

But since 1989 such warnings tend to fall on deaf ears. The European Community acts as a model and magnet to the East Europeans. Poles, Czechs, Slovaks and Hungarians in particular do not think it sinful to want to join it and to seek some share in a prosperity they have been so long denied. They are prepared to accept the austerity and discipline needed to qualify for membership.

East Germany will be the first to join by virtue of being united with West Germany. This will immediately deprive the pope of his favorite contrast between the heroic, persecuted Christians of the East and the West German church he has criticized as too worldly, too consumerist, too conformed to the modern world.

He said as much by imposing Cardinal Joachim Meisner, from East Berlin, on Cologne in December 1988. Meisner was to bring a stiffening of resolve from the East. But it is now evident that the much larger West German church will influence the East Germans, not vice versa. The East German church will soon cease to have a separate identity.

Much of what the pope habitually says about Poland will need revision. Since World War II, but especially since the abolition of Solidarity in December 1981, the Polish church provided a space of freedom where the true voice of the nation could be heard.

Not having the responsibility of power, the church was free to criticize the government, whatever it did, in the name of the common good and the Polish people.

Now that freedom has gone. The church no longer has a role as tribune of underground dissent. It has to have a more positive attitude toward a government it helped to bring into being.

What position will the church take on "communist" legislation such as abortion? If pro-life opposition to birth control and abortion is made the test, then the executed President Nicolae Ceausescu of Romania would be the model of a statesman acceptable to the church.

Solidarity was never a formally Catholic labor union, and two of its best-known leaders, Adam Michnik and Jacek Kuron, are not believers. Cardinal Józef Glemp set Christian Democrats up against them in the election. They were defeated. Is Poland, in short, to be a pluralist society?

An even graver question for John Paul is whether communism in Eastern Europe has artificially retarded the process of secularization that has gone on in the West.

So while John Paul might broadly welcome the political consequences of the events, their religious consequences are less encouraging. If Poland, because of the changed circumstances, can no longer provide a model for the church, then what country can?

In the Soviet Union, the fundamental religious liberty claimed for years by the Vatican has been achieved. But it is the start rather than the end of problems.

For the Lithuanian Catholic Church, 1989 was the year its basic rights were restored: Its cathedral was handed back, the entire hierarchy was reconstituted, a second seminary was opened, a Catholic weekly, *Katalicu Pasualis*, began regular publication, and catechism could be taught again in primary schools.

There was no particular gratitude to Gorbachev for these moves, which were merely the righting of an appalling injustice. Besides, the first fruits of *perestroika* in Lithuania whetted the appetite for more.

They highlighted the most fundamental injustice of all: Lithuania's forcible incorporation into the Soviet Union in 1940. So the fate of the Lithuanian church depends on the fate of the Lithuanian nation.

The Ukrainian Catholic church was even more strenuously persecuted than the Lithuanian: It was abolished in 1946, and its property was turned over to the Russian Orthodox church. It has emerged from the underground with great vitality.

Catholic communities may now be formally recognized, and full legislation is (or was) being prepared. After years of clandestinity, labor camps and secret ordinations of priests and bishops, that was good news.

But so far the chief effect has been that what Metropolitan Kiril, head of foreign relations for the Russian Orthodox church, called "a religious war" has broken out between his church and the Catholics. March 13, the seven Ukrainian Catholic bishops — whose existence was unknown a year before — walked out of Vatican Orthodox talks on the restoration of church properties.

"We will never," they declared as they marched out, "allow our Ukrainian Catholic church to become an object of a deal between the Vatican and the Moscow patriarchate."

The Ukrainian Catholic bishops have a case. They want the theological reality of their church to be recognized and not sacrificed to diplomacy. But these heroic confessors of the faith, preserved from the reforms of Vatican II by their remoteness, can no longer be held up as role models to Western Christians.

Lithuania and the Ukraine both have common frontiers with Poland. So does Belorussia, situated between them. But closeness does not always make for good relations.

The new bishop in Belorussia, Tadeusz Kondrusiewicz, is a Pole, and he has just received Soviet permission to "import" 40 Polish priests. There have already been murmurs about excessive "Polonization." In dealing with fellow Slavs, being Polish has its down side. The détente achieved between the superpowers is now needed among neighbors.

The pope will have a chance to give his evaluation of events when he goes to Czechoslovakia April 21-22. It would be good to hear him say that the Europe the country of President Václav Havel aspires to join represents not just materialism and hedonism, but also solid values of liberty, pluralism, democracy, tolerance.

But there will be warnings, too. He told the diplomats he hoped "the new recruits to democracy and liberty" would not be "let down by those who are, in some sense, the veterans." The ambiguities and risks of history become more evident in times of instability.

The East European Christians have gone through their Calvary; so far there are only hints of resurrection. They have become more like the rest of us. ❑

45

Excavating for foundation of infallible Humanae Vitae

(May 4, 1990) Quoting "sources in Rome and the United States," Russell Shaw, press officer for the Knights of Columbus, recently predicted that "before 1990 is out, Pope John Paul II will publish an encyclical on fundamental moral principles."

It is a rule of Roman life that documents are not admitted to exist until they actually appear. However, it is still worth asking how well founded this story is likely to be. For that, we need a potted history.

For many years, Rome has been awash with rumors that Pope John Paul would declare *Humanae Vitae* retrospectively "infallible." The aim of such a move — declared impossible by many theologians — would be to cut the ground from under those who think conscientious dissent from the encyclical defensible.

Advocating the toughest possible measures has been the Pontifical Council for the Family, headed since 1985 by French Canadian Cardinal Edouard Gagnon. Gagnon has never made a mystery of his views.

He has long believed that the church in the United States "is tolerating material schism." In 1983 he said the remedy would be "to change 90 percent of the teachers of moral theology and stop them from teaching, because they are teaching basically principles which lead to sexual abominations." He exhorted the laity to denounce errant theologians and bishops to Rome.

Such views might once have been dismissed as eccentric. But Gagnon's appointment as president of the Council for the Family showed that he had the confidence of the pope.

Gagnon it was who told the U.S. archbishops in March 1989 that ministry to the divorced was degenerating into "dating services for divorced Catholics." He warned against the tender hearts of women religious on marriage tribunals.

He has gathered some powerful allies at the Council for the Family. On the intellectual front, he could call upon Msgr. Carlo Caffarra, who won notoriety by suggesting that it would be "opportune" to return to the condemnation of contraception as homicide found in the 1917 Code of Canon Law.

For financial and practical help, Gagnon had available Virgil Dechant, grand knight of the U.S. Knights of Columbus and his wife, Ann. On the publicity level he had the services of Russell Shaw, Opus Dei member and author of our prediction.

Archbishop John Aloysius Hickey is on the board of the Council for the Family. It scored a victory Aug. 18, 1986, when Hickey, in his capacity as chancellor of The Catholic University of America, informed Fr. Charles E. Curran that action to withdraw his canonical mission to teach in the university had been initiated.

On this occasion Hickey also trotted out the Council for the Family line that no distinction could be drawn between infallible and noninfallible teachings.

Besides stopping "opponents," pushing their own men was another part of the strategy. The first two laymen on the International Theological Commission were William E. May, Curran's main opponent at CUA, and Oxford-based Australian lawyer John Finnis, a former pupil of Germain Grisez. There they joined Caffarra.

But if Curran's fate was a victory for the Council for the Family, it failed to deter the vast majority of his fellow moral theologians who continued to work as before. The Redemptorist Alfonsianum Academy in Rome organized an international conference for April 1988 in which many of the great names of postconciliar moral theology would take part.

But one cannot organize a conference in Rome without Vatican intervention. The planned program displeased the Congregation for the Doctrine of the Faith. First the paper of Italian theologian Sandro Spinsanti on the problem of AIDS would have to go.

But that was mere skirmishing. Next, it was agreed that lectures by Bonn Professor Franz Boekle and Redemptorist Bernhard Häring could be given but only on condition that they were "balanced" by lectures on the same themes by Gregorian Jesuit Bartholomew Kiely and Caffarra. Caffarra did not so much "balance" Häring as openly contradict him.

The final straw came when, Dec. 28, 1988, Cardinal William Wakefield Baum in his role as prefect of the Congregation for Catholic Education, forbade publication of the *Acta of the Redemptorist Congress*, declaring it "inopportune."

But already there had been another event that showed how determined the Vatican was to impose its own version of moral theology. In November 1988, Gagnon organized two meetings in Rome.

The first was designed to permit bishops to "celebrate 20 years of *Humanae Vitae*." Sixty attended. The second, sponsored by Caffarra's John Paul II Institute and the Opus Dei Holy Cross Academy, mustered about 300 moral theologians.

Caffarra was the keynote speaker at both meetings. He claimed that to admit any exception to the full rigor of *Humanae Vitae* was to be anti-life, anti-human and anti-God. Caffarra was also credited with being the author of the papal speeches with which the two meetings were favored.

This has its importance, for it was John Paul's words at these meetings that so struck the moral theologians because of their extravagance. One of the motives of the Cologne Declaration of Jan. 6, 1989, was to reply to the papal remarks.

The 163 German-speaking theologians said, "Recently, in addresses to theologians and bishops, the pope, without consideration for the degrees of certainty and the different weight of church statements, has linked the teaching on birth control with the fundamental truths of faith like salvation through Jesus Christ."

This disregard of the necessary hierarchy of truth, they went on, led the pope to accuse critics of the papal teaching on birth control of "attacking fundamental pillars of Christian doctrine." Moreover, their appeal to conscience was said to "make Christ's cross vain," "shatter the mystery of God" and "deny the dignity of man."

The Cologne signatories had two objections to this approach. First, it enlisted notions such as "divine revelation" and "fundamental truth" to advocate a very particular teaching. Second, they pointed out that the ban on birth control in *Humanae Vitae* did not and could not replace "the responsible conscience."

This ought to have led to a debate on the foundations of moral theology. The Cologne Declaration raised serious questions that required urgent discussion, as Häring, now sick and on the verge of retirement, told the pope.

But there was to be neither debate nor discussion. Nor was there any specific reply. Instead, there was a series of attacks on theologians as a class. The pope himself denounced those who tried to set up "an overt or surreptitious form of a parallel or alternative magisterium."

But the favorite theme, deployed by both John Paul and Cardinal Joseph Ratzinger, was that bishops, and not theologians, were the "true teachers" of the church. Ratzinger told the summit meeting of U.S. archbishops in March 1989 that bishops should cease to be intimidated by theologians and should boldly assume their role of "pastor-evangelists."

The U.S.-Vatican summit had, in any case, been preempted by the publication, in *L'Osservatore Romano* Feb. 25, 1989, of a revised profession of faith, together with an oath to be taken by theology teachers, pastors and many other officeholders in the church.

The oath included a commitment to hold whatever "the church proposes definitively with regard to teaching concerning faith or morals." Franciscan Umberto Betti, in an official commentary in the Vatican paper, said that *Humanae Vitae* fell into this category. So here, "definitive" teaching is treated as if in practice it meant infallible.

In any case, the oath said "religious submission of will and intellect" is required to the Roman pontiff and the college of bishops "when they exercise the magisterium, even if they proclaim those teachings in an act that is not definitive."

Expressing their "dismay and consternation" at this suggestion, the Catholic Theological Association of America meeting at St. Louis in June 1989 complained that it could lead to the idea that the sole function of theologians is to defend and explain the teachings of church authorities.

The International Theological Commission met in Rome Oct. 2-7. All the participants and translators were sworn to secrecy, yet there were significant leaks to right-wing papers. Although they fastidiously refused to discuss the Cologne Declaration on the grounds that it had been first published in a newspaper, they did discuss some of the issues it raised.

Their judgment was that certain theologians, "convinced in good faith, it would seem, that the church is teaching false doctrine on matters like contraception, divorce and papal infallibility, were making a tactical move in a much longer strategic campaign to change the church's doctrine on these points."

But — still according to the right-wing leaks — that is not the only aim of the protesters. Although superficially discussing contraception and moral doctrine, they are really concerned with more profound questions concerning Jesus' nature, mission, death and resurrection.

That judgment — possibly libelous and calumnious if applied to stated individuals — has the great merit of deniability.

Better-founded was the report that a subcommittee of the ITC, headed by German theologian Wilhelm Ernst, was drafting a document on moral absolutes and the nature of the moral law. Caffarra is a member of it, if not its real leader.

This brings us almost to the present. Early in February, the Pope John XXIII Medical Moral Research and Education Center of Braintree, Mass., held a workshop in Dallas. In reporting it, Shaw made his prediction about an imminent encyclical.

The workshop attacked the idea that "exceptionless norms" — that is, moral principles admitting of no exceptions in specific circumstances — do not exist. Grisez said that the bans on contraception, abortions and sex outside of marriage were such norms.

Also under attack was "modern historical-mindedness," associated with the names of Karl Rahner and Bernard Lonergan, which allegedly says "we must stop trying to define ourselves as persons by some timeless abstraction called human nature."

Shaw describes Grisez as "a leading theologian among those who support church teaching," which implies that those he disagrees with do not support church teaching — a very serious charge that begs a number of questions.

No doubt Gagnon and the Council for the Family want an encyclical on the foundations of moral theology, to act as a further loyalty test to add to the oath and the profession of faith. No doubt they want to discredit and disqualify those they have labeled as unorthodox.

But it may prove difficult to translate these positions from the polemical atmosphere of a workshop of the like-minded to the public discourse of an encyclical. Difficult but, in the current climate, far from impossible.

The latest straw in the wind is that the Holy Cross Academy, Opus Dei's Rome theological center, has just been raised to the dignity of a university.

Just a year ago, Häring quoted a fellow moral theologian on the projected text: "I only hope the document will be as bad as Carlo Caffarra wants it to be — then we can be sure of a strong reaction."

But Häring rejected this attitude. He told *NCR*, "I did not at all want something like that. It had to be prevented for the good of the church and the honor of Pope John Paul II" (April 28, 1989). ❏

46

Alternative of cowed silence strange way to defend faith

(July 13, 1990) The "Instruction on the Ecclesial Vocation of the Theologian," published June 26, says it is addressed primarily to bishops and through them to theologians. At the end it "earnestly" invites bishops "to maintain and develop trust with theologians in the fellowship of charity."

The aim of fostering trust is unlikely to be achieved. No less trusting a document can be imagined. For throughout the entire instruction, "the theologian" is presented as a troublemaker who challenges the magisterium because he does not love the church and has sold out to worldliness.

Protestant theologians, should they read it, will rub their eyes in astonishment as they come across a theological system in which there appears to be only one source of truth, that is, the magisterium (the instruction invariably capitalizes the *M* in magisterium).

They will recall the conciliar debates about the two-source theory of truth, where the two sources meant scripture and tradition. They will remember the lucid statement of *Dei Verbum* that "the teaching office (the magisterium) is not above the word of God, but serves it."

Yet, in the instruction, the magisterium takes on an independent existence. "All the acts of the magisterium," it declares, "derive from the same source, that is, from Christ who desires that his people walk in the entire truth." All? Yes, all. On this conception, the magisterium has an unmediated hot line to Christ.

This makes it a very powerful instrument, indeed. There seems to be no limit to its range. The quality of infallibility, even when not expressly invoked, extends into disciplinary matters: "Magisterial decisions in matters of discipline, even if they are not guaranteed by the charism of infallibility, are not without divine assistance and call for the adherence of the faithful."

It is difficult to know what this means, for no examples are given. Perhaps we would have to conclude that the persecution of theologians such as Yves Congar and Henri de Lubac in the 1950s was "not without divine assistance." But if everything you do has this advance guarantee, the currency of divine assistance is devalued.

Another remarkable property of the magisterium is that it is not required to be convincing: "Magisterial teaching, by virtue of divine assistance, has a validity beyond its argumentation, which may at times derive from a particular theology."

Maybe you thought the magisterium was restricted to doctrinal or moral matters involving the essentials of faith? These are its main concern, certainly. But, says the document, it can also warn the faithful "of dangerous opinions that could lead to error."

So "the magisterium can intervene in questions under discussion which involve, in addition to solid principles, certain contingent and conjectural matters." I haven't the faintest idea what that means. It could make taboo, for example, discussing women's ordination. Nothing is excluded.

But is the instruction itself an instance of the exercise of the magisterium? Although it comes from the Congregation for the Doctrine of the Faith and is signed by its prefect, Cardinal Joseph Ratzinger, it is nevertheless stamped with papal approval: "The documents issued by this congregation expressly approved by the pope participate in the ordinary magisterium of the successor of Peter." This instruction was expressly approved by Pope John Paul II May 24, 1990, Feast of the Ascension.

Thus, the document strives to vindicate its authority. The process is somewhat circular. Even more remarkably, it declares the actions of the CDF that produced it to be eminently just.

Incriminated theologians such as Hans Küng or Charles Curran should know there is nothing personal in their condemnations. It is all happening on the level of "intellectual positions." They may lose their tenure, but that is a trifle here.

However, they should not worry, for "the judgment expressed by the magisterium in such circumstances is the result of a thorough investigation conducted according to established procedures which afford the interested party the opportunity to clear up possible misunderstandings of his thought."

To complain about the lack of human rights in the church, explains the instruction, "indicates a failure to recognize the proper hierarchy of these rights as well as the nature of the ecclesial community and her common good."

That means human rights do not apply in this case. It illustrates the instruction's method. It asserts rather than argues. Its statements always take the form of "heads I win, tails you lose."

The theologian should console himself with the thought that "the fact that these procedures can be improved does not mean that they are contrary to justice and right."

But is the CDF the best judge of the fairness of its own activities? In the name of the magisterium, the CDF acts as the judge, the jury, the witness and now the interpreter of such trials.

It is the CDF's opinion that the magisterium has never, ever been wrong. But there is a problem here, as the instruction gamely admits: "It could happen, in the prudential order, that some magisterial documents might not be free from all deficiencies."

It could happen. But has it happened? Well: "Bishops and their advisers have not always taken into immediate consideration every aspect or the entire complexity of a question." True: In the 19th century they denied religious freedom and said error has no rights.

Not that the instruction gives this or any other example. It is eager you should not get the wrong impression: "It would be contrary to the truth if, proceeding from some particular examples, one were to conclude that the church's magisterium were habitually mistaken in its prudential judgments, or that it does not enjoy divine assistance in the integral exercise of its mission."

Another feature of this treatment of the magisterium is worth remarking upon. Although pastors (that is, bishops) are mentioned from time to time, the instruction does not speak of the episcopal magisterium at all. Its exclusive concern is with the papal magisterium.

There is only one sentence on episcopal conferences: "The episcopal conferences for their part contribute to the concrete realization of the collegial spirit (*affectus*)." If the episcopal conferences have any teaching to do, the instruction does not indicate how they are to do it.

Thus, the ordinary way most theologians assist the magisterial process — by being consulted by their bishops — is eliminated. Only theologians chosen as consultors by the CDF have a chance to contribute anything.

A better title for the instruction would have been "On the Ecclesial Vocation of the Magisterium." For the magisterium fills the entire scene, occupying both background and foreground.

Theologians just squeeze their way in, but not in their own right, only as the object of magisterial concern. They are allowed to exist, but only in a subordinate role. Thus the natural dialectic or interplay between the magisterium and theologians cannot take place.

True, at one point it is briefly envisaged. The instruction concedes that "tensions" (Vaticanese for conflicts) may arise even in the best-ordered church. Then: "If tensions do not spring from hostile and contrary feelings, they can become a dynamic factor, a stimulus both to the magisterium and theologians to fulfill their respective roles while practicing dialogue."

But the dialogue does not happen. It never seems to occur to the instruction's authors that they are driven by "hostile and contrary feelings" and are therefore responsible for the breakdown of dialogue. It is a simple case of projection.

Take, for example, the notion of "parallel magisterium." This consists in setting up an alternative magisterium, allegedly competing with and ousting the sole "authentic" magisterium of the bishops.

The notion of a rival magisterium is a fantasy. The twofold magisterium — that of bishops and theologians — has been much discussed, but the question has always been about their responsible relationship, not about replacing one by the other.

The debate has been about their fruitful collaboration. The U.S. bishops' peace and economics pastorals were rightly seen as instances of such collaboration. No sane theologian seeks to displace or replace the bishops.

Evidently, and without naming it, the instruction seeks to reply to the Cologne Declaration of Jan. 6, 1989. "Great harm is done to the community of the church," it says, "by attitudes of general opposition to church teaching which even come to expression in organized groups."

"Even" here presupposes that the addressee shares the writer's view. These bounders have even got up petitions. What will they do next?

But the Cologne Declaration, and the subsequent statements backing it, were not instances of "general opposition to church teachings." The Cologne Declaration warned specifically about two points: growing centralization in episcopal and theological appointments against the concordat with West Germany, and the danger to the faithful of putting the teaching of *Humanae Vitae* on the same level as fundamental truths such as salvation in Christ Jesus.

That is not, by any stretch of the imagination, "general opposition to church teachings." On the contrary, the German-speaking theologians were precise in their complaints and deeply concerned about the good and effectiveness of the magisterium, vitiated, as they saw it, by the hierarchy's neglect of truths.

To point this out is a service to the magisterium, typical of the contribution theologians can make. Time and time again, the instruction goes over the top and caricatures its imagined opponents.

Thus, those who draw attention to the ultimate role of conscience in moral decisions are presented as crypto-Protestants favoring private judgment: "Setting up a supreme magisterium of conscience in opposition to the magisterium of the church means adopting a principle of free examination incompatible with revelation."

The shift from the moral to the dogmatic sphere is quite illegitimate and unjustified. But it is symptomatic of the tendency so to exalt the magisterium that any questions addressed to it, any doubts felt about its wisdom or even scruples about its operations are seen as a devastating threat to be crushed.

Theologians are constantly accused of importing political models into the life of the church: "Standards of conduct, appropriate to civil society or a democracy, cannot be purely and simply applied to the church."

Admire the subtlety here. Admittedly, such standards cannot be applied "purely and simply." The question is: Can they be applied at all?

The tragic irony is that the "world" and the much despised "mass media" will inevitably conclude that there is an unavowed political model at work in the instruction.

Unfortunately, it is the model of the totalitarian state that suppresses every kind of dissent and expects its grateful victims to kiss the rod that beats them.

Catholic theologians are deeply embarrassed by the instruction. They are saddened, too, not so much because it curtails their freedom as because it presents an image of the church as authoritarian and totalitarian.

Theologians are in the business of commending faith and showing its reasonableness. The Vatican instruction makes the task enormously more difficult in that it confirms the stereotype of a tyrannical church that is completely at odds with the community of faith, hope and charity the theologians wish to serve.

This year is the centenary of the death of Cardinal John Henry Newman. A papal letter praising him appeared the same week as the instruction.

In his *Apologia Pro Vita Sua*, Newman, an Anglican turned Catholic, says the theologian would not be free "if he knew that an authority, which was supreme and final, was watching every word he said, and made signs of dissent or assent to each sentence as he uttered it."

That is precisely what the instruction envisages. Theologians are intimidated, denunciators are encouraged and aided by the latest electronic devices. Big Brother is constantly watching.

In such a situation, says Newman, "the theologian would indeed be fighting, as the Persian soldiers, under the lash, and the freedom of his intellect might truly be said to be beaten out of him"

The likely outcome is that the instruction will act as a self-fulfilling prophecy, driving theologians into reluctant opposition. The only alternative appears to be cowed silence. It is a strange way to defend the faith. ❏

47

Karol Jeckyll and Hyde-Wojtyla debate capitalism

(May 10, 1991) Pope John Paul's latest encyclical, *Centesimus Annus,* has at least two authors. Call them Dr. Karol Jeckyll and Professor Hyde-Wojtyla. Jeckyll believes — no, knows — that the church is always right about everything. He starts from the confident statement that "from the Christian vision of the human person there necessarily follows a correct vision of society." Necessarily? Have Christians always lived up to their lofty vision of society?

Jeckyll draws the logical consequence: Those who do not share in the Christian vision cannot have "a correct vision of society." Bad luck on secular society: doomed to be wrong.

As if this were not enough, the church apparently takes all the initiatives in the social sphere, and nothing is granted to the "labor movement." Msgr. George Higgins, please note. Once this principle is established, the next step is to exaggerate the role of *Rerum Novarum*.

Leo XIII proved "surprisingly accurate" in foreseeing the collapse of communism in 1889-90. *Rerum Novarum* had "far-reaching influence," and "this influence is evident in the numerous reforms . . . in social security, pensions, health insurance and compensation in the case of accidents."

It would be very hard to prove the influence of *Rerum Novarum* on, say, the postwar Labor government in Britain or Scandinavian social legislation — the best in the world.

Dr. Karol Jeckyll reduces all forms of "socialism" to its Marxist and atheist version. The idea of a Christian socialism that owes as much to the gospels as to Marx is not part of his experience. Now, it might be said, none of this counts for much: In a social encyclical it is not the specific details that matter so much as the general thrust of its principles.

No doubt. Yet, much of the letter is made up of historical material, and history is specific or it is nothing. The author explains why he wrote the letter: "Pastoral solicitude prompts me to propose an analysis of events of recent history." But then he adds, truthfully, that "such an analysis is not meant to pass definitive judgments, since this does not fall per se within the magisterium's specific domain."

Analysis is not about principles; it is about events. One chapter is simply called: "The Year 1989." He is going to tell us, in other words, why communism collapsed.

So it seems best to treat *Centesimus Annus* as a long editorial written by the leading Central European intellectual (only Václav Havel comes anywhere near him). He has great experience of communism. We treasure his insights and admire his philosophical acumen. He appears to be saying that he does not possess any authority in contingent matters. Not per se. Not as such.

But appearances are deceptive. What he does not officially have, he might claim informally. That's the catch. For by placing itself in the tradition of Catholic social teaching, the new encyclical now enters what some call "the social magisterium."

By the next paragraph, we read that "millions of people" have been "spurred on by the social magisterium and have sought to make that teaching the inspiration for their involvement in the world." The word *magisterium*, a word that booms like a canon, has already acquired a capital letter in the turn of a page. However, the title of

Chapter 3, "The Year 1989," makes clear we are dealing not with principles, but with the interpretation of events.

But once again, the exact question is a surprise. Not: "What was God doing in 1989?" Rather: "Who was chiefly responsible for bringing about the events of 1989?"

Answer: "An important, even decisive, contribution was made by the church's commitment to defend and promote human rights." This refers to the fall of "dictatorial and oppressive regimes" throughout the world, and not just in Central Europe. Pride of place goes to Poland because Solidarity came first, was led by genuine workers, and put right the injustices of Yalta without bloodshed or violence.

More broadly, 1989 showed that God could not be eradicated from people's hearts. It was a victory for "the gospel spirit and the willingness to negotiate" over "an adversary determined not to be bound by moral principles." This is an ungracious description of the communists who, by the time they reached their various roundtables at least, were very models of moral uprightness and kept their word in exemplary fashion.

This mud-throwing does not contribute to continuing good relations with Mikhail Gorbachev and Boris Yeltsin who will read (or have read) *Centesimus Annus* to see whether there is any place for them in the new Europe.

Chapter 4 is a commentary on *Gaudium et Spes* 69 and 71. The right to private property is asserted, but only in the context of "the universal destination of all the world's goods." This reflects the Thomist teaching that I cannot gorge myself while my brothers and sisters are starving.

The most basic form of private property is land: On this patch, I will build my hut and grow my food. But John Paul adds an interesting nuance: There is now intellectual property — the possession of know-how and technology — that is equally intended "for the good of all."

The Third World has right of access to "intellectual property." This is one of the questions at issue in the general agreements on trade and tariffs negotiations. The same principle permits an attack to be mounted on "consumerism," the ravishing of the earth's nonrenewable resources and abortion. So ecology and antiabortion are neatly linked as pro-life causes.

After the savaging of "capitalism" — understood as unreconstructed Thatcherism — it is rather disappointing to find that "the church has no models to present." In the end it is up to lay Christians, taking their cue from the social doctrine of the church, to be creative and inventive in devising models that are ever more just, fraternal and democratic.

Centesimus Annus appeared, officially at least, May 1, feast of St. Joseph the Worker. It was actually unveiled May 2, eve of a great day in Polish history.

May 3, 1991, was the 200th anniversary of the Polish Constitution. It was only the second constitution in the world, and the first in Europe. Never implemented, it gave Poles something to be proud of throughout the 19th century when the country was wiped off the map.

With great self-discipline, our author does not mention this historic event. But he alludes to it. Leo XIII, he notes, talked about the separation of powers — executive, legislative and judicial — in a way that was novel for a pope.

The Polish May 3 constitution made the same distinction, which our author rightly sees as the basis for the rule of law. But this is where Professor Hyde-Wojtyla, the Kraków intellectual, emerges. He speaks as if he were taking part in a Smithsonian Institute seminar on "the future of democracy in Europe."

He is really addressing the "peoples in the process of reforming their system." He values democracy, but also warns that "a democracy without values easily turns into open or thinly disguised totalitarianism."

The old professor addresses the West, too. He points out that our criteria for making political judgments are inadequate. The desire to get elected is at odds with the highest moral principles. Where we go wrong is in neglecting the "common good."

The common good, he says, is not just the sum total of interests, for interests diverge and conflict. The "common good" is to be sought through "an assessment and integration of those interests on the basis of a balanced hierarchy of values."

He does not say so, but I presume he thinks that in a democracy this assessment goes on all the time through public debate and editorials in the newspapers. Memo to ask him next time we meet. The professor is well-informed on current debates in the West. Familiar with the critique of dependency culture created by welfare handouts, he challenges social security arrangements that cost the earth and are "dominated more by bureaucratic ways of thinking than by concern for serving their clients." He pleads the case for the "intermediate bodies," including voluntary ones, needed to create a human space between the state and wounded individuals.

But Professor Hyde-Wojtyla is not really a believer in Reaganomics or Thatcherite economics. He would prefer to reverse the lady's maxim and say individuals do not exist, only society exists. Human persons are social beings; that is the human condition here below and will be the joy of heaven. Rugged individualism, trying to stand on your own two feet, is fine provided it does not mean trampling on someone else. That brings us back to the common good.

The professor writes a whole chapter on "The State and Culture." He is not thinking of string quartets so much as the way, under communism, the state tried to maintain tight control over education and the mass media. "Culture" in the anthropological sense means the air we breathe, the assumptions about society we take for granted.

He thinks Christians should form a counterculture, but without rejecting their national culture completely. They could not do that and, anyway, they can only convert what they love. But they have to put a question mark against the consumerist expectations of society. This is a task they can share with Jews and Muslims, their fellow monotheists.

I do not see why "all men and women of goodwill" should not join in this questioning of our society's values, even though the professor does not mention them. They are not very likely suddenly to rush off and "hold all things in common" as he recommends. Not many Christians go that far, though we could all do with "revising our lifestyle," another of his exhortations.

The trickiest point concerns "pluralism." This involves Poland very directly. He will be going home for the fourth time as pope on June 1. What will he say about abortion? Should the current "communist" legislation be retained or repealed? One can see him preparing the ground for this debate.

Step 1 is to recognize — and reject — all fundamentalisms, whether scientific or religious, that "claim to impose on others their own concept of what is true and good." It is good to have that so limpidly stated.

Step 2 is more difficult. The Polish intellectual detects a tendency to say that "agnosticism and skeptical relativism" are the attitudes most conducive to democracy.

Those who are "convinced they know the truth and firmly adhere to it are considered, from a democratic point of view, unreliable." The author is referring to himself here, and he is distinguishing his position from the fundamentalism rejected above.

Step 3 is still more difficult. Following the collapse of communist totalitarianism and — he insists on adding, that of right-wing "national security state" regimes in Latin America that he also helped shift — the democratic ideal revives together with its concomitant, concern for human rights. He welcomes this wholeheartedly.

But human rights have to be solidly grounded and established in law. Among these rights is the right to life or "the right of the child to develop in its mother's womb from the first moment of conception."

Plus a whole rackful of rights. What about the rights of the pregnant woman? The prof does not discuss this question, leaving it no doubt to other willing hands to show that it is a category mistake.

Now all this, to say the least, makes for an interesting contribution to discussion about the future of a Europe that is no longer divided by the Iron Curtain. The Krakówian thinker raises many points worth taking up.

At the same time, when he speaks he is not just another slightly older version of Václav Havel. Popes are not supposed to be interesting. They think they are authoritative. The pope has the magisterium, the teaching authority of the church, on his side. Yet the magisterium may not help him as much as he thinks, and may get in the way.

If he says something relevant and helpful, then the world, Catholic or not, will listen. There is, at the moment, a moral vacuum in international politics. President George Bush talked, for a fleeting moment, of a new world order, but it died on his lips.

What is certain is that you cannot have an NWO without a new world ethic. Where is that to come from? Last month in his first interview since resigning as Soviet foreign minister, Edward Schevardnadze wondered why "we could not approach international problems more or less in the way that democratic systems resolve domestic issues."

Schevardnadze met Pope John Paul — Humpty-Dumpty is together again at last — in February. I do not know who inspired whom, but in his encyclical the pope seems to echo Schevardnadze: "Just as the time has come, finally, when a system of private vendettas and reprisals has given way to the rule of law, so, too, a similar step forward is needed in the international community."

John Paul could give us all a lead in this direction, if only he could give his more absolute claims a rest. The world is his oyster. It would be unfortunate if his epitaph were: He would not stoop, he failed to conquer. ❏

48

Thoughts on a Slav Pope who is more Polish than papal

(June 21, 1991) Warsaw, Poland — the general resemblance between the thinking of Gen. Charles de Gaulle, sometime president of France, and Pope John Paul II has often been remarked upon. During the Pope's June 1-9 visit to Poland the comparison was irresistible, and some new traits were added.

One was stylistic. De Gaulle always spoke of himself in the third person, as if "de Gaulle" was an institution apart from himself. "You wanted de Gaulle," he would say to the massed crowds, "*eh bien*, de Gaulle is here."

In his address to the diplomatic corps in Warsaw June 8, John Paul II adopted the same device. "The election of a Slav pope," he said, as if speaking as an objective historian, "resulted in greater solidarity and responsible support on the part of the Holy See for the churches and peoples of Central and Eastern Europe."

Of course, John Paul was not speaking as an objective historian at all. He was critiquing his predecessor, Pope Paul VI, whose *Ostpolitik* to his mind was feeble and fudging, making too many concessions to the communists. With the resignation on grounds of age of Cardinal Agostino Casaroli December 1990, the last effective member of Paul's team was removed, and with him the last restraint on John Paul.

From now on he will be pope in his own way, without having Casaroli pointing out that Paul VI would not have done that. The current cardinal secretary of state, Angelo Sodano, is a "yes man" who is light-years away from Casaroli's subtlety, power of analysis and knowledge of international affairs. The only political figure Sodano knows well is Gen. Augusto Pinochet, the disgraced former dictator of Chile.

John Paul resembles de Gaulle in another way: Both of them proved to be "saviors of the nation" insofar as they incarnated not only the "spirit of the nation" but its very legitimacy and, equally important for two such proud men, its honor.

In 1940 Marshal Philippe Pétain, a World War I hero, signed an armistice with Adolf Hitler in the same railway carriage in which the Germans had surrendered in 1918. For Hitler it was sweet revenge. From London, de Gaulle issued a proclamation denouncing the armistice as treachery and saying that "Free France," the real France, would fight on. And so it did, until eventual victory.

The parallel with John Paul is astonishing. From the moment he was elected pope Oct. 16, 1978, he put pressure on the Polish government. Not only did he become overnight "the world's most famous Pole," but he embodied a truth about Poland that no communist government could possibly compete with.

The fact that in this instance, unlike de Gaulle, the "savior of the nation" wore a white soutane rather than military uniform, only made things worse for the government. For while the Polish communists had all the physical power they needed to keep the pope out of Poland, they could do nothing against his "spiritual power," which tapped into sources in the Polish psyche unavailable to them.

An anecdote makes the point. Oct. 16 the Polish minister for religious affairs, one Kasamierz Kakol, was holding his traditional noon press conference. All eyes were on Rome. "What would happen if a Polish pope were elected?" asked a reporter who later admitted that he was thinking of Cardinal Stefan Wyszinski, the primate.

Merry laughter greeted the suggestion of a Polish pope. Feeling sure of himself, Kakol said: "If there is a Polish pope, which I don't expect, I'll buy you all champagne." Later that same day, Kakol loyally treated the press to the fizzy wine the Poles call *zampan*.

In the fall of 1981, John Paul published *Laborem Exercens*, the encyclical that defended Solidarity. There was much talk then of a Soviet military intervention in Poland. We now know that this threat was real, and that the imposition of martial law, Dec. 13, 1981, was decided upon by Gen. Wojciech Jaruzelski, then Poland's leader, as the only way to avert a Soviet invasion.

What really happened can now be revealed. Jaruzelski was summoned to the Soviet Embassy, in those days the real seat of power in Warsaw, driven to a Soviet airfield and given an airplane ride during which he could see the immense concentration of forces already gathered at the Soviet-Polish border.

He was then given an ultimatum: Either you destroy *Solidarnösc* or our troops will. That was in August 1981. It takes time to plan a military takeover. When it came, it was an effective and brilliantly conducted operation. Telephone lines were cut to prevent Solidarity leaders from plotting countermoves. The army took over all aspects of the civil administration.

The pope cares passionately about what transpires in his homeland. Of course he cares, ex officio as it were, about Latin America and Africa and Asia, but when behaving spontaneously, when he consults his heart, then he is 150 percent Polish.

John Paul was the "savior of the nation" in a much deeper sense than de Gaulle. President Lech Walesa greeted him at Koszalin on the Baltic coast earlier this month and said, "Without your work and your prayer to 'renew the face of this land,' there would have been no *Solidarnösc*, no Polish August and no victory for freedom." These were not empty compliments. The blunt Gdansk electrician was saying it as it is.

The first time John Paul went to Poland, in June 1989, a huge, towering cross was set up in Victory Square, Warsaw. This had never happened in communist Poland before; the cross was dismantled as soon as the Mass was over.

John Paul quoted 16th-century Jesuit Piotr Skarga, who said the tree of faith was so firmly rooted in Polish soil that nothing could shift it. Neither the Russian czars nor the Nazis nor . . . anyone.

He did not say that he regarded the communist rulers of the time as usurpers. He did not need to say it. Our Lady was Queen of Poland, and this was a political comment. It delegitimated the communist rulers. They could deal with dissidents, up to a point, but not with this violent castration.

Why had Providence chosen a Slav pope? he asked. The answer was not altogether clear, for it was couched in a series of rhetorical questions. What emerged was that providence wished to put the Slavs on the map and to get their contribution to European history more widely recognized.

What in 1979 was only hinted at was confirmed beyond any possible doubt in 1991. Providence had chosen a "Slav pope" (he never says "Polish") to change the world.

In 1979 he ended his Victory Square homily with an invocation to the Holy Spirit: "Come down, O Holy Spirit, and renew the face of the earth!" In Polish the word for "earth" (*ziemi*) also means "land." To bring this out he cried, with an expansive gesture, "Of *this* land." It was a truly charismatic moment.

This was then used as a prayer in Polish churches. The pope is convinced that his prayer was answered: The disintegration of communism in Central and Eastern Europe began here. The new element in 1991 was that, having liberated Central and Eastern Europe, the pope was now setting his eyes on the East.

Getting as close as he could to the Soviet border in Przemyl, he prayed to the patron saints of Poland, Lithuania and the historical land of 'Rus, and then to the "Lord of History," that this miracle — concretely the collapse of the Soviet empire — might be achieved without spilling blood.

The mind boggles at the sheer audacity of this scheme. But if the Holy Spirit heard his first prayer, why should he/she not harken to this second one? When the pope prays, nations tremble. Again like de Gaulle, John Paul is a European who believes that Europe stretches "from the Atlantic to the Urals." The pope borrowed this expression from de Gaulle.

But he will not be limited by this expression. The prison camps of Siberia are beyond the Urals. When Lithuanian Jesuits (no one knew they were Jesuits) were released from labor camps, they stayed on in Siberia to work among the residents.

Some of them worked in Novasibirsk, the major Soviet university city and center of its space program. Andrei Sakharov worked there. In 1983, two years before Mikhail Gorbachev came to power, Novasibirsk academicians wrote learned papers showing the disastrous effects of trying to run a centralized economy. *Glasnost* and *perestroika* were first imagined here.

Novasibirsk University has now asked the Jesuit general, Fr. Peter-Hans Kolvenbach, for scientists to teach in the university. The Jesuits are investigating the situation, and will try to give a positive reply. The pope has already made Jesuit Fr. Joseph Werth apostolic administrator of Novasibirsk, in effect its first bishop. This ought not to upset the Russian Orthodox church for in these vast regions, it virtually does not exist.

So the pope is certainly thinking big. Perhaps he will one day realize that the Jesuits and other religious are of more use to the church in these regions than the "new movements," like Opus Dei and Communion and Liberation, in whom he puts so much trust.

The conversion of Russia demands a combination of deep spirituality and deep scholarship, which the religious can supply. So far, the "new movements" have produced no one of comparable ability.

Unfortunately, the pope thinks he has found a philosophical genius in Rocco Buttiglione, a member of Communion and Liberation and professor of political philosophy at Pescara. He flatters John Paul by saying that the churches of Western Europe and the United States have everything to learn from the suffering churches of the East and nothing to teach them.

Buttiglione confirms the pope's anti-European and anti-American prejudices.

The magazine *30 Days* is published by Communion and Liberation. In France, Cardinal Jean-Marie Lustiger abolished it after scurrilous, libelous attacks on Polish Catholic intellectuals, especially Tadeusz Mazowiecki, the first noncommunist prime minister in Poland, now out of favor with the pope.

Californian Jesuit Fr. Joseph V. Fessio, editor of the English-language version, woke up to the truth about *30 Days* when its March 1991 number was so anti-American (apropos the Gulf War) that he severed all links with the movement.

The pope has not yet discovered the limitations of Communion and Liberation. Buttiglione was the only contemporary "thinker" cited during the Polish trip. He has already written the "conclusions" to the Synod of European Bishops scheduled for Nov. 28 through Dec. 14 this year. John Paul announced in Warsaw it would take place not, as expected, in Rome, but in Velherad, Moravia.

Symbolically, this is a brilliant move. Cyril and Methodius were two brothers (*in carne*) from Thessalonika, Greece, who in the ninth century evangelized the Balkans and the fringes of the Slav world. John Paul made them coequal patrons of Europe alongside St. Benedict, who he presumably thought was dozing on the job. Cyril, after whom the Cyrillic alphabet is named, is buried in the church of San Clemente, Rome, now in charge of the Irish Dominicans. Methodius' tomb is at Velherad.

But there is not much else there, and once 200 bishops and their staff have been accommodated, there will be no room for reporters. They will have to be bused in day by day. They won't know a thing. Buttiglione's "conclusions" will be recommended by the pope on grounds of "loyalty."

Already, a reaction is setting in. Certain bishops are taking steps to ensure that the world knows what happens at Velherad. With modern electronic communications available, the pope will not be able to realize his plan of "discussing family matters in private."

One last comparison with de Gaulle. De Gaulle wanted to build a united Europe, provided it was under French leadership. He would have no truck with those who wanted a federal Europe or a United States of Europe.

John Paul wants a Europe of the nations that recognizes Poland's leading role. In an astonishing outburst on Wroclawek, Friday, June 7, the pope threw away his prepared text and told his compatriots they should thank God for making them Polish.

His face red with indignant anger, gesticulating wildly, shouting at the top of his voice, he protested at the way the European Community had taken over the term *European* as if it owned it. "The identification of Europe with Western Europe was," he declared, "an insult to Poland."

"We do not have to 'join' Europe," he raged, "because we are already there, and we created Europe. We created it incurring greater hardships than those who are credited with, or credit themselves with, being the keepers of the European spirit. What should this criterion be? Freedom? What freedom? The freedom of taking the lives of unborn children, for example?"

This played well in Wroclawek, and spontaneous applause rippled through the crowd. They were unlikely to ask themselves whether abortion was the *only* contribution Western Europe brought to Poland.

The pope half-apologized for what he called his "fiery words" by saying it was a cold day (which wasn't true). Then he said we should attribute his fierceness to the *genius loci*, the spirit of the place.

This land was drenched in so much blood. He did not say this, but already by October 1939, 40 out of the 42 priests in prewar Wroclawek were either shot or in concentration camps. It was the land of extermination camps. Fr. Jerzy Popieluszko's corpse was dumped in a lake not far away.

So don't come here, he was in effect saying, and lecture us on European civilization. How dare you say we have to "catch up" on Europe? How dare you impose on us standards of democracy and economic arrangements before allowing us into your Euro-club of the rich?

It reminded one of the saying: "He is very balanced — he has a chip on both shoulders." But it was very alarming and worrying. Said a Polish friend, "The pope is more Polish than he is papal."

But when I put this more technically and said, "He is more Polish than primatial, for Peter has the charge of the universal church," I was practically thrown out of the house. Poles may criticize him; others may not.

John Paul has forgotten what he knew when he was elected. Two days after his election he said, "The particular nature of our country of origin is from now on of little importance. As a Christian, and still more, as pope, we are and will be witnesses of a universal love."

Once he knew the theory of the Petrine office; now he has cast it to the winds. ❏

49

Europe Synod bishops pronounce on almost everything

(December 13, 1991) Rome — Rather than try to pour a quart into a pint pot, let me rather give the flavor of the Nov. 28 to Dec. 14 Synod of Bishops for Europe here by selecting a few "sayings." Do not expect dazzling wit; they have all gone through the mangle of inadequate translation, several times.

Jews, for example, are regularly referred to as our "big brothers," which was not quite what George Orwell had in mind in *1984*.

Archbishop John J. Foley, president of the Pontifical Council for the Means of Social Communications: "My four grandparents were German, English, Welsh and Irish-American."

Passionist Bishop William Kenney, auxiliary, Stockholm, Sweden: "In many part of Europe, the Good News of the gospel is no longer new and no longer news: That is why we need new ways of presenting it."

Augustinian of the Assumption Antonios Varthalitis, archbishop of Corfu and other Greek islands: "From the East we have to learn about collegial and synodal government to replace the monarchical system we have invented in the West."

Cardinal Pio Laghi, prefect of the Congregation for Catholic Education: "Europe needs many saints and priests."

Archbishop Miroslav Vlk (his name means "wolf"), Prague: "There is no exchange of gifts without the emptying out of self. This is the message of the Trinity, the fulcrum of the gospels, the norm for Europe."

Gyorgy Takubiny, auxiliary of Alba Julia, Romania, an ethnic Hungarian, warns against "linguistic imperialism" (does he mean English or German?) and concludes: "We need a language that does not have a country behind it; a practical solution would be Esperanto."

Clemente Riva, Rome auxiliary to John Paul II: "We need a choral and symphonic evangelization, not solo performances." (Is he thinking of his bishops?)

Tadeusz Kondrusiewicz, the archbishop from, but not of, Moscow: "I have no house and have to stay with friends." Does he want a palace?

Cardinal Paul Poupard, president of the Pontifical Council for Culture: "The future of Europe depends on the complete reintegration of Russia within the cultural ambit of Europe."

Ricco Buttilglione, professor of philosophy in the Principality of Lichtenstein, population, 27,000; registered companies, 83,000: "Europe can choose between nihilism and the rediscovery of Christian faith."

Irena Iluvajskaia Alberti, editor of *La Pensé russe* in Paris, runs agony column for Radio Blagovest, a Vatican station at work in Moscow for three years: "The East offers a terrible lesson in what can happen to humanity when one proclaims the death of God, but the West doesn't seem keen to take it into consideration."

Joef Zycinnski, bishop of Tarnow, Poland: "The West is given over to excessive rationality. In the East, the old babushkas saw through Marxism sooner than Western intellectuals." Spoils his effect by citing French philosopher Jean-Paul Sartre as only instance.

Josef Michalek, bishop of Gorznow, Poland: "We live in a time of truth and confrontation." Translate: Sock it to the Orthodox.

Salesian Gerardus ter Schure, bishop of Den Bosch, Netherlands: "Young people need a heart that welcomes, a face that smiles, a hand that helps." Physician, heal thyself.

Keith O'Brien, archbishop of St. Andrews and Edinburgh, Scotland: "The church must speak through the authentic teachers of the faith, the bishops, but also through articulate and dedicated laymen and laywomen, and our sincere and committed young people. . . ."

Stanislas Wielgus, rector of KUL, the Catholic University of Lublin, Poland,: "We were the only university between the Elbe and the Pacific where free politicians could think for themselves, where Ukrainian Catholics could study theology and where Jews ousted from the state universities in 1968 were made welcome."

Bishop Ivan Martyinak, Ukrainian bishop of Przemsyl in eastern Poland: "We need a separate episcopal conference for the Oriental bishops of Europe and a Catholic university other than Lublin."

Cardinal Achille Silvestrini, prefect of the Congregation for the Oriental Churches in communion with Rome and therefore a key player: "We must value the theology, spirituality and culture of the Orthodox churches while remembering that this precious patrimony is shared by the Oriental churches that still live in full communion with Peter's successor." Perhaps the most important statement of the synod so far.

Jan Hirka, Ruthenian (or Greek) bishop of Presov, Slovakia: "In our country, love not only lost its face, it lost even its name."

Metropolitan Spyridon Papagheorghiu, representing the ecumenical patriarch, Bartholemew II: "We have the impression that you have retreated from Vatican II, that you do not treat us as a sister church and that the ecumenical progress of the last decades has been gravely compromised."

Jean-Eugene Fischer, general secretary of the European Council of Churches (linking 120 churches): "We don't want a mad rush to the East, as though the church didn't already exist there. Missionaries who pay no heed to the local churches are a menace."

Bishop Mesron Krikorian, Armenian, pointed out that his church was "baptized" between 301 and 314 (sic). He quoted an early letter to Persian King Yazdagert III: "From our Christian faith, nobody can separate us. . . . Our faith is as color is to the skin: They cannot be separated from each other." ❏

50

From JPII superstar to a super surprise

(September 11, 1992) Erfurt, Germany — It would be premature to write the obituary of Pope John Paul II. Yet the operation to remove a tumor "about the size of an orange" July 15 was a reminder of mortality. A scenario of resignation has been prepared "just in case."

It envisages a John Paul II unable to carry out his duties and therefore resigning. But he could also resign in the unlikely event that he felt he had enough.

1995 would be the appropriate year. For then the bishop of Rome — the pope's fundamental title — will reach 75, the age at which all other bishops have to tender their resignations. Why should the bishop of Rome be different? Because, said Pope Paul VI, who considered resignation at 75, "One does not resign from universal paternity." Paul would have joined the Benedictines at Monte Cassino.

John Paul II would join the Carmelites in his native town of Wadowize. They turned him down in 1939 on the unspiritual grounds that he was "born for greater things."

But before withdrawing from the world and choosing the nada of St. John of the Cross (on whom he wrote his first thesis), John Paul would spend a year traveling the world to contemplate the mountains he has not yet seen. They might include Kilimanjaro and — who knows? — Mt. Rainier.

But whether he resigns or not, he has already left his stamp on the church. He does not like to be called "the first Polish pope" and much prefers "the first Slav pope." He had to correct Mikhail Gorbachev on that point.

I can now reveal that on his election Oct. 16, 1978, his first thought was to take the name of Stanislaus, after the Polish equivalent of Thomas Becket, murdered by King Bodeslaus II in 1078. Stanislaus is for him the patron of church-state relations.

Dissuaded by his electors, he took the double-barreled name of John Paul as less nationalistic and to make the point that he would continue the work of his predecessors. Yet, he does not have a high regard for either of the two popes whose name he bears, thinking them dangerously "liberal" and, in the case of Paul, feeble and compromising.

On ecumenism, the possible ordination of married men and the relationship of theologians to his magisterium, John Paul has been peremptory and negative where his predecessor was subtle, discriminating and left openings for the future. For the Brescian rapier he has substituted the Krakovian blunderbuss.

John Paul was chosen to meet what his electors saw as a crisis in the post-conciliar church. Essentially, it was a crisis of identity of the church itself. Ecumenism, it was alleged, had blurred the sharp definitions that once prevailed.

Priests and nuns no longer knew what they were about, often abandoning their common sense along with their habits. A spirituality of risk led some like Irish Bishop Eamonn Casey to the brink of disaster and over the edge.

The social and political commitment discovered in Latin America seemed to Pope John Paul a wrong track. He much prefers the boring safety of Opus Dei to the adventurous spirit of the Jesuits. Not since Pius X have we had such a personal papacy — in the sense that the pope allows his own opinions to determine what is presented as the "official line." It cannot be called church "doctrine."

Opposition to contraceptives, to the ordination of married men and even the discussion of the ordination of women has been made the criterion for becoming a bishop. No one who so much as finesses on such questions has the slightest chance of being chosen.

The result is that John Paul has created an intellectual desert and called it peace. Bishops and theologians have been cowed into silence. Synods have been reduced to papal rallies. Heads that pop up above the parapet are lopped off.

Laypeople have greater freedom than clergy, which is partly why Brazilian Fr. Leonardo Boff left the Franciscans earlier this year. St. Francis had not wanted to be a priest, he pointed out. He can be a better Franciscan as a layman. Will he run for the Brazilian presidency?

Yet, if one looks at Pope John Paul through Polish eyes, the picture is totally different. The Polish bishops think he has gone native in Rome. They cite the way he asserts a great role for the laity in the church, and especially in his encouragement of women to participate in the apostolate in all ways short of priestly ministry.

He is also the first pope to have spoken frankly and nobly about human sexuality, and surely the first to have pronounced the words "female orgasm" at a Wednesday audience. This, while puzzling the Japanese tourists with their Leicas, has not won him many friends among the married, for they can still ask: Does he know what he is talking about?

"Experience cannot contradict experience," he announced in 1980, when he recycled his 1960 Lublin lectures on sexuality. "He means experience in the phenomenological sense," explained Jerzy Turowicz, editor since 1946 of the Krakow paper *Tydognik Powszechny* and a close friend.

Whatever it means, it is not what is meant by experience in everyday language. John Paul by profession is a philosopher rather than a theologian. He sees the "essence" of the priesthood and religious life, not their historical development.

I really began to understand his Polishness in June 1987 when he stood in front of what was the people's Palace of Culture, the ludicrous "gift" from Joseph Stalin that dominates the Warsaw skyline.

He was looking eastward over the heads of the massed ranks of 7,000 crucifix-toting nuns, as many priests and a crowd of a million and a half.

With a sweeping gesture, he addressed the Slav peoples to the east and the south, the Belorussians and the Russians, the Slovaks and Czechs and Slovenians and Croatians. He beseeched the Holy Spirit to liberate them.

His vision then soared to the islands and archipelagos of the Pacific, and beyond them to the Americas, North and South. "And the rest of Europe," he added finally.

Now we West Europeans are not used to being relegated to "the rest of Europe," as though we were a mere afterthought to some grandiose Slav dream. Yet, that is the mental map the pope superimposes on the world.

When he looks at Western Europe and its cousins across the Atlantic, he sees secularization, lapsing, loss of nerve and moral fiber. Last year in Poland, he was scathing about the phrase, much used at the time, on the need to "catch up" with Europe. Catch up with Europe, he cried, his voice rising to a crescendo of passion, "We created Europe."

"What are these so-called European freedoms," he demanded, "the freedom to abort children?" Speaking close to the site of extermination camps, he was unwilling to be given lessons in "European values" from the sons of those who ran them.

Poland saved Europe three times: at the battle of Grunewald (or Tannenberg) in 1410; in 1681, when a European army led by the Polish King Jan Sobieski flung the Turks back from Vienna; and in 1920, when the Red Army was repulsed from Warsaw. This is history, not myth. Poles think the world does not appreciate them.

And now there is a fourth victory to celebrate: the collapse of communism. It was always an alien system in Poland, imposed by terror and geography rather than conviction and, therefore, ultimately doomed.

The pope's first visit home in 1979 started the rot. It gave Poles the self-confidence they needed to found Solidarity and eventually defeat the regime by peaceful means. History will judge this to have been John Paul's greatest achievement. But to bring it about, he had to have the rest of his troops behind him disciplined and in good order. No dissent is allowed up on the barricades. It proves too costly.

Yet, having unexpectedly achieved this great aim, and having outlasted the greatest persecution (his own words) since the Roman emperor Diocletian, he is unsure what to do next. Despite his stirring words about democratic values in *Centesimus Annus* last year, he strangely did not quote them when he went back home.

Perhaps he was leaving room for President Lech Walesa to install an authoritarian regime, "for the common good," of course. He is not happy with pluralism.

There is a good deal of anxiety about John Paul. John Fullenbach, a Divine Word father teaching at the Gregorian University, recounts how he concelebrated with the pope in St. Peter's last May.

The pope knelt in the sacristy afterward for 20 minutes, making his thanksgiving with great sighs and groanings. Everyone else had to kneel along with him. Someone remarked, "Either he's a saint or he's mad."

There was, as we now know, a third possibility: He was suffering intensely from the untreated tumor, trying to tough it out with that Polish virtue you call obstinacy if you do not like it, heroism if you do. The word *impossible* is not Polish. But the thoughts of the Roman curia were already turning to the succession.

Nobody knows who will be the next pope, because nobody knows when the next conclave will be. But if we assume that it will come in the next three years, whether through resignation or death, it is possible to speculate.

One sure bet is that there will not be another Polish pope. A Roman joke reveals the third secret of Fatima: "Unless you pray and do penance, you will get another Polish pope."

Another near certainty is that the next pope will come from the current College of Cardinals. Any of the 120 cardinals — the maximum complement — under 80 is eligible. So the U.S. cardinals each have a 1/120 chance. Theoretically.

For if all the cardinals are equal, some are more equal than others. I will offer a short list of three, the classic *terna* that is provided by the nuncio for episcopal appointments. The two conclaves of 1978 offer some lessons that will hold next time as well.

The easiest way to go wrong is to let one's heart rule one's head and to plump for the candidate one would like to see as pope. Ever since Carlo Maria Martini was appointed archbishop of Milan in 1980, Italian Vatican watchers have been saying he was the man most likely to become pope.

They mean that he is the best-equipped intellectually, spiritually and pastorally to succeed — which does not mean he will. Against him is the fact that he is a Jesuit — and not only has there never been a Jesuit pope, there has never been a Jesuit cardinal who was a serious candidate for the post.

In making Martini archbishop of Milan, John Paul broke with precedent. Not since St. Robert Bellarmine in the 17th century had a Jesuit been bishop of an Italian diocese, and then it was only of the minor see of Capua. It is against the rules of the Society of Jesus to accept preferment. It can only be done "by order of holy obedience."

John Paul invoked it when he named Martini to Milan, the richest and most prestigious see of Italy, the see of St. Ambrose and St. Charles Borromeo. Two popes in this century, Pius XI and Paul VI, have already come from Milan. *Jamais deux sans trois*, as the French say.

Cynics said John Paul sent Martini to Milan to make sure he could not be elected general of the Jesuits in succession to the much-loved Don Pedro Arrupe. It was better to have him kept busy in Milan rather than posing an intellectual threat as the "Black Pope" (as the Jesuit general is nicknamed).

Whatever the motive, Martini has been an outstanding archbishop of Milan. By profession an expert in the textual criticism of the Bible, he is no dusty scholar and has shown himself to be a genuine communicator.

Last Advent, he wrote three pastoral letters on "how to watch TV," one to young men, another to young women and another to their parents. He had noted how television had wrecked parish visiting.

An excellent linguist, Martini has been active on the international scene. He succeeded Cardinal Basil Hume of Westminster as president of the European bishops' conference. This spans the whole of Europe, East and West, so he cannot fairly be accused of European Community narrowness.

His deeply biblical approach makes him a natural partner in ecumenical discussions. Although relations with the Russian Orthodox church have sunk to an all-time low in the past year, because of alleged Catholic proselytism in the decomposing ex-Soviet empire, he has stayed on friendly terms with the Russian Orthodox Patriarch Alexsei. At 65, he is just the right age — now.

Last December he gave a number of curious interviews to the press. He said he wished to end his days in Jerusalem studying the Bible, his first love. This was taken to mean that he was rejecting a move to the Roman curia.

He had been tipped to succeed Cardinal Joseph Ratzinger, who had completed the two five-year terms he is allowed as prefect of the Congregation for the Doctrine of the Faith. Martini did not fancy being the inquisitor of his fellow theologians. He cooked his goose by declaring that the questions posed by the suspended German theologian Eugene Drewermann were real questions that would not go away.

Martini, as a good Jesuit, has always been loyal to the pope but without sycophancy. He has fought the good fight against Communion and Liberation, the right-wing movement that, he argues, cuts people off from their parishes and exhibits sectlike tendencies. The fact that along with Opus Dei it is Pope John Paul's favorite movement does not daunt him.

This, while it would gain Martini some votes in a conclave, might lose him as many. He is not loved by the careerists in the College of Cardinals. They have already thought about their candidate. He is your own, your very own Cardinal Pio Laghi, now prefect of the Congregation for Catholic Education.

Laghi, 70, can smile. He was nuncio in Argentina, where he played tennis with the colonels — arguably part of his diplomatic mission — and refused to condemn their crimes, which was not. He moved to Washington just in time for the election of Ronald Reagan as president.

He did much to align Vatican policies in Central America with those of the U.S. administration. He supported the contras against the Sandinistas in Nicaragua. He was rewarded by seeing his office transformed from that of a mere apostolic delegate into pro-nuncio.

His main function in the United States was to undo the good work of his predecessor, Belgian Jean Jadot, who had appointed or caused to be appointed enlightened bishops like Joseph Bernardin and Rembert Weakland.

Laghi's mission in the United States was to find conservative bishops to restore order, threatened, as Pope John Paul saw it, by dissident religious, haywire priests, uppity laity and aggressive feminists.

Typical appointments were Cardinals Bernard Law to Boston and John J. O'Connor to New York. The American cardinals, except for Bernardin, will vote for him as the man they know. It is the only way they can influence the conclave.

The curia probably thinks it has the election sewn up already. But this is a great mistake. He who enters a conclave papabile, says a Roman saw, emerges a cardinal. The very fact that Laghi is known to be running will set up a movement against him.

His critics will have plenty of material. They will recall the incident when he dismissed from the altar five women religious who were expecting to serve as eucharistic ministers on the grounds that sufficient priests were available.

They will note that he opposed the award of an honorary degree to Archbishop Rembert Weakland by the Swiss Catholic University of Fribourg. Weakland's offense? He had "listened" to the women of his diocese on the topic of abortion.

The vast majority of pastoral cardinals — those with dioceses to run — have a conscience. They will bear in mind the needs of the church as the 20th turns into the 21st century. In 1978 they elected a "strong pope" because they thought there was a need for clarity in post-conciliar fuzziness. In John Paul II, they got more than they bargained for, and some I know have regretted their choice.

But if the conservative option seemed reasonable then, in the next conclave they may well feel that it has been tried and has not delivered.

They will not need to criticize John Paul to choose someone completely different. They are more likely to argue that he was such a remarkable man, with such a bundle of talents, linguist, mountaineer, poet, philosopher, actor, that we cannot expect to see his like again. He is an impossible act to follow.

Rome needs a bishop whose first task will be to look after the Diocese of Rome. Far from being a model for the church, the city has become a microcosm of all the ills of 20th-century urban life in the developed world, from drugs to homelessness, from refugees to violence and political corruption.

The pope does not have to be a globetrotting superstar, reducing local bishops to branch managers in a multinational corporation. Yet, the papal office remains the symbol, though not the cause, of Catholic unity.

This might best be expressed by the imaginative choice of a non-European. The Latin American candidates are either burned out, like Evaristo Arns of Sao Paolo, Brazil, or insufferable, like the ambitious Alfonso Lopez Trujillo, now prefect of the Council for the Family (and we know what that means).

A sleaze factor may work against Lopez Trujillo: He was formerly bishop of Medellín, Colombia, and has never quite cleared up his relations with the drug cartel. Anyway, at age 56, he is dangerously young.

The outsider is Cardinal Francis Arinze, president of the Council for Inter-religious Dialogue. He has gathered the most competent team in the curia, listens to advice, has not been overly Romanized and has great experience of Christian-Muslim dialogue in his native Nigeria. And he is black.

He has been at the Vatican since 1984, joined the College of Cardinals a year later. Born in 1932, he was the youngest metropolitan in the world when installed as archbishop of Onitsha at age 34. So he has been on something of an ecclesial fast track.

His election would capture the world's imagination. If the future of the church depends on Africa and Latin America, Arinze, who might well revive the name Benedict, could speak to that constituency.

If the future of the world depends on cooperation between the world's largest religious groups, Christians and Muslims, then Arinze would be the man for the post-communist world just as John Paul was the right man to bring the communist world down.

It is the law of all institutions that they must adapt to survive. The Vatican is particularly good at that. To believe in the church is to believe that the Holy Spirit is still at work in it despite the vagaries of its human agencies. I only hope that by naming Arinze I have not killed his chances. ❏

51

Vatican reporting fraught with risk

(November 6, 1992) "You can tell whether you are any good as an investigative reporter," said John Pilger, an Australian exponent of the genre, "by the number of enemies you make."

This holds for writing about the Vatican, too. It means taking aboard accusations of disloyalty and ascriptions of motive. For a quiet life, the only safe course is early retirement and silence.

The reason is simple. So many hopes and so much emotion are invested in the Petrine office that judgments that would be trite or obvious in the secular sphere are here regarded as offensive or insulting. To say the pope is "Polish," banal though it is, can be a hanging matter if you mean it limits him.

Two principles offer a guide through this jungle. The first comes from Beaumarchais in "The Marriage of Figaro" (the play, not the opera): "Without the freedom to criticize, no praise has any value."

The other comes from Melchior Cano, the great Dominican theologian at the Council of Trent: "Peter has no need of our lies or flattery. Those who blindly and indiscriminately defend every decision of the supreme pontiff are the very ones who do most to undermine the authority of the Holy See — they destroy instead of strengthening its foundations."

Fine principles, but they don't work very well in practice. The first problem is that any praise of popes from the recent past is immediately taken to be critical of the reigning pope. Thus, Belgian Jesuit Marcel Chappin took me to task in *Gregorianum* for allegedly "absolutizing" Pope John in my 1984 *John XXIII: Shepherd of the Modern World*.

It was a theological error to make his opening speech to the council the yardstick of its success. "The papal magisterium is confided only to one person at a time," he shrewdly notes, "and although we may hope that any one of Pope John's successors may be inspired by his example and spirituality, the value of John's magisterial (and other) acts is to be judged by that successor, not that successor by those acts." Quite.

But when Chappin goes on to say that my praise for John XXIII "reminds him of those who invoke the authority of Pius V to refuse the liturgy introduced by Paul VI," I protest at this implied comparison with the late and excommunicated Archbishop Marcel Lefebvre.

The logical conclusion to Chappin's argument is that you can only safely praise a reigning pope. That makes history impossible. Cardinal Agostino Casaroli, secretary of state until December 1990, had the misfortune to praise Paul VI when unveiling Lello Scorzello's statue of him in Brescia Cathedral.

Casaroli presented Paul as above all a man of dialogue: "The person who does not converse with his fellows, who is shut off from reality, who neither listens nor responds, withers like a plant in dry soil."

Innocent enough? Yet the whole of the Italian press was persuaded that Casaroli was implicitly criticizing Pope John Paul II and saying that he "neither listened nor responded." All one can say is that if the cap fits, put it on.

There is a further problem in talking of the pope. The witnesses closest to him, or who see him from time to time, tell us very little we want to know about him. The casual references do not leave one much the wiser.

Heinz Schurmann, the biblical scholar from Erfurt in former East Germany, pointed out to John Paul that in the entire history of the church there had been no case of an infallible definition in moral questions. To which John Paul replied, "There's always a first time."

Was this some kind of joke? Did John Paul have a twinkle in his eye? Or should it be regarded as a threat? There is no means of knowing.

Another problem is that church officials are reluctant to speak the truth even when they know it. So Cardinal Paolo Evaristo Arns, as reported by Chicago University chaplain Willard Jabusch, "made a sharp distinction between the pope, whom he admires and respects, and the curia officials in Rome."

"Blame the curia" is a tactic that goes back to the council, when there was a good deal of truth in it under Paul VI as much as under John XXIII.

But when someone has been pope for nearly 14 years, he has had time to mold the curia in his own image. John Paul appointed these people to do whatever it is they are doing. If they are frustrating his purposes, he should sack them.

The "blame the curia" approach, designed to save the pope's reputation, in fact does the opposite. It suggests a weak, incompetent pope conducting a lame-duck papacy and incapable of imposing himself.

Another problem is that the "insiders," who ought to be able to speak with authority, invariably downplay any conflict, making history unintelligible.

John Magee served as English-language secretary to both Paul VI and John Paul II before becoming bishop of Cloyne in southern Ireland. From this privileged vantage point he says: "There are those who try to indicate that the present Holy Father is trying to rectify what may have happened because of the inactivity of Paul VI. But I think that is totally false."

Note that Magee is refuting an ultraconservative position. It holds that compared with the determined John Paul II, Paul VI was weak, vacillating and indecisive. Magee firmly rejects this view: "Having lived with John Paul II and having listened to him publicly and privately, I must say that you could never get two popes who were as close in their thinking as Paul VI and John Paul II."

This is edifying, no doubt. But if true, it totally fails to explain why John Paul has systematically undone Paul's work in ecumenism, collegiality and theological research, to take three examples.

If Magee has not noted this change, then he is remarkably imperceptive. If he has noticed it but is suppressing it for reasons of edification, he ruins himself as a witness.

The "Paul vs. John Paul" joust came to a head recently at a conference of the Paul VI Institute in Brescia. Its theme was "Paul VI and collegiality." Cardinal Carlo Maria Martini, as the local metropolitan, presided. He used the occasion to attack Cardinal Joseph Ratzinger's draft paper on episcopal conferences, sent back for further revision at the end of 1988. Martini is a member of the board of the CDF, and therefore should know where the draft is at.

"Besides being of great practical use," said Martini, firing off a salvo, "episcopal conferences are a more adequate ecclesiological expression of collegiality of great theological value."

Martini is also president of CCEE — the European equivalent of CELAM. "Our European episcopal conferences," he explained, "have purely and simply tried to let communion grow, express itself and be translated into practice among us, that communion which the Holy Spirit creates in the 'one, holy, Catholic church' in Europe and throughout the world."

So while Martini was clearly "criticizing" Ratzinger, must we say he was criticizing John Paul, who appointed him and has kept him on beyond his second five-year term of duty?

This case is slightly different, however, because this is an open question, because Martini is the intellectual equal of Ratzinger and does not need to defer to him, and because in CCEE he has a fairly solid bloc of bishops — though one cannot guarantee the Poles — on his side. Martini, in short, is not just seeking to win the argument but to change the situation.

One thing Martini was not doing was offering himself as a candidate in the next conclave. But anyone he backed would stand a good chance. Martini criticizes me, too: for being too kind to him. ❏

52

A few 'thou shalt' and 'shalt nots' for our day

(December 4, 1992) Cardinal Joseph Ratzinger, head of the Congregation for the Doctrine of the Faith, was taking no chances with his *Catechism for the Catholic Church* issued last week. Two months before the translations were due, he issued an information pack explaining how it came about and what it is for.

Although the catechism makes claims to universality, the word universal does not appear in its official title. Ratzinger describes it as "an instrument for the transmission of the essential and fundamental contents of the Catholic faith and morals in a complete and systematic manner."

You use an "instrument" if it helps toward the aim, which is the in-depth evangelization of Catholics. While remaining "a point of reference for national and diocesan catechisms," it still needs adaptation to local cultures. Ratzinger insists on the need for this "mediation" by local bishops. It seeks to assist, not replace, the work of catechists on the ground.

At the same time it is an authoritative work and a "magisterial" text, in the sense that "it was suggested by a world synod of bishops, desired by the Holy Father, written by bishops and the fruit of consultation with the episcopate, and approved by the pope in his ordinary magisterium."

Although Ratzinger does not admit it, the desire of the Holy Father both inspired the project and drove it along. Cardinal Bernard Law, who first proposed a universal catechism at the 1985 Extraordinary Synod, was a nonelected papal nominee. Had he been brought along specifically to make this proposal, which had surfaced in an Opus Dei magazine?

However that may be, once under way the draft was subjected to sharp and sometimes withering criticism from 938 bishops — about a quarter of the world's total. They proposed more than 24,000 "amendments or corrections."

The catechism, rewritten in the light of these episcopal comments, seeks to be positive rather than polemical, says Ratzinger. Its aim is to "announce Christian truth with that security which is proper to the church, while respecting the different levels of certainty the church has on particular topics, avoiding mere theological opinions."

This answers the objection that the early drafts had lacked a sense of the "hierarchy of truths." Ratzinger anticipates further objections when he contends that the catechism "draws abundantly on sacred scripture, the tradition of the Western and Eastern churches (the fathers), the liturgy, the magisterium, canon law and the lives and teachings of the saints."

Although it is not called *The Catechism of Vatican II*, because the council did not ask for one, and indeed threw out the idea, it remains true "that it reflects essentially, though not exclusively, Vatican II." This is Ratzinger's tilt at those who regard Vatican II as a wholly fresh start in church life.

In a world marked by subjectivism, relativism and fragmentation, concludes Ratzinger, "it is more than ever necessary to proclaim the Christian message of saving truth, a message that is simple and synthetic, serene and joyful, positive and demanding." It would be churlish to object to these aims. How far they are realized will only be discovered by use. This is a pudding whose proof will be in the eating.

So far, I have seen only the French version. But that is no drawback, because French was the working language of the drafting commission, and the French text is therefore normative.

Presenting it in Paris, Cardinal Jean-Marie Lustiger, archbishop of Paris, pointed out that there were many instances of "universality" in the modern world from pop music to blue jeans and foreign exchange markets that can "ruin a country in 48 hours."

The press, of course, scrutinized the catechism for new sins and were rather disappointed. The traditional bans on divorce, sex before or outside marriage, artificial contraception and abortion are reaffirmed.

But there are some new emphases on drunken or dangerous driving, drug-trafficking, the inadequacy of deterrence. Employers (including the church?) are exhorted to pay fair salaries. Under the

Seventh Commandment ("Thou shalt not steal") are denounced tax evasion, forging checks and unjust rental leases.

The catechism notes that homosexuals "do not choose their homosexual condition," adding in a remark that is bound to cause controversy: "for most of them, it is a trial." They must be treated with "respect, compassion and kindness." They should eschew genital activity.

In my view, it is a mistake to concentrate first and exclusively on the moral section of the catechism. For the commandments are set in the context of the creed, the sacraments and a commentary on the Our Father. This context illumines their meaning.

Archbishop Rembert Weakland, in his recent draft pastoral letter for the 150th anniversary of the Milwaukee diocese, recalls that "the Catholic church is a creedal church. . . . Good practice follows correct belief, and so there must be a concern on the part of all that Catholic belief be correctly stated and transmitted."

The *Catechism for the Catholic Church* will not be in vain if it meets that requirement and helps answer the questions: What do we tell the children? How do we instruct a potential convert? ❏

53

'No lame-duck papacy' and other fantasies

(January 8, 1993) Popes are never allowed to be ill until they are dead, that, at least, was the rule up to and including Pius XII. Pope John Paul II seemed different. He had very public operations in 1981, after Mehemet Ali Agca's assassination attempt. Last July 12, he himself announced that he was going into the hospital for "tests and analyses." Three days later, he had a four-hour operation that was fully and polysyllabically reported upon. No concealment there.

The manipulation of news about the pope's health began after the July 15 operation. Cardinal Secretary of State Angelo Sodano and the Pope's Polish-language secretary, Stanislaw Dziwiez, determined henceforward to keep the entire news operation in their own hands.

They implicitly blamed the papal physician, Dr. Renato Buzzonetti, for failing to detect the pope's tumor earlier. Buzzonetti has not been sacked, but from now on John Paul will be in the care of doctors from the San Raffaello Hospital in Milan.

San Raffaello is a private hospital founded by a brilliant priest-physician, Don Luigi Verse, who uses the most modern equipment, is a leading thinker in the field of bioethics and has opened hospitals in the Philippines and Poland.

The verdict of Verse's team is that John Paul has from one to four years to live. However, they keep that to themselves, and the official line is that John Paul II is fit again, full of energy and projects.

The idea is to prevent speculation about the succession, whether based on the possibility of resignation or the certainty of death. That explains why there was so much irritation in the Vatican with my September article (*NCR*, Sept. 11). There had been a moment of anxiety early in August when John Paul recovered more slowly than had been expected. The aim was to get him fit enough to go through with the somewhat reduced Santo Domingo program. Just as that objective was achieved, an article that talked of a "scenario of resignation" was distinctly unwelcome — especially because the source for the resignation-at-75 story was the French Cardinal Jacques Martin, who in the meantime had himself died.

So no resignation. But also, no handicapping illness. And consequently, no talk of a lame-duck papacy. This is the official line being peddled by the cardinal secretary of state and his staff. The highest-placed Briton in the secretariat, Msgr. Bryan Chestle, sticks faithfully to it, assuring everyone that the pope is well. Because the secretariat of state coordinates news, that is all one will ever hear. Anecdotal evidence from people who have audiences is ambivalent: There are good days and bad days. Joaquín Navarro-Valls, the Vatican spokesman, who has medical training and whose reports on the July operation were distinguished by their detail and completeness, has been struck dumb.

All his time has been devoted to reorganizing the press office. The open-space plan, which dates back to the council, has been replaced by a series of isolated little booths. The big table laden with newspapers has gone. Smoking is banned. "The place has been given the Opus Dei treatment," said Bruno Bartoloni of Agence France-Presse. "You work here without knowing whether anyone else is here at all. The idea seems to be to stop any kind of collective action or protest."

Bartoloni, the son of a distinguished Vaticanologist, wondered what would happen next time there was a major event — a synod or a conclave. Where would everyone be put? Would there be room for 500 people?

The answer is no, but it doesn't matter because there will be no conclave for a while. Meantime, only good news emanates from the Vatican press office.

The Flow of Fantasies

The *Catechism of the Catholic Church* is eagerly awaited by the whole world. Somehow, it will magically solve all our doctrinal problems, settle all doubts, clarify the obscure.

Other fantasies flow from the same source. Introducing a conference on natural family planning, Cardinal Alfonso Lopez Trujillo, president of the Pontifical Council for the Family, declared that the subject was "of enormous interest for the Russian authorities."

The final phase of the pontificate should be dated from December 1990, when Angelo Sodano replaced Agostino Casaroli as cardinal secretary of state.

Casaroli represented the best traditions of Vatican diplomacy. When he signed the Charter for Europe at the Paris Conference in 1990, his swan song, he knew personally all the leaders who were his fellow signatories, from Mikhail Gorbachev to George Bush. His first missions to Eastern Europe dated back to the time of Pope John.

"If you want diplomatic longevity," he said with a twinkle in his eyes behind those rimless glasses, "it helps to serve an absolute monarch."

Casaroli never believed that the coordinating function of the secretariat of state meant that it should try to control everything that happened in the curia. In any case, he had to compete with the alternative power center of the Congregation for the Doctrine of the Faith and did not always come off best.

But constitutionally, he believed in the separation of powers. It was not the business of the secretariat of state to interfere in the work of the Justice and Peace Commission, for example.

Sodano has a different concept of the role of Secretariat of State. His years as nuncio in Chile were not the best preparation for the job. Gen. Augusto Pinochet is the only world ex-leader whom he knows well.

"Cardinal Sodano is a gray, gray man," said a Rome staffer, "and everything about him is conservative: his theology, his mindset, his approach to diplomacy."

He has demoralized Justice and Peace, headed by French Cardinal Roger Etchegaray. Gianni La Bella of Rome's progressive San Egidio community has recently resigned from Justice and Peace in protest at Sodano's high-handedness. A delegation that reported to Etchegaray on the situation in Haiti was thanked and told to say it all again in the Secretariat of State. Sodano's role at the Santo Domingo CELAM conference was far from the evenhandedness his office requires.

The chief result of coordination by Sodano is confusion. It is Sodano who has been talking of using force in Bosnia — the right of *ingerenza* or interference. It has been denied or at least qualified by Archbishop Jean-Luis Tauran, head of the foreign relations department of the Vatican, who remembers the pope's "rejection of war as an instrument of justice" during the Persian Gulf crisis.

A whole year has been wasted in the vain quest for "new structures" to replace CCEE — the Europe-wide equivalent of CELAM. Pope John Paul called for them at the conclusion of the Eurosynod a year ago.

Twelve months later the only change is that the delegates to CCEE will no longer be elected by their peers but will be the presidents of the episcopal conferences. In the case of Italy, this means that Cardinal Camillo Ruini, unelected and appointed directly by the pope, will replace Cardinal Carlo Maria Martini. Some say that was the point of the entire operation. In which case, it is scandalous as well as petty-minded. Martini represents the hope for ecumenism in Europe; he is the only official Catholic side who is trusted by Protestants and the Russian Orthodox.

Ruini, by contrast, has no understanding of ecumenism. Karl-Christoph Epting complained that the presence of Protestant observers at the synod was merely "cosmetic."

Ruini replied that the synod was an instance of Catholic ecumenism, and you could not expect it to indulge the Protestant version.

Yet Ruini is the favored son of John Paul, who made him vicar of Rome — the man who looks after the diocese of Rome on his behalf — and president of the Italian episcopal conference. Ruini thinks of himself as papabile and tends to follow behind the pope at audiences, imitating his gestures and attitudes, patting the sick on both cheeks, kissing them on the brow before sketching a vague blessing.

So Rome and Italy are in the hands of Ruini while the rest of the church depends on Sodano.

Meantime, John Paul contemplates fresh journeys. The Jan. 8 ecumenical prayer meeting at Assisi is all that survives of a bold but unrealizable plan to meet in Sarajevo.

A six-hour visit to Khartoum in the Sudan has been tacked on to the end of the next Africa trip to Uganda in February; it is not clear what good, if any, it will do to the persecuted Christians in the south of the country.

The Baltic republics are scheduled for September. Beyond that Moscow still tantalizingly beckons and, the supreme goal, Jerusalem. ❏

54

In Assisi, religious leaders deplore cruelties

(January 22, 1993) Dare one say it? For the first time in his pontificate, Pope John Paul II was upstaged by another speaker.

At the vigil for prayer and penance at Assisi Jan. 9, Ra'is ul Ulama Jakub Selimoski, religious leader of the Bosnian Muslims, delivered a powerful indictment of the Serbian onslaught on his people.

Standing alongside John Paul in the Basilica of St. Francis, beneath Giotto's frescoes of the life of the saint who tried to stop a crusade, Selimoski rehearsed the grim statistics of Serbian aggression: "200,000 Muslims exterminated; 100,000 in concentration camps; 35,000 women raped (including seven over 80); 650 mosques destroyed or ruined."

These crimes make a mockery, said Selimoski, of "all Europe's claims to civilization, its democratic declarations, its humanistic achievements, its respect for human rights and liberty."

"How can such a Europe," he angrily asked, "allow an entire nation to disappear, and how can it wash its hands, with tranquillity and indifference, of this problem, adopting only ineffectual solutions?"

"We beseech Allah," was Selimoski's prayer of petition, "to illumine the minds of those responsible so that they may call a halt as soon as possible to the killing of so many people and the destruction of their property.

"We ask Allah that the Geneva Conference may lead to a just and lasting peace which does not condone crimes by rewarding violence and aggression."

John Paul's tone was less accusatory. He spoke more in bewildered sorrow than in righteous anger. "How can it be that such enmity and hatred exists in the world?" he demanded. "How is it possible to kill each other in this way?"

For him, as for Selimoski, what is at stake is the survival of Europe itself. Europe can only survive if it respects difference and "otherness."

Borrowing a theme dear to the Lithuanian-born Jewish philosopher Emmanuel Levinas, he declared that "it is never allowed to deprive someone of the right to life and security simply because he is not one of us, because he is *other*."

"It is never allowed," he thundered, "to deprive a woman of her right to integrity and dignity simply because she is not one of us, because she is *other*."

He went on, "Nor can one deprive a child of the right to a roof over its head and food to sustain it simply because it is a child of the *others*."

Where all are children of the one God, the God of Abraham, concluded John Paul, then the distinction "us-them" has no meaning and solidarity should prevail.

He invited all monotheists — Christians, Jews and Muslims — to pray each according to their own tradition to the God of Abraham, the Lord of history, for the gift that only he can give, "the precious gift of peace."

For "this is our strength, this is our weapon. Faced with violence and cruelty, we have no other recourse than God. We are neither strong nor powerful, but we know that God will not leave us without an answer."

John Paul then departed for an early bed — it was after 9:30 p.m. — leaving Cardinal Carlo Maria Martini, archbishop of Milan, to continue the prayer vigil with young people in the Basilica of St. Clare until well after midnight.

Christian and Muslim leaders from all over Europe were present in strength. Jews were represented by Rabbi David Rosen, from

Jerusalem, and Lisa Palmieri of the Italian branch of the Anti-Defamation League. There would have been more, but it was the sabbath, and the prayers for peace were echoed in all Italian synagogues.

The absence of the Orthodox was disquieting. The only one to attend was Metropolitan Timothy from Skopje, Macedonia, who was scoring a Macedonian nationalist point against the Serbian Patriarch Pavle of Belgrade.

Pavle himself replied to the papal invitation. He explained that he could not come because it was the Orthodox Christmas — celebrated on the Western feast of the Epiphany, because sanctions made travel difficult and for unspecified "other reasons."

But Pavle's negative response was not unfriendly. He referred to "this crazy and fratricidal war" which he has condemned along with Cardinal Franjo Kuharic of Zagreb and Selimoski in a meeting organized by the Council of European Churches in Switzerland. The Serbian patriarch said he did not reject "the pope's outstretched hand" and announced he will be sending a delegation to the Vatican to prepare a meeting with John Paul.

The ecumenical patriarch of Constantinople, Bartholomew, wrote the Pope regretting his absence and saying he would be "spiritually present." The responses of Pavle and Bartholomew did not amount to the "snub" from the Orthodox that some news agencies detected in their absence.

Inner Orthodox factors constrain them. Bartholomew has to look over his shoulder at the Russian Orthodox patriarch, Alexis, who did not deign to reply to the papal invitation and complained in his Christmas message, yet again, of "the advance of foreign confessions and sects which seek to fill the vacuum left by the collapse of communism."

The isolation and weakness of Patriarch Pavle in Belgrade should be recognized. His good will and sincerity are not in doubt, but he is an old man of 78, is regarded as pious but a bit naive, and is not supported by his synod.

On a recent visit to Belgrade, Jan ter Laak, secretary of Pax Christi Netherlands, was shocked to discover that Serbian Orthodox bishops (though not Pavle) are utterly convinced that the Arab world wants to exploit the situation in Bosnia-Herzegovina to carve out a fundamentalist Muslim state in Europe.

Even a "moderate" Orthodox bishop told ter Laak he considers it his duty to warn the West about "the Islamic threat." "Why do you not see this danger?" was the refrain.

The Serbian Orthodox base their fears on the nasty experiences of the Copts in Egypt and other "brothers in faith" in the Arab world. Their Greek Orthodox neighbors fan the flames of hatred with their traditional anti-Turkish feelings.

Anyone steeped in this atavistic ideology and conditioned by the Belgrade media is bound to perceive the Assisi meeting as the treacherous ganging-up of the Vatican and Islam against gallant little Serbia.

There is a relation between prayer and politics. Orthodoxy has never had a Second Vatican Council which saw positive values in Islam and non-Christian religions. In Sarajevo Christian-Muslim relations were exemplary, better than anywhere in the world according to U.S Jesuit Fr. Tom Michel of the Vatican's Council for Inter-religious Dialogue. And that included the Orthodox.

The Catholic-Muslim alliance in Bosnia (which to some extent overlaps with the Croat-Bosnian alliance) is the best defense against the creation of a fundamentalist Islamic state which the Orthodox say they fear.

For the Bosnian Muslims — this was the gist of Selimoski's statement in Assisi — are European by tradition, would prefer help from Europe to that of Muslim fundamentalists from the Middle East, and share in the European values of respect for the "other" which John Paul stressed.

Les absents ont toujours tort (The absent are always wrong), says a French proverb. The sooner the Serbian Orthodox Church — and the nation — can bring themselves to rejoin the international dialogue, the better. It is more difficult to kill the "others" when you know them and have prayed with them. But it will need an act of repentance. ❏

55

Vatican takes over European bishops

(March 5, 1993) At Santo Domingo last October, an attempt was made to bring CELAM, the council of Latin American bishops, to heel. The African bishops, scheduled to meet in synod in Rome April 10, 1994, appear next for the treatment.

Largely unnoticed, without fuss or publicity, the European bishops were brought under control just before Christmas last year.

To understand this move, one needs to backtrack to the special synod on Europe in November-December 1991. The synod was a chance for the European bishops, from East and West, to assess the state of Europe after the dramatic events of 1989. Not that they were meeting for the first time. Since 1975 the CCEE (Latin acronym for the Council of European Bishops' Conferences) has held regular symposia.

In this time it has had only three presidents: Cardinal Roger Etchegaray, now president of International Justice and Peace, whose brainchild it was; Cardinal Basil Hume, archbishop of Westminster, England; and the current president, Cardinal Carlo Maria Martini of Milan, the Italian press' hot tip for the next conclave.

One might have expected Pope John Paul II, who, as archbishop of Kraków, had been a member of CCEE, to thank the European bishops for their good work and urge them to welcome aboard the new members from Romania, Ukraine and the Baltic republics as they emerged from the catacombs.

The practical way to help CCEE would have been to strengthen it in personnel and finance so it could become a real expression of European solidarity.

At the synod, Cardinal Martini made the obvious but neglected point that collegiality, the *affectus collegialis*, depends on friendships between bishops, including the bishop of Rome, himself another "European" bishop.

Personal contacts between church leaders can help build the unity of the wider Europe. It can help to make Europe whole again. It will do this, in the famous phrase *cum Petro et sub Petro* (with and under Peter).

The fantasy that the European bishops were trying to set up some kind of alternative or parallel magisterium deserves booting into the Tiber. The Eurosynod proved it.

Yet, this picture of harmony all round was rudely disturbed by a passage in Pope John Paul's final address to the 1991 synod. Searching for understatements, it could only be described as a snub to the CCEE.

John Paul explained, "So that the *affectus collegialis* and the *communio hierarchica* (*Lumen Gentium*) between the head and the members of the episcopal college so admirably experienced during the synod assembly may be strengthened for the benefit of evangelization in the continent of Europe, I ask the president delegates, the general relater, the secretary general and the special secretaries to present me with a concrete proposal for a structure, dedicated to the implementation of synod aims, analogous to the activity of the General Secretariat of the synod, within the year."

Why seek to invent a new "structure" when one already exists to do precisely this job? The CCEE had a Secretariat, hitherto at Sankt Gallen in Switzerland, competently presided over by Msgr. Ivo Furer. It was perfectly capable of implementing the Eurosynod's conclusions, especially since these merely recommitted it to what it was already doing. It was difficult to see the point of the exercise.

Mark Santer, Anglican bishop of Birmingham, with the clear eye of the "fraternal delegate," surmised that "some parts of the Roman curia are suspicious when local church speaks to local church." He admitted this was an odd thing to have to say.

Asked what was going on, Jesuit Fr. Giovanni Caprile, who knows many Vatican secrets, told *NCR*: "The Holy Father doesn't really know what he means by this proposal, so it is up to others to say what it should mean." Caprile, of the prestigious Rome fortnightly *Civiltà Cattolica*, is not known as a joker.

It was enough to consider who was on the committee to suspect the truth. The key people were the relater and the special secretary; Cardinal Camillo Ruini, vicar of Rome; and Archbishop Jan Schotte, secretary of the synod council.

Of the three president delegates, Cardinal Eduardo Martinez Somalo, prefect of the Congregation for Divine Worship, was in Rome: the others were Cardinals Jean-Marie Lustiger of Paris and Joseph Glemp of Gniezno-Warsaw. There was not a man among them who by experience and languages could be said to have a European vocation.

After a year's cogitation behind locked doors, this body produced a plan shattering in its simplicity, devastating in its effects. The quest for "new structures" having proved vain, it was decided simply to take over CCEE.

When the CCEE members arrived in Rome on Dec. 1, 1992, they saw for the first time what was proposed and had to "react" off the cuff.

Pope John Paul explained in his introductory address why they were there: "From the new situation which arose after 1989 came the necessity for CCEE to make a fresh start since this council now included churches from the whole continent of Europe. During this meeting, the conclusions reached will be expounded on and discussed so that, from next year, the council can already work in this more complete dimension."

But that was not the rationale offered for the changes in 1991 when the stated purpose was to strengthen the bonds of collegiality, in particular the *affectus collegialis*.

Moreover, these conclusions had been decided upon before the meeting, so there was nothing to discuss. How was the new aim to be achieved? "In its institutional activity," said the pope, "the council will acquire new strength and greater authority if its members are the presidents of episcopal conferences."

The notion that presidents of episcopal conferences have greater authority will appear to be wishful thinking to many. Conferences in the past have elected as their Eurodelegate the bishop who was the best equipped for this role culturally and linguistically.

Presidents of conferences, already overburdened, are not likely to have the leisure to pay attention to the Eurodimension. So their meetings may possess "greater dignity," as the pope requires, but they will also be more superficial and more formal. The *affectus collegialis* will be diminished rather than strengthened.

The change from elected member to president of the conference is crucial in the case of Italy. Hitherto the elected Italian delegate has been Martini. To oust Martini and replace him as Italian delegate with Cardinal Ruini is a fine instance of shooting oneself in the foot.

Besides, unlike all other presidents of episcopal conferences, Ruini was not elected by his peers but simply appointed by the pope — "a great honor," says Ruini.

A second "decision" suggests an even greater role for Ruini. Henceforward, the CCEE Secretariat will no longer be in Sankt Gallen, Switzerland, but in Rome. Where should it be housed? Why, conveniently enough in the building from which Ruini already presides over CEI (the Italian episcopal conference) as well as the Rome diocese.

Then it would be "logical" for CCEE to elect Ruini as its president. The East Europeans would certainly conclude that such is the desire of the Holy Father.

Even if a Ruini presidency were averted and Glemp filled the post, the move to Rome would be unfortunate. It would reduce CCEE in practice to a department of the Roman curia, incapable of initiative or enterprise.

It would mean a loss of credibility in ecumenism. At the moment, CCEE is the only forum in which Catholics and Orthodox meet in friendly fashion. It would reduce collegiality in Europe to a formality if not a sham.

Worst of all, if one draws attention to these disadvantages, one is accused of disloyalty or being "anti-Roman." Probably, there is not much point in noting that the statutes of CCEE, last approved in 1981, cannot be changed unless there is a two-thirds majority. ❑

56

World Youth Day tied to 'culture of pilgrimage'

(July 2, 1993) "My visit to Denver," Pope John Paul II told the bishops of Iowa, Kansas, Missouri and Nebraska, May 28, "will be truly a pilgrimage which I, along with so many young men and women, am preparing for through reflection, prayer and penance." He invited the bishops to join him in this exercise.

Addressing the bishops of New Mexico, Utah, Arizona, Colorado and Wyoming, June 8, John Paul further explained: "This is a pilgrimage of faith and friendship to encounter Christ in the city — in his eucharistic self-offering, in the sufferings of our brothers and sisters, in the prayers of his people."

John Paul is probably the first person to have spoken of a visit to Denver as a pilgrimage. He thinks of all of his globetrotting trips in this way. He sees them as "pilgrimages to the heart of the church."

The idea of "going on pilgrimage" comes naturally to him and owes a great deal to his European background. Moreover, in communist Poland the church was denied any public visibility. Catholics were confined to the church building and the sacristy. The only exception to this rule was the annual pilgrimage to Czestochowa to venerate the "Black Madonna" — an icon that mysteriously arrived there some time in the 14th century.

Slashed by a Swedish Lutheran sword in 1665 and saved by the warrior monks, the Madonna of Czestochowa became a symbol of Catholic resistance to foreign tyranny. In the early 19th century Czar Alexander I razed its fortifications to the ground.

For John Paul, the pilgrimage is not some kind of accessory to the spiritual life; it is at the very center of it. On becoming pope, he tried to transfer this same attitude first to Italy, then to Europe and finally to the whole church.

His international trips should not blind us to the fact that he has traveled more freely within Italy than any previous pope. And he has reanimated ancient pilgrimage centers.

June 19 he was in Macerata, a city 27 kilometers from Loreto. There John Paul said Mass for several thousand young members of the Communion and Liberation movement who then set out on pilgrimage throughout the night, arriving, as dawn broke, at the hilltop shrine of Loreto.

Legend says that the house at Nazareth where Jesus, Mary and Joseph lived, was miraculously transported from the Holy Land and deposited here on this rocky eminence overlooking the Adriatic. Antedating Lourdes and Fatima — not to mention the upstart Medjugorje — by several centuries, Loreto is the chief shrine of Italy.

Dioceses organize bus trips there. Pope John XXIII went to Loreto to pray for the Second Vatican Council — the only time he left the Vatican. It is moving because it is a place where many people have prayed hard. It has an atmosphere independent of the legend of its origins.

As an Englishman, I much prefer the shrine of Our Lady of Walsingham. For the medieval pilgrim it was more important even than Canterbury, about which Geoffrey Chaucer wrote his tales. Kings went there to do penance. Erasmus visited it on the eve of its dissolution. Now, though Anglican and Catholic pilgrimages have been revived in the 20th century, medieval Walsingham lies in ruins.

The origin of Walsingham was a dream or a vision in which Our Lady revealed the exact dimensions of her house at Nazareth so that it could be rebuilt in the English countryside according to her specifications.

But the real point of Walsingham, what it said to the medieval English man or woman was this: You do not have to go gallivanting off to the Holy Land in search of the traces of Jesus and to walk in his footsteps. Your Holy Land is here, amid the lanes and hedgerows of Norfolk. This is where you find your holiness, your grace. The "holy family" is your family.

But I don't really want to set Walsingham and Loreto in com-
petition. Loreto has a continuity that Walsingham cannot boast. Yet
since tragedy is always more affecting than success, better poems
have been written about Walsingham. Anon wrote in the mid-16th
century:

Bitter, bitter, O to behold
The grass to grow
Where the walls of Walsingham
So stately did show.
Such were the works of Walsingham
While she did stand.
Such were the wracks as now do show
Of that holy land.

Though I now have a high regard for Walsingham, I was in
Loreto first. It became the home of Msgr. Loris F. Capovilla, Pope
John's secretary in Venice and in Rome. He was the official "guard-
ian of the shrine."

But my first pilgrimage ever was to Chartres in the 1950s,
when I was a student in Paris. It started on the Friday before Whit-
sunday.

It involved serious physical effort. We traveled from Paris by
train to three different towns within 60 kilometers of Chartres. We
then marched along the road in "chapters" of 60, singing the rosary.

Having sung it thousands of times, I can still render the tune of
Je vous salut, Marie, pleine de grace.

Each "chapter" had a chaplain. For some reason, I have forgotten, I marched with the Paris School of Agriculture — known familiarly as *les fumiers*, the dung heaps. Our chaplain was a brilliant
young Jesuit patristic scholar called Jean Daniélou.

We spent the night in barns, sleeping on the hay. On the Saturday morning, we met in a natural amphitheater where 200 priests
said Mass simultaneously. It was the best they could do in pre-con-
celebration days.

Of course the pilgrimage to Chartres, which in those days gathered 20,000 students, owed a lot to the Catholic poet and socialist
patriot Charles Péguy, killed on the first day of World War I.

I wrote my first-ever published article about the pilgrimage to
Chartres, heavily laced — no doubt — with the thoughts of our chaplain. I remember writing that St. Paul's words — "Carry one another's

burdens, and so fulfill the law of Christ" — came literally true on the pilgrimage, where the strong came to the help of the weak.

What emerges from all this is that in Europe there is a "culture of pilgrimage" in which it is taken for granted, even by someone like myself who lives in "Protestant" England. If that is true of me, how much more is it true of Karol Wojtyla, now Pope John Paul II.

In communist Poland the pilgrimage to Czestochowa in the month of August was the only way in which the church could have any contact with youth, let alone influence.

Going on pilgrimage to Czestochowa was a serious business. It took a week of backpacking. Friendly farmers along the route put you up in barns — just as in France.

Priests mingled with the students, heard confessions at halts, dispensed spiritual advice. It was like going on retreat. Then Vatican II discovered that the church was a "pilgrim church." That was what we had all learned, with much sweat and toil, on the dusty roads that led to Loreto, Walsingham, Chartres, Czestochowa.

We — no, to tell the truth, I — thought Protestants worse off because they had internalized, spiritualized and moralized the grand idea of pilgrimage. I refer to John Bunyan's *Pilgrim's Progress*.

It is a wonderful book. But it all "goes on in the head." It has turned the pilgrimage into a symbol. There is no sweat in Bunyan, except in anxiety about salvation. I much prefer the bunch of sinners, half-saints and scoundrels whom Chaucer depicts on the road to Canterbury.

Now John Paul has tried hard to recapture the genuine spirit of the medieval pilgrimage in his World Youth Days. In 1989 it was held at Compostela in northern Spain at the shrine of St. James — site of the greatest medieval pilgrimage.

John Paul said that "awareness of Europe" was the result of pilgrimages: "In the centuries when a homogeneous and spiritually united continent was being shaped, the whole of Europe came here to the 'memorial' of St. James. It was one of the places that favored the mutual understanding of the so very different European peoples, the Latins, the Germans, the Celts, the Anglo-Saxons and the Slavs."

"The pilgrimage," John Paul went on, "brought together, put in contact and united all those peoples who throughout the centuries, once touched by the preaching of Christ's apostles, accepted the gospel, and at the same time were born as peoples and nations."

First the nations were "baptized" — Augustine in Canterbury in 597, Adalbert in Poland in 966, Vladimir in Kiev in 988 — and then

Europe itself was baptized and acquired its identity through its baptism.

After Compostela in 1989, the next World Youth Day was a pilgrimage to — obviously — Czestochowa. It was the first time that John Paul had been able to invite the youth of Europe and the world to the shrine that meant so much to him. No doubt it did wonders for the Polish tourist industry, but it didn't quite recapture the spirit of the pilgrimages in the communist era. There were too many wild swings between "consumerism" on the one hand and chaos and discomfort on the other for minds to concentrate on prayer.

Not everyone understood "pilgrimage" in John Paul's ennobling sense. The result was that Czestochowa 1991 was more like a youth rally of right-wing supporters of the pope than a genuine pilgrimage.

If that happened at Czestochowa, which has a long tradition of pilgrimages, what will happen at Denver, where there is none? ❏

57

Infallibility boosted in leaked encyclical

(August 13, 1993) Unlike *Humanae Vitae* in 1968, which was not allowed to exist until it appeared, Pope John Paul's next encyclical, *Veritatis Splendor* ("The Splendor of Truth"), has been in the air a long time.

It was first announced by John Paul himself in 1987, the 200th anniversary of the death of St. Alphonsus Liguori, patron of confessors and moral theologians. Cardinal Joseph Ratzinger told a cardinals' meeting in 1991 that it would attack the Enlightenment notion that "the good was undiscoverable and inaccessible." But still it did not come.

Last month, Norbert Greinacher, moral theology professor at Tübingen in Germany, claimed direct knowledge of the upcoming encyclical. He denounced it in a July 3 interview in the Italian daily *La Repubblica*.

"It's not sensational as far as sexuality is concerned," said Greinacher, "but its main point is a still more rigorous and restrictive emphasis on papal infallibility. The whole thing is very negative."

He added that *Veritatis Splendor*, concerned with "principles," was only a first installment. A later encyclical would apply it to practical cases and everyday life. An enterprising Rome news agency, ADISTA, got hold of a copy of Greinacher's version of the encyclical and leaked extracts from it July 31, feast of St. Ignatius.

Dr. Joaquín Navarro-Valls, Vatican press officer, treated the leak with lofty disdain. The text available to ADISTA, he declared, is "partial and nonauthentic," and "primitive, three years out of date, and very largely superseded."

The language, structure and style of this 3-year-old draft, Navarro-Valls went on, is very different from that of the true encyclical which, anyway, the Holy Father had not yet signed. Asked about a report in the Spanish daily *El Pais* that the pope would sign it Aug. 6, feast of the Transfiguration and 15th anniversary of the death of Pope Paul VI, Navarro-Valls testily replied, "It's on the pope's desk."

Of course, there is usually a gap between signature and publication, so don't expect it in time for the papal visit.

Who wrote it? ADISTA named two Communion and Liberation theologians: Angelo Scola, bishop of Grosseto, Italy, and Rocco Buttiglione, professor at the Liechtenstein International Academy of Philosophy.

Two Polish theologians allegedly completed the team: Jozef Tischner, an old friend of the pope, and Salvatorian Fr. Tadeusz Styczen, the pope's successor in the chair of moral theology at the Catholic University of Lublin, Poland.

Navarro-Valls dismissed all this as speculation. "The Holy Father wanted to hear," he claimed, "the views of a great number of pastors and theologians of various nationalities." But he did not vouchsafe any further information.

ADISTA did not invent these names. They were lifted from the Communion and Liberation monthly, *Trenta Giorni*, and may therefore be considered reliable. The right-wing review added the Swiss Dominican, Georges Cottier, theologian to the papal household.

The magazine said that the draft had been cut down from 300 to 150 pages, claiming also that it was written in Italian and Polish. If true, this would confirm that the consultors were limited to one narrow theological school. The moral theologians of the Jesuit Gregorian University and the Redemptorist Alfonsianum had no part in it.

No one doubts that the purpose of the encyclical is to insist on the existence of an "objective moral order" in which certain actions are of themselves right or wrong. Any form of ethical relativism is rejected.

The "unofficial" version begins: "The splendor of truth shines forth in all the works of the Creator, leading and inviting us to seek our human freedom in his divine love."

Its polemical purpose is plain from the start. It sets itself against ethical trends found within the church itself — and found for years, it adds, referring to Pius XII's 1956 condemnation of "situation ethics."

"Some have even asserted," it complains, "that the church can say nothing magisterially on general moral questions and can only stimulate the conscience of individuals and mediate moral values."

It seeks to refute such positions in three substantial chapters. Chapter 1 establishes the scriptural basis of morality. It begins from the question of the rich, young man in Matthew 19:16: "Teacher, what good deed must I do to obtain eternal life?" There follows a discussion of the beatitudes and the "new commandment" of love.

Chapter 2 lays down "The Principles of Moral Teaching." It defends the concept of "natural law" as based on the truth that the human person is made "in God's image." Universally applicable natural law is the basis of human solidarity.

It declares that certain acts are "intrinsically evil" and admit of no exceptions. They cannot be "redeemed" by good intentions or good consequences. In a long and sophisticated discussion of "conscience" it stresses that the human conscience needs to be "formed" or "trained" to know the good.

Chapter 3 on "Moral Theology in the Mission of the Church" draws the practical consequences. It says that the authority of pope and bishops extends even to "moral teachings that have not yet been finally defined." It demands that bishops should sack dissenting moral theologians and rigorously supervise Catholic universities and publications.

Media attention has concentrated on the disciplinary measures of this final chapter. Theologians will be more interested in Chapter 2 which is most likely to bear Pope John Paul's personal stamp.

According to *Trenta Giorni*, the publication delay was due to the papal desire to harmonize his own "philosophical anthropology" (based on the phenomenologist Max Scheler) with traditional Thomism.

This, then, will be the most weighty theological encyclical of the pontificate. A writer in the Italian daily *Corriere della Sera* described it as "a kind of spiritual testament of a now old and exhausted pope." If it makes moral theologians unemployed, it will keep ecclesiologists busy for a long time. ❏

58

Encyclical nails objective right and wrong

(October 8, 1993) *Veritatis Splendor,* Pope John Paul II's encyclical on moral theology, was to have been promulgated Oct. 5. Days before the U.S. bishops had the 170-page document in their hands, excerpts were appearing last week in European newspapers.

What is the new encyclical for?

The introduction describes the "specific purpose" of the encyclical thus: "To set forth the principles of a moral teaching based upon Sacred Scripture and the living apostolic tradition, and at the same time to shed light on the presuppositions and consequences of the dissent which that teaching has met (with)" (paragraph 5 in text).

That suggests a positive and a negative aim: to expound the foundations of Christian morality in the light of scripture and tradition, and to denounce errors either of disagreement or dissent.

The encyclical is written in a crisis atmosphere. For "it is no longer a matter of limited and occasional dissent, but of an overall and systematic calling into question of traditional moral doctrine, on the basis of certain anthropological and ethical presuppositions" (4).

The encyclical is addressed specifically to bishops. Everyone else is, in a sense, eavesdropping. Pope John Paul is trying to stir up his fellow bishops to action.

"Dear brothers in the episcopate," he cries, not without a note of pathos, "we must not be content merely to warn the faithful about the errors and dangers of certain ethical theories" (83).

So mere warnings about dangerous moral theologians are not enough. Bishops should adopt "appropriate measures to ensure that the faithful are guarded from every doctrine and theory contrary to it" (116).

What measures are appropriate? Sackings and oustings seem to be called for. The same episcopal vigilance is to be extended to institutions bearing the name "Catholic." Mentioned are church-related schools, universities, health care facilities and counseling services. They must forfeit their "Catholic" title if they "seriously fail to live up to it" (116).

Archbishop Luigi Barbarito, pro-nuncio in London, has already declared that there is "nothing new" about *Veritatis Splendor*. It is true that since the start of his pontificate Pope John Paul has been defending the positions outlined in the encyclical. That is why he quotes himself more than any other pope.

For example, the doctrine that certain acts are "intrinsically evil" (*intrinsece malum*), the key to the entire operation, was forcefully stated in *Reconciliatio et Penitentia* in 1983. That document can be regarded as a dress rehearsal for *Veritatis Splendor*.

John Paul also refers repeatedly to the *Catechism of the Catholic Church*. It has already become a "source," even though not yet available in English. *Donum Veritatis*, the 1990 instruction of the Congregation for the Doctrine of the Faith on the ecclesial vocation of the theologian, is another source.

Yet *Reconciliatio et Penitentia* is the crucial foundation document on which the encyclical builds. It was the official papal reply to the 1980 Synod on Christian Marriage, which suggested that not all those who dissent from official church teaching on contraception are necessarily "unfaithful" or "insincere."

It was also a reply to those bishops who pointed out at the 1980 synod that Paul VI in *Humanae Vitae* described artificial contraception as *intrinsece inhonestum*, which, however translated, means something less than "intrinsically evil." (I have heard it rendered by a cardinal as "not quite the best thing to do").

But *Reconciliatio et Penitentia* was largely ignored. Hence the restatement of its themes in more solemn form in *Veritatis Splendor*. It is an attempt to close down, once and for all, all loopholes or escape hatches. For if an act really is intrinsically evil, that is, evil by its very nature, then it can neither be palliated by good intentions nor mitigated by good consequences.

Casuistry is no help because, says *Veritatis Splendor*, casuistry is concerned only with "doubtful or uncertain matters" (76). But there can be no doubts or questions about what is intrinsically evil.

What about compassion, what might be called the Graham Greene quality — the sense that God's mercy is so much greater than our weakness?

This stern moralist replies that "it is human for the sinner to acknowledge his weakness and ask mercy for his failings; what is unacceptable is the attitude of one who makes his own weakness the criterion of the truth about the good" (104).

Nor does the appeal to "conscience" help. The untutored or uninstructed conscience does not know the truth on which the good is based. John Henry Newman is quoted to the effect that "conscience has duties as well as rights."

Conscience is not infallible. Its function is not, as many suppose, to decide what to do, but to discern the good. The fact that an "erroneous conscience" must be followed does not make it any less erroneous (62).

The theory of "fundamental option" is also given short shrift. Developed by Hungarian Jesuit Ladislas Boros in the 1960s, it said that what mattered most in Christian life was the "fundamental choice" for God. If one was genuinely turned Godward and trying to live a charity-inspired life, then individual acts could not basically affect that orientation.

But — once again — this is ruled out by the "intrinsically evil" view. At this point *Veritatis Splendor* also "restores" the notion of mortal sin by refusing to reduce it to a fundamental option rejecting God (70).

"For mortal sin," it urges, "exists also when a person knowingly and willingly, for whatever reason, chooses something gravely disordered" (107). There is a practical pastoral aspect here: Many a pedophile priest may have excused himself on the grounds that his "fundamental option" was okay.

The same argument based on intrinsically evil acts excludes one from presenting, say, *Humanae Vitae* as an ideal: "It would be a serious error to conclude that the church's teaching is essentially only an 'ideal,' which must then be adapted, proportioned or graduated to the so-called concrete possibilities of man, according to the balancing of the goods in question" (103).

We need to stand back a little from the detailed exegesis of the text and ask what is going on here. There are two basic forms of teaching in the church. There is the pastoral magisterium, which belongs to bishops and the pope. It is concerned with the practical application of Christian truth to everyday life. It answers the questions and doubts thrown up by life. The theological magisterium is the systematic and scholarly working out of the articulation of Christian truths and their relations between each other.

What happens in *Veritatis Splendor* is that the pastoral magisterium has usurped the function of the theological magisterium. It does precisely what it says it is not doing: "Certainly the church's magisterium does not intend to impose upon the faithful any particular theological system, still less a philosophical one" (29).

That is hard to credit. *Veritatis Splendor* reflects the teachers of Karol Wojtyla's youth, especially the French Dominican Réginald Garrigou-Lagrange under whom he wrote his thesis on St. John of the Cross.

There is the same emphasis on "timeless or immutable truths," which are incapable of development. Garrigou-Lagrange also influenced the 1950 encyclical *Humani Generis*, which led to countless sackings among French Dominicans and Jesuits.

That is an encouraging precedent: The ousted theologians of 1950, the casualties of *Humani Generis*, made a comeback at Vatican II. They included Henri de Lubac and Yves Congar.

So in *Veritatis Splendor*, we have a reversion to the timeless Thomism of the 1940s. It is indeed a document so timeless as to be almost out of this world. In the context of AIDS and the population explosion, it provides a marvelous example of "thinking in centuries."

Christians are not alone in witnessing "to the absoluteness of moral good" (94). Who are their allies? The Latin satirical poet Juvenal is quoted in support, and then the Stoics who, according to second century St. Justin, "at least in their teaching on ethics demonstrated wisdom, thanks to the seeds of the Word present in all peoples."

Another historical reminiscence is wheeled up to support the contention that "God does not ask the impossible." Some gay persons may say (this particular example is not given) it is impossible for them to live other than as they do. The thundering reply is that "sins can be avoided because together with the commandments the Lord gives us the possibility of keeping them" (102).

Impossible is not a word in John Paul's vocabulary. Everything is possible with grace. One might suspect that although John Paul is formally talking about "morality," his real theme is heroic holiness — which takes us, or most of us, into another order altogether. This suspicion is confirmed by two features of the encyclical.

First, the scriptural section insists that "following Christ is the essential and primordial foundation of Christian morality" (19). It is not enough for the Christian to hear and assimilate the word of God; he/she has to obey it.

John Paul denies, with great vehemence, the idea that Christian faith can be separated from Christian morality. He repudiates the notion that the magisterium can intervene only to "exhort consciences" or "propose values . . . in the light of which each individual will independently make up his or her decisions and life choices" (4). Orthodoxy and orthopraxy go hand in hand.

Second, holiness is presented as the summit of morality in a long section (90-94) on martyrdom. The readiness for martyrdom is seen as "affirming the inviolability of the moral order."

There is nothing wrong with presenting Christian morality in the context of the heroic following of Christ put forward in the gospels. However, it could be said that this belongs to spirituality.

At any rate, it is not an approach to morality that makes possible dialogue or discussion with secular ethicians. Indeed, the encyclical asserts that "modern culture" is so profoundly de-Christianized, and so many people live "as if God did not exist," that any such dialogue is vain (88).

Moreover — and this is why John Paul sets the alarm bells ringing — "in a widely de-Christianized culture, the criteria employed by believers themselves in making judgments and decisions often appear extraneous or even contrary to the gospels" (88).

Does he fear that this "prevalent and all-intrusive culture" has invaded Poland and other countries of Central Europe? No doubt, but there is a lack of specificity.

We touch here on the key to the whole document: In the papal view there is not just a gap but a huge chasm between a morality based on God's divine intention (heteronomy) and one based on the best we can do according to human reason (autonomy). Since nonbelievers work outside this system, they will inevitably be puzzled, to say the least, about the source of the moral principles the encyclical propounds.

One of its main themes is that there can be no knowledge of the "good" (which is what ethics is about) without knowledge of the "truth" about the human condition. Unless you know where the human person is heading — in faith toward the beatific vision — you can say nothing useful about how to get there.

This puts the secular ethician at a disadvantage. Secular ethics is self-contained or autonomous by definition. That the human person has a final goal or end is not a thought he/she entertains. So he/she is bound to be disconcerted on learning that the "natural law," as defined by St. Thomas Aquinas in the 13th century, is "nothing other than the light of understanding infused in us by God, whereby we understand what must be done and what must be avoided. God gave this light and this law to man at creation" (12).

So the "natural law" has nothing whatever to do with observable behavior. In this scheme, natural law is a manifestation of the eternal law, lodged in the mind of God.

Adopt this (heteronomous) standpoint, and the encyclical makes powerful sense. So, for example, it is quite wrong to think of freedom as meaning independence and autonomy. On the contrary, human freedom is fulfilled in submission to God's law (17). True freedom lies in obedience. So freedom itself needs to be set free (87). A quotation from St. Augustine comes in handy here: "In the house of the Lord, slavery is free" (87).

This is where the encyclical is most at odds with "modern thought." It rejects utterly the Jean-Paul Sartre notion that "reason itself creates values and moral norms" (40).

It pooh-poohs the idea that "freedom is the absolute source of values," and that in the absence of knowable truth, "sincerity and authenticity" are the proper criteria of action (42). It will have no truck with "behaviorism," which "misuses scientific research": "Arguing from the great variety of customs, behavior patterns and institutions present in humanity, these theories end up, if not with the outright denial of universal human values, at least with a relativistic conception of morality" (33).

Likewise dismissed, and for the same reason, are opinion polls: "Some ethicists . . . are tempted to take as the standard for their discipline and even for its operative norms the results of a statistical study of concrete human behavior patterns and the opinions about morality encountered in the majority of people" (46).

But counting heads is not the way to discover the good. This is indeed a traditional problem in moral theory. How does one get from an "is" to an "ought," from the description of human behavior to an obligation of conscience?

Some have accused the church of falling into the "naturalistic fallacy," by regarding biological laws as determining morality: "It was, they maintain, on the basis of a naturalistic understanding of the sexual act that contraception, direct sterilization, autoeroticism, premarital sexual relations, homosexual relations and artificial insemination were condemned as morally unacceptable" (47).

The encyclical rejects this charge, insisting that biology is taken up into the personal sphere because the person is a body-soul unity, a *compositum*. Sexual activity has a God-given meaning in itself.

Veritatis Splendor sees in the modern "dissociation of the moral act from its bodily dimension" a revival of the ancient heresy condemned by St. Paul in 1 Corinthians 6:9: "The immoral, idolaters, adulterers, sexual perverts, thieves, the greedy, drunkards, revilers, robbers" are all excluded from the kingdom of God (49).

St. Paul is quoted here not in a fundamentalist manner as a proof text. The text is cited because of its importance in tradition. It was taken up by the Council of Trent, which condemned as "mortal sins" such "immoral practices." John Paul already stated this in *Reconciliatio et Penitentia*. But apparently no one was listening.

John Paul knows his message will be unwelcome to many, both within and without the church. It is "a stumbling block to the Jews and folly to the Gentiles" (85 quoting 1 Cor 17:23-24). But he has thrown down the gauntlet. From his own perspective, opposition will merely prove how right he is.

One of the most revealing passages contrasts democratic methods with those of the church: "While exchanges and conflicts of opinion may constitute normal expressions of public life in a representative democracy, moral teaching certainly cannot depend upon respect for a process; indeed it is in no way established by following the rules and deliberative procedures typical of a democracy" (113).

What follows? *"Dissent, in the form of carefully orchestrated protests and polemics carried on in the media, is opposed to ecclesial communion and to a correct understanding of the hierarchical constitution of the people of God"* (113, emphasis in the text).

So it is now up to the bishops to take "appropriate measures." The final section leaves no room for doubt: "In carrying out our task, we (bishops) are all assisted by theologians; even so, theological opinions constitute neither the rule nor the norm of our teaching. Its authority is derived by the assistance of the Holy Spirit and in communion *cum Petro et sub Petro* (with Peter and under Peter), from our fidelity to the Catholic faith which comes to us from the Apostles" (113).

That account suggests that episcopal teaching somehow swings clear from theological teaching and has another source. Yet it will surely be pointed out that the papal teaching itself is based on the views of a narrow group of theologians, some of them linked to Opus Dei.

No theologians are named. So another line of defense from moral theologians will be to say that their views have been caricatured in the encyclical, and therefore that "they have not been hit, not even grazed."

That may not be enough to save them. ❏

59

Pope soldiers on, carries weight of seven decades

(October 22, 1993) Karol Wojtyla, Archbishop of Kraków, was elected pope Oct. 16, 1978 — 15 years ago. He doubtless would say that the anniversary of his priestly ordination, Nov. 1, 1946, was more important, for he insists that he remains first and foremost a priest.

John Paul was 73 May 18. Last time he was back in Poland, he heard people singing the traditional Polish greeting, *Sto lat* — meaning "May you live to be a hundred years." He quipped: "If this pope lives so long, your grandchildren will be coming to see him. And what could be done with such an old pope? I can see only one solution: He'll have to run away and live in a monastery."

He was not entirely joking. He might one day go back to the Carmelite monastery he tried to join in 1939. ("You're born for higher things," they said: *Ad majora natus es*, which sounds very worldly coming from Carmelites.) In 1995 he will reach 75, the age at which bishops must tender their resignation — to him. But to whom can the bishop of Rome offer to resign?

Official Vatican sources insist the pope's health is fine and that he suffers no ill effects from his July 15, 1992, operation. Suggest the contrary and you will be accused of "wishful thinking" — wanting him dead. I expect he will soldier on, health and God permitting, until the year 2000, a date which fascinates him like the eye of the basilisk. The Vatican objects to resignation talk because it suggests a lame-duck papacy.

Everything the pope does — especially his energetic travels — refutes the speculation. Though the foreign trips are a little less demanding than they once were, they still take a heavy toll on the accompanying cardinals and journalists, who return whey-faced saying, "never again."

The pope's intellectual stamina is no less astonishing. His 10th encyclical, *Veritatis Splendor*, is his most substantial, soporific and weighty to date — and that's saying something.

The response to it, like the response to his pontificate generally, has been mixed. Some think Pope John Paul is saving the church from 1960s wimpishness, while others believe his utter rejection of modernity is undermining its credibility. Compromise is hardly possible between such contradictory views.

But one can still try to figure him out. One way to do this is to snapshot him as the decades of his life roll by. Was he destined to write *Veritatis Splendor*?

1930. At 10, Karol — "Lolek" as he was known — is about to move on to high school. April 13, 1929, tragedy had struck: His mother, Emilia, died giving birth to a stillborn daughter. So at a stroke Karol lost his mother and the sister he would never know. For all his admiration for "family life," he hardly knew it personally.

He is alone in his one-parent family with his disciplinarian father, a junior officer in the Polish army. His brother Edmund, a medical doctor, is 14 years older and absent. Edmund will die two years later in a scarlet fever epidemic.

His father's earlier service in the Austro-Hungarian army and his mother's family origins in Silesia mean that German is already his natural second language.

During World War I, his father heard propaganda lectures from Max Scheler, the phenomenologist. Scheler claimed the Central Powers were defending Christian civilization against the Godless French, the autocratic Russians and the mercantile Protestant English.

1940. At 20 Wojtyla has just seen the collapse of his hopes, personally and nationally. His university is closed down, its professors hauled away to concentration camps. Poland is humiliated and enslaved after a mere 20 years of independence.

Wojtyla's response: a play (now lost) on the Book of Job. His Job suffers atrociously, but ends up with a resurrection vision. Hope is born on the other side of despair; faith is the only antidote to the absurd.

1950. At 30 Wojtyla has been a priest for just over three years, and is back from Rome with a thesis on St. John of the Cross. The "liberation" brought to Poland by Marxism (in fact by the Red Army) is a cheat, the rhetoric of progress a lie.

He writes a play about Adam Chmielowski, an artist who gave up painting to serve the poor of Kraków. It is the key to his own vocation: The poet-actor became a priest to lead a spiritual resistance movement.

1960. At 40 Wojtyla, moral philosophy professor in the Catholic University of Lublin, has written a thesis: Can one base a moral system on the value ethics of Max Scheler? He answers no. He becomes auxiliary bishop of Kraków in 1958, shortly before John XXIII succeeds Pius XII. But he keeps his Lublin chair.

He teaches a rejigged Thomism based on the dignity of the human person. He claims that artificial contraception degrades women by turning them into sex objects. His lecture notes — translated into French in 1965 — will affect *Humanae Vitae*.

He defends human rights in Poland. But Leszek Kolokowski asks whether he attacks communism because it is "godless" or because it is "totalitarian."

1970. Wojtyla, now a cardinal, is more widely known thanks to Vatican II (1962-65). He defends religious liberty stoutly, but more as a right the church claims against atheist regimes than one it concedes to fellow Christians or nonbelievers.

He finds some of the council's statements in *Gaudium et Spes* about the omnipresence of grace in the world to be wildly optimistic. He believes that the shadow of the cross falls across all human endeavors. Chapter 3 of *Veritatis Splendor* exhorts us "not to evacuate Christ's cross." Perhaps that is why, although a member of the Pontifical Commission on Population Problems, he never attends a single meeting.

Still, in comparison with Poland's primate, Cardinal Stefan Wyszinski, who thinks Vatican II breaks the cohesion of the Polish Catholic church, Wojtyla is committed to the council. In Kraków he supervises its gradual, prudent and controlled implementation. But he is already suspicious of the Dutch church and theologians like Hans Küng who are linked with the journal *Concilium*. He accuses them of emptying the churches of the West with their secularizing theology. They show insufficient subordination to papal teaching authority.

For him *Humanae Vitae* dramatizes the crisis of authority. He privately called for a special synod to denounce "dissident" theologians or even bishops. Nothing in his Polish experience prepares him for the concept of "loyal opposition."

1980. Wojtyla is now pope after the brief interlude of the smiling John Paul I. He adopts his predecessor's double-barreled name, which neatly sidesteps the question of whether he is going to be more like John XXIII or Paul VI. He would have preferred the name Pope Stanislaus I, but this was rejected as "too nationalistic" — rather like an Irish pope calling himself Patrick.

There is early euphoria, an ecstatic honeymoon. His election is a triple surprise: the first non-Italian since 1523, the first Slav ever, the youngest since Pius IX in 1846. He also brings a formidable array of talents and experience to the post: poet, philosopher, linguist, actor, quarry worker.

But most of all he is Polish. Though he tries to downplay this, and declares that from now on he will be "witness to a universal love," his Polish experience colors all his thinking. His return home in June 1979 is a triumphant royal progress, illustrating the reality of spiritual power.

The Polish government has all the physical power needed to keep him out, but it cannot do so without a revolution. Solidarity was born of the self-confidence he inspired in Polish workers. He tells them his election was "providential" — God's way of letting the Slav voice be heard in the church, compensation for all those years of torment and suffering, Job's consolation, a hint of resurrection.

His message is the slogan of all Polish revolutions: "For our freedom — and yours!" To the world he says: Open wide your frontiers, cast down your barriers.

1990. By now he can feel that the frontiers of the impossible have been pushed back. In Prague he rejoices with fellow intellectual President Václav Havel that a free Central Europe has been restored to the map.

Yet if his message to the nations has won some sort of hearing, especially east of the River Elbe, his message to the church is not always so gratefully received. He comes down particularly hard on two groups a church leader is ill-advised to tangle with: bishops and theologians.

Veritatis Splendor represents a determined effort to get bishops to wake up to the danger of loose-cannon theologians. If the "appropriate measures" it calls for are implemented, there will be sackings in seminaries and other Catholic institutions.

Not all bishops will take the relaxed, laid-back approach of Cardinal Basil Hume in Westminster. Crisis? What crisis? There may be one somewhere else, but here we get on well with our moral theologians.

But Hume was named by Pope Paul VI. It does nothing for episcopal morale today to know that bishops are being appointed for their readiness to toe the most rigid party line. As for theologians, whose task is to think for the church as well as with it, credibility is not served by keeping men like Hans Küng, Leonardo Boff or Charles Curran in intellectual limbo.

They have shown their loyalty in adversity. They differ on noninfallible questions. They have no other home but the church. An amnesty would be in order. But the message of *Veritatis Splendor* is that it will have to wait for the next pontificate. Meantime, vigilance will be increased rather than diminished.

Two quotations spring to mind. Aldous Huxley: "You can do anything with bayonets — except sit upon them." And Benedictine Christopher Butler, formerly abbot of Downside Abbey and auxiliary bishop of Westminster: "An authority that does not address the conscience, will soon cease to be an authority." ❏

60

Pope gives interview, decries capitalism

An interview with Pope John Paul II, which appeared in recent editions of *La Stampa*, *Liberation*, and the *Guardian*, is only the second substantial interview with the pope. It was conducted by an old friend, Jas Gawronski, a Polish émigré who for many years was a Moscow correspondent for RAI (Italian television).

Only two questions touched on personal matters. The pope does not keep a diary ("I have other things to do") and, unlike Pope Paul VI, never feels lonely: "Perhaps I have another temperament, and besides I always have near me people who are close to me and are my friends. Neither do I make the decisions alone. I work collegially with the episcopates, with the curia." Note the two senses of "collegiality."

Asked what difference "being Polish" has made to his papacy, John Paul gave a rather surprising answer: "Having lived in a country which has had to struggle for its freedom, in a country vulnerable to aggression and the dictates of its neighbors, I have been led to sympathize with the plight of countries in the Third World which also are subject to another type of dependence, especially an economic one."

A more revealing passage about his homeland concerned its fatal weakness: "In part it is Poland's vice, a kind of atavistic vice: an exaggerated individualism which leads to the fragmentation and division of the sociopolitical scene. Its forte lies in opposition and not in constructive proposals that lead to successful government." That is his explanation of why Solidarity, in particular, failed to make the transition from opposition to government.

But he does not accept that the communists in Poland and Lithuania have "made a comeback." He thinks their electoral success was "a reaction to the ineffectiveness of the new governments." It should not cause surprise. The former communists are the only people "who know how politics works, how the parliament operates."

Gawronski, having informed the pope that he was perhaps more popular today than at any time since he became pope, asked about "criticisms" occasionally heard even in "your" Poland. It would have been better not to have introduced Poland at this stage, for it meant that John Paul replied only to the rather specialized "Polish" critique of his pontificate. He dealt sternly with those who say Poland should "catch up" with Western Europe: "Naturally I am not opposed to Poland's so-called entry into Europe, but I am against turning this endeavor into a kind of idol, a false idol." For him Poland does not have to "rejoin" Europe; it is already there, at the heart of Europe, part of its definition.

For these idolatrous "Westernizers," "Poland's entry into Europe would mean the introduction into Poland of that ultraliberal, consumeristic system devoid of values, introducing it through the force of propaganda. It all goes back to this."

Poland has to keep its own values and, above all, identity, toughened in the crucible of communism, but now threatened by the desire "to adopt in an uncritical and blind fashion the customs of the West."

The critique of "savage" capitalism comes in at this point. As in Latvia, he spoke of the "kernel or seeds of truth" in Marxism: "In communism there was a concern for the community, whereas capitalism is individualistic." Of course communism demanded a high price in loss of human freedom and trampling on human rights, but "we should not overlook the good things achieved by communism: the efforts to overcome unemployment, the concern for the poor."

That magnanimity toward a defeated foe contrasts with the pope's toughness on unreconstructed capitalism. He conceded that capitalism had changed since the days of Leo XIII and *Rerum Novarum*: "Today's capitalism is different. It has introduced social safety nets, thanks to the trade unions; it has enacted social policies and is monitored by the state and the unions." However, "in some countries of the world it has remained in its 'savage' state, almost as it was in the past century." A pity no examples were provided.

Pope John Paul says he is doing no more than denouncing, with Leo XIII, the opposing temptations of unrestrained capitalism (or liberalism) and unrestrained collectivism. Yet he rejects the notion of presenting the church's social doctrine as "a third way," as "utopian." That makes it hard to know what models of society, if any, he is proposing. He makes, for example, no mention of democracy.

There is only one oblique reference to *Veritatis Splendor*. It comes in a very specific context. After saying that his Polish experience of oppression gave him a special sympathy with the Third World, he went on: "The powerful of this world do not always look with favor upon such a pope. At times they even deprecate him for his stance on moral principles. They ask, for example, for license to practice abortion, contraception . . . things that the pope cannot grant because the charge handed down to him from God is to defend the human person, his dignity, his rights, among which the right to life is foremost."

Pope John Paul frequently speaks of himself in the third person. He says not "I" but "the pope." Even so, he does not claim that "the pope" had a hand in the fall of communism. He attributes the "decisive role to Christianity as such, with its tenets, with its religious and moral message, with its intrinsic defense of the human being and his rights." ❑

61

Uneasy pope eyes joyous dance of African church

(April 22, 1994) Rome — Opening ceremonies for the particular synod for Africa began on the octave of Easter, April 10. It was "solemnly inaugurated" by Pope John Paul II with a high Mass in St. Peter's Basilica.

Never before have Africans — priests, sisters, laypeople — taken over St. Peter's with such uninhibited musical joie de vivre. There were drums and handclaps and dancing and joyous singing in 15 African languages. There was ululation — a kind of high-pitched wailing, a sign of happiness.

It all seemed very strange in the baroque setting of St. Peter's. The bits of Gregorian chant that were sung — the Sanctus and Agnus Dei — sounded effete and halfhearted in comparison.

African music sets the feet tapping and the whole body in motion. It is intended for the open air. The proof is that in the Ethiopian rite used for what we redundantly call the "responsorial psalm" (what other kind of psalm is there?) the three kings (from the Epiphany) were shielded by a multicolored umbrella.

The even more ancient Coptic rite, which uses clashing cymbals rather than drums, introduced the gospel of the day. It was about the doubting apostle Thomas who, though not a witness of the resurrection, yet proclaimed his faith: "My Lord and my God."

This brought a response from Jesus, which Rudolf Bultmann — the great if at times misguided exegete — called the "ninth beatitude": "Blessed are those who have not seen, and yet have believed." That enshrines a lesson for all, not just for Africans.

While African music sets the feet stomping and the whole body moving, this does not work for everyone. Swiss Guards with their halberds looked impassively on — but they were merely doing their duty.

Cardinal Joseph Ratzinger, sitting in the front row, twitched not and looked ill at ease as though he wished he were someplace else. John Paul seemed to be waiting for the music to stop so he could get on with the serious business of his homily. But you can't hurry Africans.

The most astonishing thing, however, was the complete immobility of the 14 African cardinals and 122 bishops, sitting or standing there in serried ranks.

That Ratzinger and the pope should regard African singing and dancing as something to be observed as a spectacle "out there" is understandable. But that African bishops should do the same is surprising and perhaps sinister. Is not this their synod?

No is the only honest answer. The synod is officially described as a Synod for Africa. It is not really a Synod *of* Africa.

In his homily John Paul tried to answer this and other objections. Surely the natural setting for an African Synod is Africa.

This truism has been answered in three stages over the last few months. First, Cardinal Joseph Arinze, the Nigerian head of the Council for Inter-Religious Dialogue, said it could not be held in Africa for that would have been to privilege one or other of several theological schools.

Belgian Archbishop Jan Schotte, synod secretary, in a great press conference on the eve of the synod explained that Rome was the place for "first division" synods, and only "second class" synods were held someplace else.

John Paul, to put it bluntly, talked in riddles: "This synod has a totally African character and, at the same time, participates in the full universality of the church, as she is represented by the ministry of the Successor of St. Peter. Therefore, we wish this to be a real African Synod that goes to the roots. Hence, the church in Africa is African and at the same time universal."

I cannot claim to throw light on this. It seems to mean that African bishops have to behave with docility. Otherwise their funds will be cut off. They are entirely financed by the Congregation for the Evangelization of Peoples, whose head is the Slovakian Cardinal Jozef Tomko.

Tomko does not seem to be very smart. In a recent interview he explained the reluctance to introduce a permanent diaconate into Africa by the fact that "in the prolonged absence of a priest, catechists have been known to take over both the priest's powers and authority."

How frightfully shocking. Ordain the catechists, and the pseudo-problem disappears.

What happened, therefore, on the octave of Easter was this: With significant participation of women, the Africans were allowed to be themselves, let their hair down and let it all hang out for two and a half hours. But what happens next is none of their business.

The sprightly African women will dance off the scene and screen. Some will say the singing and dancing never happened. The chaps will take over. A chance will have been missed. And that's that.

Yet if the African Synod's end is in its beginning, then the portent for the future is that the Africans will dance their way into inventing an African church in which their liturgy is appreciated, not as an occasional concession but as a birthright. ❏

62

Synods, meetings are prelude to conclave

(May 20, 1994) Rome — Not long after the synod for Africa, actually in mid-June and once delayed because of Pope John Paul's accident, comes the fifth meeting of the entire college of 141 cardinals.

Until this pontificate, the cardinals never met as a body except when they came together in a conclave to elect the pope.

These regular meetings with the cardinals are one of Pope John Paul II's most striking innovations. It meant upgrading the College of Cardinals, sometimes known as the "senate" of the church.

Yet the office of cardinal is not scriptural. It was invented only toward the end of the first millennium. After Vatican II it seemed to be on its way out, having little place in a church that stressed the importance of bishops as pastors of local churches.

Paul VI toyed with the idea of entrusting the election of his successor not to the traditional College of Cardinals but to a special synod of presidents of episcopal conferences (some of whom would be cardinals, but most would not).

But then he took fright at this departure from tradition and restricted his reform to excluding from the conclave cardinals over age 80.

That made the over-80s furious back in 1972. Cardinal Alfredo Ottaviani's jowls wobbled, Cardinal Eugène Tisserant's beard bobbed as they went on TV to denounce this move. Yet it was an important step. For in such matters, a small departure from precedent is as important as a big one: It says that change is possible.

John Paul II has not restored the over-80s to the conclave. On the other hand, all 141 cardinals, whatever their age, are invited to the June 13 and 14 meeting to discuss the next encyclical — according to Cardinal John J. O'Connor an antiabortion blockbuster — a wider role for retired bishops, and "the church's preparations to mark the year 2000."

No doubt they will have earnest discussions on these worthy topics, whatever they turn out to mean. But they will surely give some thought to the succession, given John Paul's age — 74 on May 18.

These meetings of cardinals have often been described as "dress rehearsals for the next conclave." Though only doubtfully true of previous meetings when there were no scares about the pope's health, it seems likely to be verified this time around. With this in mind, I looked through the contributions made by the cardinals who were present at the Synod for Africa. All 20 heads of Roman dicasteries, or departments, were present, and two of them are African. Then there were 12 more African cardinals still working in their home countries.

Was the next pope among them? I have already given my reasons why Nigerian Cardinal Francis J. Arinze seems the most plausible African candidate. He has run a tight ship in Rome since 1985 as president of the Council for Inter-Religious Dialogue. He has shown himself a good talent spotter.

His main area of interest — dialogue with Islam — will be of the utmost importance throughout the next two decades. Only through dialogue can moderate Muslims be weaned from fundamentalism. Confrontation can only make matters worse. For Arinze "spiritual emulation" is the only permissible form of rivalry. In preparation for the Lebanon synod, he consulted local Muslims about the preparatory texts that concerned them — a unique instance of practical dialogue.

But would the 13 other African cardinals vote for him? They might well. For he is clearly the outstanding "African" candidate. Arinze was one of the three presidents of the Synod for Africa. He had a "good synod," in the sense that he did not put a foot wrong. Maybe some Africans think he is too "Romanized." But others would see that as an advantage. Born Nov. 1, 1932, he is just the right age.

Moreover, there are no other serious African contenders. Cardinal Bernardin Gantin, 72, prefect of the Congregation for Bishops, is a friendly man. He provided the following summary of his speech to the synod: "In the evangelization of Africa, the first and irreplaceable responsibility of the bishops goes to the poor of every kind: the disinherited, elites and intellectuals, the young, women, our distant brothers in the Americas, soldiers."

That was the full text. Provided by the author. No expansion. No comment.

Most of the Roman cardinals confined themselves to saying what their office was doing or might do for Africa. Thus, Australian Cardinal Edward Cassidy talked about ecumenism, which began in Africa as the irrelevance of divisions derived from 16th century Europe appeared.

Argentinian Eduardo Pironio talked about lay movements. Bavarian Cardinal Joseph Ratzinger threw in some learned doubts on the concept of "inculturation."

This prepared the ground for the Spaniard Antonio Maria Javierre Ortas, prefect of the Congregation for Divine Worship and the Sacraments — the man who gave us altar girls. Immediately before the synod he produced the document on "Inculturation in the Liturgy" that seemed to preempt the synod debate. He addressed this topic in Spanish — not one of the main languages of Africa. He said his document was written "by mandate of the Holy Father." One cannot say he was outstandingly well-received.

This was routine bureaucratic stuff. What would be the message of Angelo Sodano, cardinal secretary of state, usually considered the most important man in the Vatican after the pope? He offered a fascinating glimpse of the Roman mind. His world is entirely pope-centered.

Sodano said: "Pope John Paul II has already made 10 pastoral visits to Africa and Madagascar and has been to 39 countries. This synod is a fresh proof of the pastoral solicitude of the successor of Peter for Africa. Besides, to make for ever-closer bonds with the local bishops, the Roman pontiff has in Africa 24 diplomatic representatives, whether nuncios or apostolic delegates."

Sodano, as head of the Vatican diplomatic service, might be expected to make that point. But he seemed to judge the African churches as flourishing because they received the nuncios so well.

Further proof of vitality, Sodano suggested, was the increase in the circulation of the weekly edition of the Vatican newspaper, *L'Osservatore Romano*, and the ever greater popularity in Africa of Vatican Radio.

Cardinal Eduardo Martinez Somalo, prefect of the Congregation for Institutes of Consecrated Life and Societies of Apostolic Life (it was much simpler when it was called "for Religious and Secular Institutes"), views the Synod for Africa as a dry run for the synod on religious life next October.

What he said does not bode well. He claimed to be worried by "certain trends of Western culture that would seek to mitigate the observance of the evangelical counsels, regarding them as an imposition on the modern mind." That's new.

The October synod on religious life is "providential," he explained, "because it will enable the church to deal with the ambiguous modernization of religious life." One can foresee a synod that will be much livelier than the Synod for Africa.

Cardinal Achille Silvestrini, prefect of the Congregation for Oriental Churches, is usually interesting. An Italian dark horse candidate, he pointed out that there already existed two ancient "African" rites with their own liturgy and canon law. The Coptic church in Egypt links up with the tradition of the Greek fathers like Origen and Clement of Alexandria. It somehow survived the assaults of Islam, and is the last survivor of the once-proud church of North Africa. It is of special importance for the dialogue with Islam.

The tradition of Alexandria drifted down to Ethiopia where it gave rise to the Ethiopian church, another survivor from antiquity. Silvestrini suggested that it could serve as the model for a genuine African rite, and therefore that the whole of Abyssinia should move from the Congregation for the Evangelization of Peoples (formerly Propaganda Fide) to his congregation.

This would not be to the liking of the prefect of propaganda, Slovakian Cardinal Jozef Tomko — the man who masterminded the synod and insisted it be held in Rome.

But Silvestrini's suggestion raises some wider questions: At what point are the local churches of Africa to be regarded as mature and adult sister churches, entering the ordinary administration of the church under the Congregation for Bishops? Is it only financial considerations that keep them tied to the apron strings of the Congregation for the Evangelization of Peoples? And should finance prevail over theology?

The conclusion is rather bleak. It seems unlikely that the next pope was present at the Synod for Africa. But 32 or a quarter of his electors were. That thought is even more alarming. ❏

63

New catechism is safe, patristic, predictable

(June 17, 1994) I have been dreading writing this article ever since the day too many months back when I picked up a copy of the French edition of the *Catechism of the Catholic Church* at the Paris airport. How could my feelings of irritation be kept in check?

Perhaps the best way would be to concentrate on Part 4, devoted to Christian prayer, which concludes the volume. Here, I told myself, we can avoid theological controversy and test whether the book is really communicating.

Moreover, this section has been praised by Bernard Häring who declared that he "would like to see it published separately in a handsome format, accessible to everyone."

I wish I could share his enthusiasm. Most of what this section has to say is unexceptional. And there's the rub. For what is obvious and unexceptional is also unexciting. One is very conscious that it is translated from the French, and that it has been thought in French. This is the best of French spirituality of the 1960s.

Here it is on *le coeur*, the heart, echoing the admirable *Vocabulaire de la théologie biblique* published in 1962. It is the heart that prays. If our hearts are far from God, the words on our lips are vain. Then: "The heart is our hidden center, beyond the grasp of our reason and of others; only the Spirit of God can fathom the human heart and know it fully. The heart is the place of decision, deeper than our psychic drives. It is the place of truth, where we choose life or death. It is the place of encounter, because as image of God, we live in relation; it is the place of covenant" (2563).

A deep insight is struggling to come to birth here through the Gallic rhetoric: something to do with the way we relate to God on the deepest level of our being. Some religious literary allusions might have helped. Such as Blaise Pascal: "The heart has its reasons that reason does not know." John Henry Newman's motto: *"Cor ad cor loquitur"* ("Heart speaks to heart"). And maybe the Prayer of the Heart in the Russian Orthodox tradition.

But instead after the passage about the heart, where women can feel included and perhaps superior, we are brought down with a bump: "Christian prayer is a covenant relationship between God and man in Christ. It is the action of God and man, springing forth both from the Holy Spirit and ourselves, wholly directed to the Father, in union with the Son of God made man" (2565). Man, man, man: pounding away three times in two sentences. Even I, who have not always been particularly sensitive to the need for inclusive language, find that very painful, unnecessary, and gratuitously offensive.

So the promising theme of the "heart" as the God faculty is abandoned. Much later on, however, the text of 1 Corinthians 12:3 is quoted, which would have made a natural transition: "No one can say 'Jesus is the Lord' except in the Holy Spirit." That means that the ability to say "Jesus is the Lord" — which is the very essence of Christian faith — is only possible in the Holy Spirit. Therefore, to begin to pray at all attests to the presence of the Holy Spirit as God in our hearts.

One could say that the rest of prayer is a working-out of the implications of that statement. The CCC knows this in theory, but spoils it by sexism again, describing the Holy Spirit as "the interior Master of Christian prayer," adding that "he is the artisan of the living tradition of prayer." Considering that the Holy Spirit is the one member of the Trinity who has been given some feminine titles, this is rough.

The CCC is a tissue of quotations, mostly from patristic authors. Some of them no doubt sounded better in the Greek or Latin but they come out in English with considerable banality. Here is St. Ambrose, patron of the Ambrosian rite and bank in Milan, urging Christians — that is, us — to frequent reading of the scripture: "Let them remember, however, that prayer should accompany the reading of sacred scripture, so that a dialogue takes place between God and man. For we speak to him when we pray; we listen to him when we read the divine oracles." The divine what? Quotations can adorn, illumine, enrich. But CCC uses patristic quotes as padding. It is as though nothing, however banal, can be said without patristic authority. It would have been much better just to quote Pascal again: *"Dieu parle bien de Dieu"* — "God (in the Bible) speaks well of God."

Matthew 7:7 advises the would-be prayer to knock and knock again. This immediately prompts the authors to think of Guigo the Carthusian who observed: "Seek in reading and you will find in meditating; knock in mental prayer and it will be opened to you in contemplation."

These notions are later explained, somewhat laboriously. But Guigo the Carthusian, I feel, should have been left in the decent obscurity from which he was dragged. It seems to be monastic forms of prayer that are being recommended. Is this what the kids need?

True, the teacher is advised to "mediate" this material. But I find it very difficult to imagine any path from Guigo the Carthusian to the contemporary classroom.

The CCC states an admirable principle, which it ascribes to Jesus: "The wise teacher takes hold of us where we are, and leads us progressively toward the Father" (2607). That wise example should have been followed by the CCC itself.

Of course, one has to admit that teaching people to pray is not, on the whole, something that can be done from books. How-to books tend to fail because the starting point of prayer is openness to the Holy Spirit, and no one can predict what will happen next. But what we so often get here is exhortation, pulpit rhetoric. Commenting on "pray for us now and at the hour of our death," we are told: "We give ourselves over to her now, in the today of our lives. And our trust broadens further . . . to surrender the hour of death wholly to her care. May she be there as she was at her Son's death on the cross. May she welcome us as our Mother at the hour of our passing" (2676).

Maybe a fine peroration. But it illumines nothing. But such is the stylistic inconsistency of the work that this bout of exhortation is immediately followed by what can only be called a page torn from an encyclopedia: "Medieval piety in the West developed the prayer of the rosary as a popular substitute for the Liturgy of the Hours. In the East, the liturgy called the Akathistos and the Paraclesis remained closer to the choral office in the Byzantine churches, while the Armenian, Coptic and Syriac traditions preferred popular hymns and songs to the Mother of God" (2676). OK, this piece of liturgical learning is in small print. But having raised the point, the CCC might have explained where these traditions are today. The Armenians, Copts and Syriacs are all hard-pressed to survive in the Mideast.

They are symbolically important as instances of that "inculturation" that is recommended as the next stage, the adaptation to local circumstances that the CCC recommends. But they have had hardly any influence in the West. The CCC notes the existence of "schools of spirituality" but does not say much about them.

Having boldly said that the charism or special talent for spiritual direction can be found in both men and women, it then quotes St. John of the Cross as saying that "the person who wishes to advance toward perfection should take care into whose hands he entrusts himself, for as the master is, so will the disciple be" (2690). This notion of "advancing toward perfection" betrays a very monastic view of prayer.

Where does this all come home today? Where are the schools of prayer? "Prayer groups" are somewhat nervously commended, provided "they drink from the authentic wellsprings of Christian prayer" and remember that "concern for ecclesial communion" is the real test (2689).

The family as the "domestic church" is the first school of prayer. There young children learn to pray "as church" and to persevere in prayer. A "prayer corner" is recommended "with the sacred scripture and icons" and "this kind of little oratory fosters prayer in common" (2691). Do they really mean icons? Or just images?

One can't be sure. But as every parent knows, while young children may have a feeling for prayer, adolescents do not respond so readily to the "domestic church," however prayerful their parents.

The liturgy is the other great school of prayer. The psalms are commended for the way they combine the personal and the communal. The "Jewishness" of Jesus is stressed here, and with it an incipient, balanced Mariology. This part is excellent. Jesus "learns to pray from his Mother, who kept all the great things the Almighty had done and treasured them in her heart" (2599).

The world and justice break in only fitfully. "Give us this day our daily bread" prompts the reflection that in the beatitudes "poverty" is the virtue of sharing. We need to share "so that the abundance of some may remedy the needs of others." It is all rather timid. Even the *audemus dicere* or "boldness" with which the Our Father is introduced in the liturgies of East and West is scaled down. The Greek word *parrhesia* means, it says, "straightforward simplicity, filial trust, joyous assurance, humble boldness, the certainty of being loved" (2777).

That is bland and reassuring. But another interpretation of *parrhesia* is that it means rather courage in speaking out in the church. It is a virtue much needed today.

You wouldn't think it from this treatment. It turns prayer into a carefully controlled gas jet rather than an all-consuming fire of the Spirit. It prefers conformity to empowering and responsibility.

I notice that in the new and revised edition of Fr. Richard McBrien's *Catholicism*, a totally new Chapter 29 ("Worship, Liturgy, Prayer and Devotions") covers much the same ground as the CCC.

I know which work I would recommend to someone looking for guidance on prayer. Or anything else for that matter. An alert mind always does better than a committee. ❏

64

Catholics try to digest papal bombshell

(July 1, 1994) Vatican bombshells are often timed to coincide with the start of the summer vacation, when the opposition is unable to organize. So it was with *Humanae Vitae* in 1968. So it is now with *Sacerdotalis Ordinatio*, the apostolic letter of Pope John Paul II declaring that priestly ordination is for men (males) only.

The most frank and brutal response has been that of Tübingen, Germany, canon lawyer Norbert Greinacher. He calls on the pope to resign on the grounds that he has "separated himself from the faith of the church." He describes the letter as "theological nonsense."

His bishop, Walter Kasper, former professor of theology at Tübingen, alleged that, on the contrary, it was Greinacher who was separating himself from the faith of the church. Greinacher replies that he has statements up to January 1993 in which Kasper accepted that "there is no theological argument against women's ordination."

Down under in Australia, Dominican Fr. Philip Kennedy, who has a doctorate in theology from the Catholic University of Fribourg in Switzerland, wrote an article in the Melbourne daily, *Herald Sun*.

"Thomas Aquinas wrote," says Kennedy, "that when it came to the truth, it did not matter who was speaking. I am no Aquinas, but having carefully studied the pope's latest letter, I think his argument is invalid and does not square with the historical evidence."

Kennedy has had two letters from the archbishop of Melbourne, Thomas F. Little, asking him to promise in writing not to "preach against the pope."

A casuist might point out to both Little and Kennedy that acceptance of the papal letter does not entail accepting its arguments as valid. Admittedly this leaves the decision swinging in the wind, entirely dependent on papal authority.

In the United States, scattered academics were slow to respond, but an open letter to the pope was passed and signed by 23 who affirmed the "indispensable importance of intellectual debate and discussion in the ongoing process of faith and spiritual development." The academics stated the pope's letter "may have dire consequences for the life of the church."

Bishops are less free than theologians. Hansjörg Vogel, 43, was elected by the cathedral chapter bishop of Basel, Switzerland, only last February.

He starts with a resounding platitude: "The apostolic letter of Pope John Paul II about priestly ordination being reserved to men merely puts down in writing the tradition of our church, and declares it to be definitive."

But then Vogel picks up courage: "This decision shocked many of us. In the eyes of many, the theological discussion of this topic is not yet concluded. To my mind, this apostolic letter raises more new theological questions than it solves old ones." One of the problems to which *Sacerdotalis Ordinatio* gives rise is that it seems to have invented a new category of teaching that is deemed "definitive" without being infallible. Hitherto, in the exercise of his ordinary magisterium the pope was thought to speak "authoritatively," but in a non-definitive way. His teaching carried weight, but it was not the absolutely last word. Only clearly flagged ex cathedra statements were thought to be "irreformable," that is, not subject to revision. The concept of "non-infallible but definitive" is confusing, perhaps intentionally so. A lot of theological firepower will concentrate on the meaning of "definitive." There will be room for canonical and theological quibbles.

The process has already begun. An example comes from the Belgian bishops who are faced with a particularly disturbed laity. The theology faculty at Leuven University expressed its "consternation" at the papal letter.

Fifty-nine members of the Flemish-speaking pastoral council passed a resolution inviting their bishops to urge Rome to "reopen" this question. (There was one negative vote and five abstentions). The Belgian bishops agreed to make representations to Rome. In their statement, they finesse on the word *definitively*. In ecclesiastical jargon, they explain, it means that something belongs to the received doctrine of the church as pope and bishops have proposed it; but to modern ears, to call something definitive sounds like a ban on thought or an attempt to impose silence.

Far from accepting that, the Belgian bishops say there's still much theological work to do. They suggest starting with "Authority and the Magisterium," and "Tradition as Norm."

These need translation. The first topic means: Yes, we accept that the pope can act in this way, but should he have done? The second means: Is tradition really the sole norm of faith, and if so what is the meaning of the Spirit's guidance? More generally, are there no new questions that have not been answered by tradition because they have not previously been asked?

Also relevant are questions about "the biblical conception of man and woman, and the value and relativity of our own culture." French Dominican Hervé Legrand says there are two ways in which one can "disobey" *Sacerdotalis Ordinatio*: the first is by minimizing its importance, the second is by exaggerating it.

According to this view, it would be equally wrong to dismiss the apostolic letter as the last threshings of a doomed patriarchy as to use it as the litmus test of Catholic orthodoxy. The question for theologians is what kind of assent does the document call for? What space does it leave for further discussion?

Sacerdotalis Ordinatio itself says that "this judgment is definitively to be held by all the church's faithful." This wording is important.

For there is a crucial distinction between saying that something is to be believed, for then one is in the realm of divine revelation, and saying that something is to be held, even if "definitively."

In the second case, there is no question of proposing something as a doctrine of faith, or expecting a response of faith to a dogma divinely revealed. Is that the loophole?

Very few have shown much enthusiasm for the apostolic letter. It has been not so much damned with faint praise as praised with faint damns. ❏

65

Pope discusses millennium with cardinals

(July 1, 1994) "It is good to be together again," quipped Pope John Paul II at lunch June 14 with the 114 cardinals in Rome for the special consistory, "without having to hold a conclave." That was close to the bone. The unspoken thought was that next time they meet it will be at the conclave to elect his successor.

The consistory was called to discuss the papal proposals for the celebration of the year 2000. John Paul revealed that he had personally written a 10,000-word letter issued in advance, described by one U.S. bishop as "off the wall."

Yet he repeated its main themes with even greater emphasis:
- The jubilee of the year 2000 is the culminating moment of the church, prepared by 20th century popes and anticipated by Vatican II.

- Preparations will include "continental" synods for North and South America, Asia and the Far East.

- The composition of a "new martyrology" of 20th century saints, with emphasis on the "younger" churches.

- A defense of his canonization policy: He has beatified 596 people and canonized 267 — more than all his 20th century predecessors combined. He was merely responding to Vatican II's teaching on the "universal vocation to holiness."

- Ecumenism, yes, but between "the Catholic West and the Orthodox East. . . . We cannot present ourselves divided before the lord of history in the year 2000." By ordaining women, the Anglicans have "indubitably created an obstacle to unity."

- The ecumenical movement is not stalled. The proof: During the way of the cross on Good Friday he had used prayers composed by Bartholomew, the ecumenical patriarch of Constantinople.

- The church needs *metanoia*, defined as "the discernment of its historical failings and the way its children have fallen short of the gospel."

The speech was a jumble in which it was difficult to distinguish theological attitudes from precise proposals. But neither was really up for debate. It is fair to say that the pontificate is increasingly perceived as idiosyncratic.

Yet Cardinal Hyacynthe Thiandoum, who succeeded the excommunicated Marcel Lefebvre as archbishop of Dakar, Senegal, in 1962, said at a press conference afterward that the regular consistories, revived by John Paul, were a good example of "participation" in the life of the church. It meant that cardinals were no longer "bystanders or spectators."

After this experience, one wonders.

The consistory is only a consultative body, highly secretive, and it did not really have time to develop any significant ideas or make alternative proposals. It broke up into eight language-based groups. The francophones emphasized that celebrating the millennium was not another D-Day commemoration. "We are not celebrating an event in the past," they declared, "but the ever-present fact that is at the heart of Christian faith: Jesus Christ, the same yesterday, today and tomorrow."

Cardinal Jean-Marie Lustiger, archbishop of Paris, said the model for any jubilee celebration was that proposed by Jesus in the synagogue at Nazareth: good news for the poor, freedom for captives, remission of debts, sight for the blind, liberation of the oppressed (Lk 4:18).

English-speakers emphasized the need for in-depth preparation of events. Such preparation should involve the episcopal conferences and the laity. It was not a matter of organizing great religious spectaculars. The jubilee concerned all Christians on the ground, where they live.

The English speakers also tried to finesse on the "courageous idea of a confession of the church's faults" proposed by John Paul. It is all too easy, they suggested, to deplore the errors of the past — Galileo and Jan Hus — rather than consider those of the present. But there was no time to pursue this interesting thought or make a list.

Much easier to denounce the faults of the modern world. The francophones ominously alleged that "it is not so much the authority of the pope that is rejected today, but the authority of Christ." They talked of the "moral darkness" that engulfs us. The idea of a pan-Christian meeting at Bethlehem or Jerusalem was generally welcomed.

But the prospect of a meeting with Jews and Muslims on Mount Sinai "in the footsteps of Abraham" bristled with diplomatic and theological difficulties. John Paul had emphasized the need for Muslims to grant religious liberty.

Cardinal Francis J. Arinze, responsible for dealings with Islam, said that Mount Sinai was a "symbol" of the interfaith path the church had to tread in the next millennium, not an event that could be fixed for the year 2000.

The consistory passed only two resolutions, both proposed by Americans.

Cardinal Bernard Law, archbishop of Boston, presented an appeal for Rwanda, adopted unanimously. It urged the nations of the world to "apply the principle of humanitarian intervention," which should prevail over notions of national sovereignty.

Cardinal John J. O'Connor, archbishop of New York, proposed a resolution, also adopted unanimously, on the U.N. population conference, scheduled for Cairo, Egypt, in September. It declared that the Cairo conference should not be approached with "an attitude of despair and of exaggerated fear concerning population trends." It warned that the measures proposed would legitimate "abortion on demand, sexual promiscuity and distorted notions of the family."

O'Connor took the lead in denouncing "cultural imperialism" and said that "the failed social policies of many developed countries should not be foisted on the world's poor."

It was all very predictable. John Paul uses meetings of cardinals to orchestrate support for his own pet projects. After the pope's disappointing meeting with President Clinton, the campaign against the Cairo conference is being conducted with great intensity.

The presidents of the Latin American bishops' conferences were summoned to another meeting June 25-26 on this theme; July 4-5 it will be the turn of the European bishops. The key role is being played by Colombian Cardinal Alfonso Lopez Trujillo, president of the Pontifical Council for the Family.

The cardinals who met in consistory had very little room for maneuver and not enough time to raise doubts. Their moment of freedom will come in the conclave. For a pope's projects die with him. ❏

66

Pope's book makes debut amid glitterati

(November 4, 1994) Italian book presentations typically involve some distinguished person lauding the work to the skies, and then the bashful author answering nonthreatening questions about it.

Pope John Paul II, however, missed the launching of his book, *Crossing the Threshold of Hope*, because it was Wednesday, audience day in the Vatican. (Six million copies were simultaneously released worldwide. The U.S. publisher is Knopf, 244 pages, $20).

The unveiling took place in Milan, not in the historic center of the city but far out in the suburbs in the Mt. Thabor conference center, part of the San Raffaele Hospital complex.

This was the very hospital, founded by the brilliant priest-physician Don Luigi Verse, where the pope was operated on in July 1992 for the removal of a growth "the size of an orange." It is curious that this hospital should have been chosen for the presentation of the papal book.

All the glitterati of Milan were there — some of the "clean hands" judges, top industrialists and bankers not in jail, civic dignitaries, society hostesses, film stars and so on. San Raffaele nurses in gray completed the list of 650 specially invited guests. It was like an opening night at La Scala, the famous Milan opera house.

But where was Cardinal Carlo Maria Martini, the local archbishop?

He was very definitely "uninvited." One reason for this slight was that Irena Pivetti, 32, speaker of the Italian Parliament, was on the podium. Indeed, apart from Cardinal Joseph Ratzinger, who gave a predictable lecture, she was the star of the show. Pivetti has been at odds with Martini, whom she considers a dangerous man. He has criticized the Lega, the northern federalist party to which she belongs.

She responded to Martini by saying she wanted to found a truly "papal party." Meanwhile, she has to make do with the Lega. It forms one pillar of the Silvio Berlusconi coalition. (The other pillar is the fascists). To call her excessively right wing would be a charitable understatement.

She has founded a movement called Faith and Justice designed to show that emphasis on justice should not undermine faith. Most of the time, it does, she implies.

Pivetti praised the papal book as "bread for the simple faithful," one of whom she claimed to be. When she asks some clerics for bread — could she conceivably have been thinking of Martini? — she gets merely a stone, she said.

John Paul has been pope for half of Pivetti's life — since she was 16. During his papacy, she moved from the school bench to the speaker's chair.

And there was the handsome, smiling Joaquín Navarro-Valls, psychiatrist, spin doctor and bullfighter, the man closest to the pope. Of course, that was it. This whole project, from conception to presentation, has the markings of an Opus Dei scheme.

Proof is made difficult because Opus Dei members do not reveal themselves. But Vittorio Messori, who lobbed those easy questions to which the book, supposedly, is a reply, has also written a book about Opus Dei so fulsome that suspicions are bound to be aroused. For no one outside Opus Dei ever praises Opus Dei. Except Pope John Paul.

Messori starts with a series of statements about the papal primacy that come close to heresy. "The pope is considered," he confidently pontificates, "the man on earth who represents the Son of God, who 'takes the place' of the second person of the omnipotent God of the Trinity." That is why, he concludes, Catholics call the pope "Holy Father" or "Your Holiness."

"You are either," says Messori, addressing John Paul and evoking Blaise Pascal's wager, ". . . the mysterious living proof of the Creator of the universe or the central protagonist of a millennial illusion." More bluntly: You either prove the existence of God or you are a fraud.

John Paul responds to this hype with skillful dialectic. "Vicar of Christ" is indeed dangerous language, going to the very edge of blasphemy. But as Vatican II teaches, every bishop is the "vicar of Christ" for his diocese. And "in a certain sense" every Christian is a "vicar of Christ." Just imagine: Let me introduce my wife, a vicar of Christ. A new order: the VCs.

On the less significant titles, "Holy Father" and "Your Holiness," John Paul quotes the powerful words of Jesus himself: "Call no one father on earth; you have but one Father in heaven. Do not be called master; you have but one master, the Christ" (Mt 23:9-10).

That is one of the clearest statements of the New Testament, and one of the rare instances where we have what St. Paul calls a *verbum Domini*, an express command of the Lord. Yet it is ignored.

Having reminded us of it, John Paul's next move is cavalier: "These expressions, nevertheless, have evolved out of a long tradition, becoming part of common usage. One must not be afraid of these words either."

But a pope should fear them. Pope John XXIII knew that, like any Christian, he would be judged and saved by the gospel. After six weeks as pope, he told the alumni of his old seminary: "Very slowly I'm getting used to the forms of speech involved in my new ministry. Yes I am, though most unworthily, 'the servant of the servants of God,' because the Lord willed it, not I. But every time I hear someone address me as 'Your Holiness' or 'Holy Father' you can't imagine how embarrassed and pensive it makes me."

John Paul knows no such embarrassment. Yet he quotes the magnificent phrase of St. Augustine: *Vobis sum episcopus, vobiscum Christianus* ("For you I am a bishop, with you I am a Christian"), adding "*Christianus* has far greater significance than *episcopus*, even if the subject is the bishop of Rome."

That's the way to do it. John Paul's former student, Halina Bortnowska, told him just before the Synod on the Laity in 1987: "We need a Copernican revolution. Most people think the laity are there to help the priests do their job. In fact, it is the other way round. The priest is there to help the laity do their work in the world."

"And that includes all offices in the church," she concluded.

"Including mine?" asked the man his students called *wujek* ("uncle").

"Including yours," replied the Joan of Arc of Nova Huta. John Paul seems not to have taken the lesson to heart. Messori does not even know what the question is.

Crossing the Threshold of Hope is not and cannot be an act of the magisterium. Therefore one is free to criticize it. As Figaro says: "Without the freedom to criticize, no praise has any value."

John Paul is interesting on youth. One understands why he wants above all to be fit for the January 1995 World Youth Day in the Philippines. He admits to feeling old and can reminisce. In his day, young people's idealism was expressed in the form of duty; today it takes the form of criticism. Today positivism prevails; in his day "romantic traditions" still persisted. No native English-language speaker could ever say that.

John Paul tells the story of the brilliant engineer, Jerzy Ciecielski, who decided after much prayer that he should get married. What to do? Instead of going to the local disco or the parish ball, "he sought a companion for his life and sought her on his knees, in prayer."

That is the difference between the Polish "romantic traditions" in which he was brought up, and not only our Western societies but today's Poland. But how hard he tries to bridge the gap. His message to youth is always: "What I am going to say to you is much less important than what you are going to say to me." He may believe that. But no one about him does.

John Paul has often quoted French novelist Georges Bernanos: "The church doesn't need reformers; it needs saints." Maybe so. But when in his book he talks of martyrs, as the true heroes of the faith, he lists only the victims of communism starting with the politically incorrect "martyrs" in the Spanish civil war. Nearly all the martyrs in his pontificate have been the victims of Latin American dictators who went to Mass every Sunday.

But the pope can't see that. It is his Polish blind spot. Like any Catholic, he starts out from a national culture that provides a strong sense of identity, and then tries to rise to the level of the universal church. With his knowledge of languages he has succeeded better than most of us in this enterprise.

But when he comes to talk of human rights he has two paradigms unknown to the rest of the world. The Kraków Theological Faculty, he tells Messori, "condemned the violence perpetrated against the Baltic peoples" at the Council of Constance in 1414. They condemned, in other words, forced conversions. Later, he adds, the Spanish theologians of the Salamanca school condemned the forcible conversion of the Native Americans on the same grounds. But Poland scored a first. Bravo.

John Paul has thought deeply and prayed about every question that Messori pitches at him. His reading is a little out of date — he introduces Albert Camus to illustrate a "bleak vision" of the world, as though Jean-Paul Sartre were still smoking Gauloises in the Café Flore. This "conversation with every home" implies a very sophisticated household. They are expected to know the difference between the young Ludwig Wittgenstein and the mature ditto.

These Catholic households may appreciate the truth that "man's existence is always coexistence." But they may choke on the notion that "it is not possible to affirm that when something is transempirical, it ceases to be empirical."

Messori asks: "Was God at work in the fall of communism?"

The answer is rambling. John Paul begins with a meditation on John 5:17: "My Father is at work until now, so I am at work." But much of the meditation has little to do with the communism question and is more about how God works generally.

He tells us again that young people are still having the experience of God-at-work in their history.

How otherwise can one explain the many movements flourishing in the church? He means movements like Communion and Liberation and the Neo-Catechumenate.

How else, John Paul asks rhetorically, "could the experience of World Youth Day in Denver be understood, if not as the voice of God being heard by young people in a situation which, humanly speaking, offered no hope of success, also because much was being done to prevent that voice being heard?"

Enemies are on the prowl, John Paul goes on. If people do not hear the voice of God in history, that is partly because they have blocked their ears and partly because they have been deafened by society, the mass media, and the ideological foes who, since the 18th century, have led "the struggle against God."

That sounds like another swipe at the Enlightenment. John Paul reduces it to an anti-God movement whose aim is "the systematic elimination of all that is Christian." Marxism appears as a cut-price version of this scheme. Now that it has gone, "a similar plan is revealing itself in all its danger and, at the same time, in all its faultiness."

However, there was some merit in Marxism. It began as "part of the history of protest in the face of injustice," a genuinely justified workers' protest that was then, alas, turned into an ideology.

Fortunately, this "protest" against injustice seeped into the life of the church. It led to *Rerum Novarum* in 1891. Indeed, Leo XIII "in a certain sense predicted the fall of communism, a fall that would cost humanity and Europe dearly, since the medicine . . . could prove more dangerous than the disease itself."

John Paul next exploits the Fatima story, claiming that the three children could not have invented the predictions that "Russia will convert." They simply "did not know enough about history for that." The attempt on his life was "necessary." It occurred on the feast of Our Lady of Fatima in 1981. This happened "so that all could become more transparent and comprehensible, so that the voice of God, which speaks in human history through the 'signs of the times' could be more easily heard and understood."

This comes close to disclosing the "providential meaning" of his pontificate: "Perhaps this is also why the pope was called from 'a faraway country.' "

However, he declares it would be "simplistic to say that Divine Providence caused the fall of communism." It crumbled under the weight of its own mistakes and abuses. The causes of its collapse were internal: "It fell by itself, because of its own inherent weaknesses."

This is interesting, but a little "thin." He dealt more fully with this theme in his interview with Jas Gawronski in *The Guardian* and in his address to Latvian intellectuals in Riga in September 1993.

In the preparation for the Eurosynod, he remarked profoundly that "now that communism has gone, we have to be on the side of the poor; otherwise they will go undefended."

This remark, implying some merit in Marxism, caused distress to Michael Novak when Rocco Buttiglione quoted it at a presentation of the Italian translation of *The Spirit of Democratic Capitalism* in Rome in September.

In 1983 Cardinal Basil Hume, archbishop of Westminster, England, was presenting a book titled *Searching for God* that collected together his weekly talks to the monks of Ampleforth where he had been abbot. He was asked: "Do you think your Ampleforth talks would have been published had you not become cardinal archbishop of Westminster? And if not, what does this tell us?"

Without a moment's hesitation, Hume replied: "They would certainly not have been published. What does this tell us? That being a cardinal is a good commercial proposition." Being a pope is an even better commercial proposition. After all, as Archbishop Paul Marcinkus used to say: "You can't run the church on Hail Marys." ❏

67

Pope stacks school of cardinals

(November 11, 1994) In the sixth consistory of his pontificate, Pope John Paul has rewarded his friends and left potential "dissidents" out in the cold. By creating 30 more cardinals, 23 of them under 80 and eligible therefore to vote in the next conclave, he has done everything possible to ensure that his successor will be "sound."

I deliberately use the old words — "creating cardinals" — because it is so accurate. The pope makes cardinals out of nothing. He need consult nobody. They are entirely dependent on his will. Agency reports speak of him as "installing cardinals" Nov. 26. There is no such ceremony.

Many appointments are "obvious." A cardinal's hat — also now symbolic — goes with certain major sees. The two Americans, Joseph Maida, 64, archbishop of Detroit, and William Henry Keeler, 63, archbishop of Baltimore, fall into this category.

But then one has to ask why Justin Rigali, 59, since January archbishop of another see that normally carries a hat, failed to get one. Perhaps he is in this context "too young." We need to see how he performs in St. Louis before moving him to New York when Cardinal John J. O'Connor tenders his resignation Jan. 15, 1995. But not all the obvious nominations are ideologically neutral. Pierre Eyt, archbishop of Bordeaux, France, is close to the "new movements" and possibly Opus Dei.

Opus Dei members may imagine they have the next conclave sown up thanks to the sympathy shown it by the *camerlingo* or chamberlain, Spanish Cardinal Eduardo Martinez Somalo, 67, appointed in 1991. On the death of the pope, his task will be to arrange the funeral and organize the conclave.

Cardinal Carlo Maria Martini, 67, archbishop of Milan, does not stand a chance in this company — although he was at the top of the list of European bishops in the election for the synod council.

Then there are "political" appointments in communist or semi-communist countries. John Paul's Polish experience persuades him that cardinals — men in red — are best equipped to deal with reds. Thus the archbishop of Hanoi, Paul Joseph Pham Dinh Tung, 75, gets the nod. So, too, does Jaime Luca Ortega y Alamino, 58, archbishop of Havana whose task is to wave farewell to President Fidel Castro.

There are four cardinals from ex-communist countries. Miroslav Vlk (his name means "wolf"), archbishop of Prague, needs it to strengthen his authority. John Paul maneuvered him into the presidency of the European bishops' conference. The ex-window cleaner did not want the job since it meant ousting Martini.

Prague is at the exact center of Europe. Vlk is a pious man, most of whose new clergy have come out of Focolarini, founded by Chiara Lubich, the best of the new movements.

With excellent theologians like Dominik Duka, provincial of the Dominicans and friend of President Václav Havel, and Tomas Halik to help, Vlk can make Prague the crossroads of the church in Europe.

The surprise here — the joker in the pack — is Vinko Puljic, 49, archbishop of Sarajevo. John Paul saw a lot of him in the past six months as the pope prepared for his aborted trip to Sarajevo. Puljic, in his intervention at the synod on religious, reported on some sociological field work. Sixty-two percent of the religious he interviewed in Zagreb and Spoleto said they could justify disobedience to their superiors in the name of human rights.

He feared that some religious were more concerned to defend "the collective ideology of their congregation" than the founder's charism. Obedience, virtue and sacrifice had been exchanged, he opined, for "democratic values."

The two others from ex-communist countries are both over 80: Kazimierz Swiatek, archbishop of Minsk, Belarus, stayed on after 75 because there is no one else; and Fr. Mikel Koliqi who miraculously survived the harsh atheist regime in Albania.

Then comes a little group of Jesuits, indispensable when it comes to the crunch.

Augusto Vargas Alzamora, 72, archbishop of Lima, Peru, has played a useful role in the post-Shining Path situation. Julius Riyadi Darmaatmadja, 59, archbishop of Semarang, Indonesia, knows about life under Islam. The other Jesuit cardinal, Fr. Alois Grillmeier, theologian from Sankt Georgen, Frankfurt, is a man of copper-bottomed reliability whose account of the early councils and Christological controversies is the standard work.

The obvious German candidate, Karl Lehmann, bishop of Mainz, was passed over. He made the mistake of helping write the letter on the pastoral treatment of the divorced and remarried that caused a furor. Such deliberate snubs are worrying.

No Brazilian was thought worthy of becoming a cardinal. Yet the president of the conference, Jesuit Luciano Pedro Mendes de Almeida, came first in the election to the synod council. (Cardinal Joseph Bernardin of Chicago came second.) That the country with the world's largest Catholic population should get no new cardinals looks like a deliberate slight.

If Mendes de Almeida, archbishop of Mariana, raises alarm by being a Jesuit — he would presumably be another vote for Martini — then Hélder Câmara Pessoa, 85, formerly bishop of Recife, could have been honored in old age.

In the 1970s Hélder Câmara was a name to conjure with. He had defied his military regime and was the most "prophetic" bishop in Latin America. As such he stood alongside Mother Teresa at the bicentennial celebration in Philadelphia in 1976. His mistake was to suggest that theologians today should do for Marx what St. Thomas Aquinas did for Aristotle in the 13th century.

While Brazil gets no cardinals, Mexico gets two: Adolfo Antonio Suarez Rivera, 67, archbishop of Monterrey, and Juan Sandoval Iniguez, 61, archbishop of Guadalajara.

Chile's new cardinal, Carlos Oviedo Cavada, 67, archbishop of Santiago, addressed the synod on one-parent families or, as he put it, "families not created through matrimony."

Having a cardinal puts small nations on the map. So Tom Winning, 69, archbishop of Glasgow, Scotland, just shades it ahead of Edinburgh — or St. Andrew's as it is known. Winning has always tried to stress his man-of-the-people differences with patrician Cardinal Basil Hume down in Westminster.

Like Scotland, Catalonia, a region of northeast Spain, counts as a nation within the European Union. It is right that Ricardo Maria Carles Gordó, 68, archbishop of Barcelona, should get a hat. Maybe Jean-Claude Turcotte, of Montreal, Canada, a youthful 58, belongs here.

The curialists form another distinct group. Carlo Forno, 72, was such a disaster as nuncio to Brazil that he was kicked upstairs as Vatican ambassador to Italy, a post he will now relinquish, since a cardinal cannot be a nuncio.

Luigi Poggi, 77, was once the Vatican's troubleshooter for Central and Eastern Europe. He has now retired into the Vatican Library. He should write his memoirs.

No reporter is known to have ever seen the Swiss Gilberto Agustoni, 72, head of various tribunals in the Vatican. Belgian Jan P. Schotte, 66, has been relatively visible if rather silent as synod secretary since 1984. He must now give up this job, deemed unworthy of a cardinal.

Vincenzo Fagiolo, 76, is president of the Pontifical Council for the Interpretation of Legislative Texts. He solemnly warned the synod that "subsidiarity," of which he approved, did not mean smuggling democratic practices into the church.

Three more complete the list. Emmanuel Wamala, now 67, archbishop of Kampala, Uganda, is the only African, unless we count Armand Gaetan Razafindratandra, 69, of Madagascar. Peter Seiichi Shirayanegi, 66, archbishop of Tokyo, is definitely Asian. From the Mideast is Nasrallah Pierre Sefir, 74, patriarch of the Maronites in Lebanon. The Maronites number 900,000 of the 1.1 million Lebanese Catholics.

"Honorary" cardinals are Ersilio Tonino, formerly archbishop of Ravenna, Italy, star of Italian TV; and French Dominican Yves Congar, who is practically confined to his bed in the Invalides where *les grands français* end their days. He will most certainly refuse to be ordained archbishop, as did his friend, the Jesuit Henri de Lubac.

Before this exercise, there were 97 cardinals eligible to vote in the next conclave. After it, and if no one dies in the meantime, the maximum complement of 120 will have been reached. They would be very crowded and possibly asphyxiated in the Apostolic Palace. However, in 1993 work began on a new hotel-like building on the Piazza Santa Marta just inside the Vatican to the left of St. Peter's. It will cost $15 million, said to have been provided by U.S. benefactors. Officially the purpose of the new building is to house long-term guests to Rome. But with its 130 rooms "complete with every amenity" it could well be used for the next conclave.

The building will be ready by 1996. Is this a clue? ❑

Part IV

Postscripts

68

Why I love the church

by Peter Hebblethwaite

(January 6, 1995) *Human no less than divine elements are part of the church's constitution. It must be taken both for what it is and what it could be, if it is to be truly loved. These thoughts are from a lecture delivered in 1984 in the state of Washington.*

Vatican II's document on the church, *Lumen Gentium*, has a helpful phrase: "The church, or in other words, the kingdom of Christ now present in mystery, grows visibly in the world through the power of God." We cannot say this of any other human group or association. People band together for all kinds of reasons — to collect stamps, to advocate causes, to defend themselves, or simply because they need someone else. The church is a unique association because of what it does to time and in time. It becomes, as T.S. Eliot says, the point of intersection of time with timelessness.

Now, there are people who abuse this idea. The church is a mystery, they say, therefore you must not criticize it. Cardinal Joseph Ratzinger has been known to suggest this.

Or they say: Modern Catholics are so tied up with the nuts and bolts of the church, with electing bishops or ordaining women, that they lose sight of its deep underlying reality.

These half-truths point to the fundamental problem in thinking about the church and consequently in loving the church. For we can always speak in a double register.

The church is divine, yes, in its origin, sustenance and goal; the church is human, all too human, in its membership and leadership. We cannot yank these two apart and say: I am going to concentrate on loving the divine component while loathing the human one. That would be a kind of schizophrenia.

We do not love the church for its own sake nor sacralize the institution, putting it beyond reach of criticism, or even debate. "We do not 'confuse the institution of the papacy with the kingdom of God,' " said Henri de Lubac in his great work *Catholicism* of 1974.

De Lubac knew what he was talking about, for he suffered at the hands of the church. At the height of the modernist crisis, at the start of this century, a French Dominican, Humbert Clérrisac, said, "It is easy to suffer for the church, the difficult thing is to suffer at the hands of the church." The gospel teaches one to expect persecution. But when it comes from those within the church, then it is demoralizing. We looked for support; we got a slap in the face. De Lubac hung in there.

But what about today's dissidents? What about feminists, for example, who find the church so patriarchal as to deserve rejection or at least reexamination until further notice? What about a theologian like Hans Küng, who has lost his license to teach as a Catholic theologian, yet remains a priest in good standing, and yet again manages to criticize the pope in vituperative fashion in the most recent issue of *Concilium*?

This *Concilium* article prompted me to ask the question: Does Hans Küng love the church? So I sent him a fax to ask, explaining that I was giving a lecture, and my hearers would want to know. I got an immediate reply — but from his secretary, he himself being in Budapest for the *Concilium* board meeting.

So Eleonore Henn sent several pages from a book called *Reforming the Church Today: Keeping Hope Alive*. The particular chapter, called "Why I am Staying in the Church," was written immediately after Dec. 18, 1979, when the Congregation for the Doctrine of the Faith issued a declaration on "some major points in the theological doctrine of Professor Hans Küng." He was charged with "contempt for the magisterium of the church," particularly on the issue of infallibility and, it was said, "could no longer be considered a Catholic theologian or function as such in a teaching role."

Now this was a terrible blow. True, it did not prevent Küng from teaching graduate students in Tübingen, or traveling the world giving lectures to thousands, or moving with great distinction into the study of Judaism and Islam and from there fanning out into the urgent need for a new world ethic for a new world order.

But none of that was evident in early 1980 when the ax fell and he lost his immediate job as dogmatic theologian in the University of Tübingen. How did he react?

People said to him: You should obviously leave a church that treats you so badly. Charles Davis up in Canada had already done so. But, says Küng:

I have received too much from this community of faith to be able to leave so easily. I have been too involved with church reform to be willing to disappoint those who have been involved with me. To those opposed to renewal, I do not want to give the pleasure of my leaving; to the partisans of renewal, I do not want to give them the pain.

Küng goes on to stress that he received his faith not from books or even the Bible but from ordinary Christian communities of faith:

This would be my decisive answer: I am staying in the church because I have been convinced by Jesus Christ and all that he stands for, and because the church community, despite all its failures, pleads the cause of Jesus Christ and must continue to do so.

Die Sache Christi is the phrase translated as "the cause of Jesus Christ." It is more than that: It is everything Jesus stands for.

This still is not quite an answer. Why I stay in the church is not quite the same as why I love the church. In terms of marriage, one can choose to stay with one's wife because there is nowhere else to go, just as a religious might stay where he or she is because there seems no better hole to go to. Hilaire Belloc's verse applies about "holding fast to nurse, for fear of finding something worse."

Just when I was thinking these thoughts, Küng began to move beyond mere "staying in the church" to "loving the church."

I love this church for what it is and what it could be. I love this church not as a mother but as a family of faith. It is for the sake of this family that the institutions, constitutions and authorities exist at all. Sometimes one simply has to put up with them.

I hope he would still say this in 1992, for this is a splendid formulation. If one were merely to say, "I love this church because of what it could be," then one would leap out of the real world toward an ideal, invisible church of which anything could be said because it does not exist except on the drawing board. Küng does not say with John Stuart Mill, the British utilitarian thinker, "My love for an institution is in proportion to my desire to reform it." He says he loves it both as it is and as it could be.

The Catholic "and" — the importance of holding both ends of the chain — applies supremely here. You do not pharisaically dissociate yourself from this community of sinners that prepares the communion of saints. If we are talking about ministry — all of us, wherever we stand, have some sort of ministry in the church — there is no opposition in ministry between working for holiness and working for reform.

Hans Küng says he loves the church not as a mother but as a family. I wonder what he means by this distinction. I suppose he is rejecting the idea of "Mother Church" — the *ecclesia Mater* which is part of tradition — on the grounds that it keeps us in an immature state, prolongs adolescence, implies dependency. A church made up only of brothers and sisters feels much more comfortable and democratic.

Yet, whoever heard of a family that consisted only of coequal brothers and sisters? Is it not possible that in rejecting Mother Church and all fatherhood, including that of the Holy Father, we are losing an essential dimension? The church exists not only horizontally, in space, but vertically in time as tradition and handing on. There is a danger in throwing out not just the baby with the bathwater but the grandmother as well.

Mothers — literal ones — do not have to be perfect to be loved. What is required of a parent is that he or she be "good enough." We are disappointed when we do not find perfect faith, perfect hope and perfect charity in the church. But that is asking too much. We have a right to expect enough faith, enough hope and enough charity to sustain us as we stumble along our pilgrim way.

Perfect faith, hope and charity will come only at the end, at the great eschatological blowup. "We are named, and are truly, God's sons and daughters," says the first epistle of St. John, "but what we shall be has not yet been revealed." In that tension between what has already been achieved in us and what remains to be accomplished lies the possibility of growth.

But there remains a problem. The difficulty of loving the church — or loving anybody — is that love is incompatible with power relationships. So it is when the hierarchical church appears intent chiefly on imposing its power, as when in Europe and Brazil the pope appoints wholly unsuitable bishops, that people like Hans Küng are inclined to speak with great harshness and talk about the pope as the last of the European dictators.

Personally, I think this is to dig a pit for oneself, for there is no way out of this — unless the pope decides on a change of heart, which will not happen. Yet, the point remains: Power drives love out. A Jungian psychiatrist once asked: What is the opposite of love? Most people say hatred, the more sophisticated say indifference. The psychiatrist's answer was: The opposite of love is not hatred or indifference but power.

It is very difficult to conclude with any practical advice for those having difficulties with loving the church. It would be comforting to think that experiences of suffering at the hands of the church or the people we love were a way of being led from love to deeper love. But that presumes a mystical temperament that we cannot always expect to find. So I conclude with the words of Mark Twain: When you don't know what to do, do what is right. ❏

69

He gave new theological genre to church: An appreciation
Arthur Jones

(January 6, 1995) Washington — the tiny elevator at the hotel Columbus would be too slow, so I ran up the marble staircase, hurried along the faded red carpeting and knocked on the dark, varnished door with its bright brass numerals. It was just after 7 p.m. on Aug. 25, 1978.

There was some grumbling and snorting from within until, finally, the door opened slightly and the round, flushed face of Peter Hebblethwaite, roused from a late afternoon nap after an extended Roman lunch, smiled in recognition and amused anticipation.

"Arthur. Yes."

"Better go, Peter," I said. "We may have a pope." In St. Peter's Square, the conclave smoke was an uncertain gray. Hebblethwaite didn't hazard a guess as to who it might be and disappeared behind the door. He probably hoped it was not Cardinal Giovanni Benelli, whom Jesuit Fr. Peter Hebblethwaite had attacked in the *London Observer* five years earlier as a deputy secretary of state who was "repressive . . . secretive . . . mysterious (and whose) methods obfuscate the message of the gospels."

In the intervening five years, Hebblethwaite had passed from the Jesuits to the role of layman/journalist.

"Coming?" he asked, as he emerged from his room. "No," I replied. "Your story."

Earlier in 1978, Hebblethwaite had introduced the upcoming papal election this way: "The 111 cardinals carried their suitcases into the world's most exclusive club and the world's most expensive polling booth: the conclave area of Vatican City."

And of the scene that took place not five minutes after he arrived breathless at St. Peter's Square, he wrote, "When Cardinal Pericle Felici called out (the new pope's) Christian name from the balcony of St. Peter's, there was a moment of ominous silence . . . the first reaction was one of disappointment . . . Albino who?"

When, two months later, Cardinal Karol Wojtyla was elected Pope John Paul II, Hebblethwaite's third paragraph began, "No one would call him an adventurous theologian." And a month later, Hebblethwaite said, introducing his book, *The Year of Three Popes*, "I have often thought that we needed a new theological genre which would combine observation of what was going on with theological reflection upon it; in this way, the theology springs from the event and constantly refers back to it."

Having invented the genre by describing it, Hebblethwaite proceeded to practice it for the rest of his life. He had the gift of verisimilitude: You were there; you heard what was said and thought — or might have been or, at times, ought to have been.

He would file his story, banged out on a tinny British-made Lion portable with threadbare ribbon. Often enough, hours later, when they still had to file their stories, other reporters would seek him out for insights, background, facts. And he loved, in such settings, to hold forth. He signaled his views with a puff of disgust, a hiss of regret or a snort of disdain.

Three weeks before his death — the reason for the call completed — we talked about our children. Oh, how he loved his three, Dominic, Cordelia and Benedict.

Their dad was a wizard with words, but it was the children he loved. And those were the words he most wanted to say — words which, in all probability, he never found time for. He was always so busy elsewhere.

As he told *NCR* readers in July 1975, just before he came aboard as a correspondent: "Is there no (Vatican) accountability, other than to God, in the church? There is need for constant evaluation of the church's policies, especially in its central administration. Who is to do it? Unofficially, the task is left to journalists, who put their heads on the block every time they write."

And that he did. Very well indeed. ❑

70

Peter Hebblethwaite wrote of church he knew, loved: An obituary

Thomas C. Fox

(January 6, 1995) Oxford, England — NCR Vatican Affairs writer Peter Hebblethwaite's life, death and new life were celebrated in a Mass here Dec. 23, punctuated by the consoling chant of the *Dies Irae* and a chorus from Fauré's "Requiem." The service took place in a packed, small church once pastored by the Jesuit fathers with whom Peter felt a special kinship.

Peter is survived by his wife, Margaret, and three children, Dominic, Cordelia and Benedict.

Hebblethwaite, 64, died Dec. 18 after his heart gave out, paying the final toll for years of smoking and drinking. He had a passion for life and brought it to every aspect of his faith, love for the church and for his work: a unique form of journalism that combined keen observation, scholarship, wit and understatement into a mix of unparalleled reporting. His weekly analysis pieces have been a regular component of *NCR* since he joined the staff in 1978.

Two dozen priests along with the local Roman Catholic bishop concelebrated the Mass. The local Anglican bishop also participated in the service that was attended by family members and several hundred colleagues and friends.

Jesuit Fr. Edward Yarnold, one of Hebblethwaite's oldest friends, recalled him in a homily as a man who had a special love for his family as well as for the Jesuit order to which Hebblethwaite once belonged. Said Yarnold: "The (Anglican) bishop of Oxford (Richard Harries) on the radio this morning recalled Peter's personal credo: 'I love my wife, I love my children, I love the Society of Jesus.' "

On a chilly, misty day, Hebblethwaite was buried in Wolvercote Cemetery in Oxford, his home for these past dozen years. His grave is just a stone's throw from that of British author J.R.R. Tolkien.

Hebblethwaite was a prolific writer, the author of at least 15 books, including the monumental works, *John XXIII, Pope of the Council* (1984), and *Paul VI, the First Modern Pope* (1993), acts of lasting scholarship and love. During the past decade he became best known in Catholic English-speaking circles for his work in *NCR* and his regular contributions to *The Tablet* in Britain.

His death represents a great personal loss. During 15 years of collaboration, he became a kindred spirit. His passing represents a major loss to this paper and to Catholic journalism.

Hebblethwaite was a man of deep faith, a loving husband and father. It was an unusual week when he, in conversing on the telephone about some article he was working on, did not speak of his wife and three children. He was very proud of his family.

He was also an accomplished musician and loved to play the piano to entertain friends.

The key to his success, I think, will be found in his enormous love for the church, both as institution and as a quarreling family on a journey, carrying a banner inscribed "people of God."

He possessed a towering intellect. It included an immense grasp of history, philosophy and theology. It was, though, an Ignatian spirituality which guided him. Hebblethwaite was conservative by instinct, which may confound his critics. He had no qualm about criticizing a bishop or a pope, but had little patience with those who talked about discarding the episcopacy or papacy. His Catholic faith grounded him and at the same time gave him great latitude to write as loving critic.

While working for *NCR*, Hebblethwaite went on dozens of papal journeys, including those to Poland and to Africa. He enjoyed analyzing all sorts of church-related documents, and, because of his powerful memory and church background, more often than not found in them penetrating insights others would simply miss. He was a gifted storyteller, wrote entertainingly and was an editor's dream, showing great detachment from his writings once they left his desk. You could take or leave what he had to say; he was on to the next task.

Born into the working class near Manchester, England, he was educated at the Xaverian college there. He joined the Jesuits in 1948.

After finishing his novitiate, he was sent to study philosophy near Paris where he mastered the French language, one of many he would learn to read and speak. He was ordained to the priesthood in 1963 and later became assistant editor of the Jesuit journal *The Month*.

As a young Jesuit, he had the good fortune to attend the final two sessions of the Second Vatican Council to report on it for that publication. Those energetic years empowered Hebblethwaite with fresh hope for a church he saw breaking into renewal after centuries of dormancy; the possibilities for God's people were endless, he believed.

His curiosity kindled, journalism began to suit him well and helped channel his idealism.

In 1967, he became editor of *The Month* and began to travel widely in Europe. It was during that time he took a special interest in Eastern Europe. But by then a post-conciliar letdown was spreading within the church. He was still a Jesuit when he published two outspoken articles attacking the record of Cardinal Benelli, the Vatican conservative. Hebblethwaite had become convinced that it was Benelli who was holding back the implementation of the reforms of Vatican II.

His comments were always reformist and laced with a healthy arm's-length approach to Rome (he loved Fr. Ronald Knox's bon mot, "Never go down to the engine room; you'll only feel sick").

In 1974 he left the Jesuits, obtained a dispensation from his vows and married Margaret Speaight, then still a student at Oxford. He was 43, she was 23. However, it is said by those who best know him that he never stopped being a Jesuit priest.

The Hebblethwaites set up house in Oxford, where in 1976 he became a lecturer in modern languages at Wadham College. Two years later, in August 1978, then *NCR* publisher and editor Arthur Jones, familiar with Hebblethwaite's works, invited him to go to Rome as the paper's correspondent there. He worked out of Rome until moving back to Oxford in 1981 where he continued as the paper's Vatican affairs writer.

Hebblethwaite's book writing began in 1965 with a study of Georges Bernanos, the French novelist. The council, of course, had captured his imagination and directed his focus upon the church. It showed in his authorship of *The Council Fathers and Atheism* (1966), *Theology of the Church* (1968), *The Runaway Church* (1975), *Christian-Marxist Dialogue and Beyond* (1977), *The Year of Three Popes* (1978), *The New Inquisition?* (1979), *The Papal Year*

(1981), *Introducing John Paul II, the Populist Pope* (1982), *Synod Extraordinary* (1986), *In the Vatican* (1986), and his much acclaimed biographies of John XXIII and Paul VI. His latest book, *The Next Pope*, was published in England (HarperCollins) the week of his death and is due out in the United States this spring (HarperSanFrancisco).

Hebblethwaite was never happier than when sitting with friends expounding, explaining and investigating the latest news from Rome, the future political shape of Europe or discussing rugby with his children.

His health began to fail intermittently in recent years. He recently suffered from asthma and at the end of November spent a week in the hospital, rushed in as an emergency patient having trouble breathing. He rallied but within two weeks was failing again. An autopsy revealed that he died of an enlarged heart that could no longer cope.

He was at home at the time of his death. Among his last words were "Maranatha" — "O Lord, come." ❑

Index